Four Accounts of Terry's Texas Rangers

Four Accounts of Terry's Texas Rangers
The 8th Texas Cavalry, Confederate Army During the American Civil War

The Life Record of H. W. Graber
H. W. Graber

Terry's Texas Rangers
L. B. Giles

Reminiscences of the Terry Rangers
J. K. P. Blackburn

Diary of Ephraim Shelby Dodd
Ephraim Shelby Dodd

LEONAUR

Four Accounts of Terry's Texas Rangers
The 8th Texas Cavalry, Confederate Army During the American Civil War
The Life Record of H. W. Graber
by H. W. Graber
Terry's Texas Rangers
by L. B. Giles
Reminiscences of the Terry Rangers
by J. K. P. Blackburn
Diary of Ephraim Shelby Dodd
by Ephraim Shelby Dodd

FIRST EDITION

First published under the titles
The Life Record of H. W. Graber
Terry's Texas Rangers
Reminiscences of the Terry Rangers
and
Diary of Ephraim Shelby Dodd

Leonaur is an imprint of Oakpast Ltd

Copyright in this form © 2022 Oakpast Ltd

ISBN: 978-1-915234-82-7 (hardcover)
ISBN: 978-1-915234-83-4 (softcover)

http://www.leonaur.com

Publisher's Notes

The views expressed in this book are not necessarily those of the publisher.

Contents

The Life Record of H. W. Graber	7
Terry's Texas Rangers	165
Reminiscences of the Terry Rangers	227
Diary of Ephraim Shelby Dodd	299

The Life Record of H. W. Graber

H. W. GRABER

Contents

Preface	11
My Earliest Recollections	13
I Abandon the Printer's Trade and Take Up Surveying	16
Indian Troubles—My First Venture in Business	21
My First Military Experiences	25
Our First Engagement	34
An Accidental Injury—Shiloh	41
I am Wounded and Captured	51
The Escape of Major Ousley	61
In Prison at Louisville, Where I was Honoured with Handcuffs	65
I Change My Name for the First Time and am Finally Exchanged	70
The Inhumanity of the Federal Government	87
I Rejoin My Command	91
Middle Tennessee and Kentucky	93
Bardstown Engagement—I "Swap" Horses with a Federal	100
The Battle of Perryville	108
I Refuse to Become a Teamster	112

Omissions in Preceding Chapters	118
General Johnston's Failure to Strike—Sherman	121
Georgia Service	132
I Sell a Ten Dollar Gold Piece for Fifteen Hundred Dollars	145
My Service with Captain Shannon	149
We Receive Notice of Johnston's Surrender	153

Preface

The purpose of this narrative is to hand down to my children, and to present to my friends, an intimate, personal account of a life which has not been without interesting episodes, and which has been lived during the most eventful period that this Nation will, in all probability, ever know.

Though a large portion of my story will deal with incidents which occurred during the great sectional strife of the sixties, it is not intended as a history of that great calamity, but is meant, simply, to be an account of incidents with which the writer was personally associated.

The Great Strife which so nearly disrupted our country is over. For many years we of the South have been dwelling amicably with those of the North—this is as it should be. We are, united, the greatest country on the face of God's footstool. And to both the North and the South belongs the credit.

The mistakes of certain Northern fanatics, which were not, I believe, dictated by general Northern sentiment, have long been rectified. The Government at Washington today is, I know, truly representative of the entire country. The tragic blunders which were evident in the South during what has been called the "Reconstruction Period" would not be possible today. The country has become a unit.

In perfect love and friendship for all the good people of the United States, irrespective of location, and with no sectional feeling other than an abiding love for my South, I write this story. I hope it may be found to be not without interest.

H. W. Graber.

CHAPTER 1

My Earliest Recollections

I was born in the city of Bremen, Germany, on the 18th day of May, 1841. My father was a native of Prussia, and my mother of the Kingdom of Hanover. They were married in the city of Bremen in 1839. There were five children born unto them; a daughter, the oldest of the family, died in Bremen; the others moved with the family to Texas. I was educated at a private school, starting at six years old, up to the time of our removal to Texas in 1853.

In connection with the ordinary literary course, the French and English languages were taught in the higher grades in which I had just entered, but when father decided to move to Texas, he had me drop the French and employed an additional private teacher to come to our home and give me English lessons, which enabled me to speak the English language on our arrival in Texas.

Our father was a manufacturer of fine mahogany furniture and established a profitable trade on this with New York, exporting more of his furniture than was sold at home, though he had quite an extensive local trade, as his styles and work were very popular, all of his furniture being hand carved.

The great Revolution of 1848, which caused great stringency in financial affairs of the country, forced him to mortgage his home, and from this he never recovered. It was this condition that induced his removal to Texas.

Father and I came to Texas a year in advance of the balance of the family, for the purpose of getting acquainted with the country and its conditions. Then, the year following the rest of the family came over. We settled in Houston, Texas. We came over on a large sailing ship, as steamships were very few, and we came by way of New Orleans, where we found a great yellow fever epidemic, though we escaped it this year.

I forgot to mention that, when a child about four years old, I was playing on the river front, sliding up and down on a plank with one end in the water, the other end on the steps leading down to the water, when I lost my hold, slid into the river and under the bottom of a schooner, coming out on the opposite side, where one of the sailors caught me by the hair just as I started under the third time. I was carried home unconscious. This proved my first narrow escape from death, of which I had many during life.

Soon after our arrival in Houston, father worked in an undertaking establishment for a man by the name of Pannel, but during the first summer, both father and mother were taken sick with typhoid fever and died within one week, leaving me, the oldest of the family, then thirteen years old, to take care of the rest of the children.

We had an uncle, father's brother, living on Spring Creek, in the upper part of Harris County, who took charge of our sister and a younger brother until I could make provisions for them to come back to Houston, there to get the benefit of the schools.

During the yellow fever of that fall my brother, next to me, died with yellow fever.

I forgot to mention that soon after arrival in Houston I secured a position in the large retail grocery establishment of F. Bauman, and, subsequently, in the wholesale grocery establishment of C. E. Gregory, where I soon became shipping clerk and an expert marker of freight, with the marking brush; so much so that when a lot of freight was turned out on the sidewalk (to be shipped by ox-wagon, which was the only means of transportation out of Houston before the day of railroads) and when marking this freight, passers-by would stop and watch me, as I was the youngest shipping clerk in Houston, which of course made me feel very proud.

After a year or more in the service of this wholesale establishment I was offered a position in a retail dry goods establishment of G. Gerson, where I became familiar with the dry goods business. After about a year, Gerson decided to open a general merchandise establishment at Waxahachie and place his cousin, Robert Angleman, in charge of the same, and, for this purpose, loaded about a half dozen ox-wagons with part of his Houston stock and employed me to go to Waxahachie and clerk for Angleman.

In place of going up to Waxahachie on the stage, our only means of travel then, I begged them to allow me to go with the wagons, as I was anxious to camp out and hunt on the way, but I took a great fancy to driving one of the wagons, the driver of which permitted me to learn, and I became somewhat expert in handling six yoke of oxen, each one of which had a name, such as "Red" or "Ball," or "Jerry." The oxen seemed to know their names when called on to move up, followed by the crack of the big whip, and it is hardly necessary to say when this outfit entered Waxahachie, preceded by this team, this little boy was driving, popping his whip as loud as any of the men. I felt I was the biggest man among them.

Angleman's business proved a great success—selling goods for cash and also taking pecans in trade for goods at fifty cents a bushel. These pecans were shipped by wagon to Houston and from thence to New York, where they netted from sixteen to eighteen cents per pound. Angleman's business was the first Jewish establishment in Waxahachie, and ultimately grew to be the largest business in that section of the country.

My sojourn at Waxahachie of about two years proved the most pleasant of my life, as everybody seemed to be my friend, and took a special interest in me because I was the only orphan child in the place and was without a home. While there I boarded at both hotels; first at the Rogers House and next at the Ellis House.

Chapter 2

I Abandon the Printer's Trade and Take Up Surveying

After two years in Waxahachie, I decided to move back to Houston, where I concluded to learn the printer's trade, and for this purpose secured a position in the office of the Houston Telegraph, which, at that time, perhaps, had the largest circulation and was the leading paper in the State. It was published by Allen & Brockett. Soon after entering this office and acting as printer's devil for a while, they promoted me to the job office, where I became expert in doing fancy work, such as marriage notices, ball invitations, etc., but I was unable to collect any salary; these people were always hard up for money, and I never got anything out of it but my board and sufficient money for clothing.

I finally became disgusted and went to Galveston, where I had an offer from a man by the name of Spratt, who published a little paper called the Ignis Fatuous or Jack o' the Lantern. As the name indicates it was a humorous paper, containing criticisms in a humorous vein, of leading politicians of the city and the State. It was one of the most popular periodicals then published, selling at ten cents a copy, by newsboys, without having any left over each week. Here, too, I failed to get my pay, though I set up the whole paper and made up the forms, which were sent up to the Gazette's office on Friday, where it was struck off ready for the sale of the paper on Saturday. I did my work at Spratt's home, where he had set apart a room containing cases. I had board at the same place.

Spratt was a billiard fiend and, as soon as he got the money for his papers on Saturday, he would stay in town, play billiards until his money was exhausted, come home about Tuesday, and then prepare to furnish matter for the next issue. I worked with him for about sixty days. Failing to get my pay, I became disgusted and concluded that the printer's trade was a good thing for me to drop. I then went back to Waxahachie and again went to work with the Angleman house and formed the acquaintance of an old land surveyor by the name of James E. Patton, who employed me to go with him on surveying expeditions, just for company, paying me a good salary.

I furnished my own horse and arms, the latter of which he never carried. He was firm in the belief that Indians would never trouble him, although it was said that he was taken prisoner by the Indians, having been caught surveying lands down on Chambers' Creek in Ellis County. They turned him loose, which was considered one of the most remarkable cases of Indian generosity ever known on the frontier, as they always killed surveyors whom they caught locating land.

It was also related of this old man, that, in the early days, when he surveyed lands in Ellis County, he substituted chain carrying by hobbling his ankles just the length of a *vara*, and stepped off the land, in place of measuring it with a chain. Colonel Patton was one of the most popular surveyors and land locaters in Texas. His compensation for locating headright certificates was one-half of the land, which made him one of the richest men in lands, at the time of his death, in that section of the State.

My first trip with Colonel Patton was to Fort Belknap, Texas, where he had formed the acquaintance of a man by the name of Gibbons, who moved there from Arkansas and owned about a dozen negroes, with whom he cultivated a considerable plantation just across the river from Fort Belknap. Gibbons had an Indian wife, a Delaware, who was dark complected like other Indians, but she had a younger sister, who married General Tarrant, an old Texas pioneer and Indian fighter, after whom Tarrant County is named. General Tarrant made his home in Ellis County and he and Colonel Patton were great friends. General Tarrant happened to be on a visit at Gibbons' when we arrived there on our first expedition, and we were made to feel at home before starting out surveying.

It was the custom there for surveyors to make up a party of a half dozen or more to go on these expeditions, for protection against Indians who were then roaming over that whole section of the country. There was an Indian agency about twelve or fifteen miles below Belknap, in charge of Captain Shapley Ross, the father of General L. S. Ross, then a boy like myself. This agency was composed of remnant tribes of Indians, probably a half dozen or more, whom the Comanche Indians had run in off the range. These Indians had the protection of the United States Government and, of course, pretended to be friendly.

The most uncivilized Indian in this agency was the Tonkawa, who, it was claimed, were cannibals. I remember as we passed through Keechie Valley, on our way to Weatherford, we stopped at a store for about an hour, resting and talking, when the storekeeper told us of a trouble he came very near having the day before. It seems a Tonkawa Indian had offered to trade him a pony for a young Kentuckian, who had just come out from his State and was clerking in the store. He asked the Indian what he wanted to do with the Kentuckian if he accepted his offer. The Indian told him that he wanted to eat him. The young man got a gun and was about to shoot the Indian, when the storekeeper stopped him and made the Indian leave.

There was another Indian agency at Camp Cooper, about forty miles west of Belknap, presided over by a man by the name of Neighbors. This agency had a tribe of the Southern Comanches, who were also run in by the Northern Comanches, or Apaches. These Southern Comanches claimed to be friendly with the whites in order to have the protection of the United States Government, but they, and occasionally the Ross Agency Indians, were believed to be responsible for many of the raids on our exposed frontier; especially the Indians at the upper agency at Camp Cooper. These raids became frequent; one of them culminating in the murder of two families in Jack County, and the carrying off of a little boy and girl as prisoners.

Being hotly pursued by Rangers and citizens, they were forced to abandon the boy, whom they threw into the brush to be found by the pursuers. He made the statement that he was taken upon a horse, behind a red-headed white man, who seemed to be the leader of the band. This red-headed white man was seen in the Indian camp, located up on the Canadian River, at different times, by scouts.

Major Neighbors, while on a visit to Fort Belknap, became involved in a dispute with one of the citizens, who charged that his Indians were responsible for many of the raids on our frontier. The dispute resulted in a fight and Major Neighbors was killed by the citizen. His death created quite an excitement on the frontier, as he was a United States officer and the Government asked an investigation of the affair, but there was never anything done about it.

While on my first trip with Colonel Patton, while we were making our headquarters at Gibbons', we found General Tarrant and his wife, the sister of Mrs. Gibbons. This lady, by the way, was as fair as most of the white women on the frontier. Their adopted son, Jesse, was about my age. Gibbons had two sons, one about my age, the other a year younger. We boys became great friends, and sometimes engaged in hunting and fishing.

One day we four decided to go fishing at the mouth of a creek, where it emptied into the Brazos, about three-quarters of a mile below the house. We cut fishing poles at a thicket near the creek. After fishing a while without any result, we got tired and commenced shooting with our pistols, of which each had one. All boys of our age always then went armed with six-shooters, the custom of the frontier. After shooting at a log in the creek, thereby emptying our pistols, we did not reload, not deeming it necessary just then, and decided to go in bathing in the river.

The river being very low, was only running on the Fort Belknap side, and we had to walk a considerable distance on a sand bar to the water. Having just stripped ourselves of our clothing, ready to go in, we heard voices calling on the south bank of the river and discovered a group of men beckoning to us to come over to them. These proved to be General Tarrant, Colonel Patton, Gibbons, his overseer and a blacksmith, who, with his wife, occupied a log cabin on Gibbons' place, he being at work for the troops at the fort.

When we reached this party of men we were asked where we had been. When we told them that we had cut our fishing poles at a thicket, they commenced laughing and guying this blacksmith, telling him that his wife had mistaken us for Indians and concluded that this was a sufficient explanation of the alarm about Indians that she had created. This blacksmith insisted on going down to this thicket, saying that he was satisfied that his wife was not frightened and made no mistake; that she must have seen Indians there, but they would not hear to it, and in going up to the house, stopped at the cabin and told this woman that it was us boys that she saw, in place of Indians. She, too, insisted that they were mistaken, that there were surely Indians in that thicket, but they paid no further attention to the matter and went home.

It was the custom there to tie all horses in the yard, around the house, which was done that night. When we woke next morning, we found all of our horses gone. When they then investigated the thicket where we boys cut our fishing poles, they found plenty of Indian signs, such as small pieces of buffalo meat and *moccasin* tracks. The matter, of course, was reported to the *commandant* of the fort, who got his troops ready to start in pursuit the next evening. This was about the character of protection afforded by the United States troops. If Rangers had been stationed there, they would have been in the saddle in less than an hour and continued the pursuit until the Indians were caught up with.

CHAPTER 3

Indian Troubles—My First Venture in Business

This bold raid of these Indians stirred up General Tarrant and he determined to raise about five hundred volunteers in the frontier counties, to break up a big Indian camp, under a celebrated chief, Buffalo Hump, that was known to exist on the North Canadian, and for this purpose he canvassed the frontier counties and had no trouble in having volunteers sign to go out on the expedition. He fixed the time of departure from Fort Belknap on the fourth day of July, which was most unfortunate, as the time of his canvass was in the early part of May, when during the long interim the Indians had been quiet, and had made no raids into the settlements. The volunteers who subscribed had lost interest in the matter and would not go.

I was one of twenty who subscribed to go from Ellis County, and believe I was the only one that ever started. About this time Colonel Patton had arranged to start on another surveying expedition, in conjunction with a party of surveyors, in charge of Gid Rucker, who had a contract for running the centre line of a twenty-mile reserve, granted by the State to the Memphis & El Paso Railroad Company. This centre line was run on the thirty-second parallel. Colonel Patton went along to locate land certificates, of which he had a great many, and was anxious to see the country up on Hubbard's Creek in Young County. Hubbard's Creek is a tributary of the Clear Fork of the Brazos.

When we reached Weatherford, we found General Tarrant very sick, not expected to live, and he died a few days afterwards, which, of course, broke up the expedition for which I had enlisted. Colonel Patton then induced the railroad company's surveyors to make me a proposition and pay me two dollars per day to simply go along as company, they being anxious to have a sufficient crowd to overawe any attack Indians might contemplate.

After reaching the eightieth milepost, Colonel Patton had them run down ten miles to the southern boundary of the reserve, which was done, and a most magnificent country developed. It seems Colonel Patton had requested Mr. Rucker to get a sketch of that section of the country from the General Land Office at Austin, and gave him money to pay for such sketch, and when he asked for this sketch Rucker told him that they told him at the Land Office that the whole country was vacant; that there had been no surveys recorded in that section. Colonel Patton then struck out alone, riding around and, after a few hours' investigation, became disgusted, having found quite a number of rock piles and blazed trees, indicating that the country was not vacant and had been well surveyed over by others.

Colonel Patton then told me that he was going back home, his whole trip was a failure, that he wouldn't stay with a crowd that had deceived him so grossly. He planned to go back by himself, but I told him he should not do so—if he was going back, I would go with him. The whole party started back to the centre line, where we quit work. It was now late at night, the moon shining brightly, and we were about ten miles away from water, which we needed for our horses, before we could go into camp.

After riding over the high, rolling prairie on this beautiful night, some seven or eight miles, coming over a ridge we discovered a few camp fires in the bottom of Hubbard's Creek, which, of course, were thought to be Indian fires by our party. After consultation, we decided to make a charge on them and scatter them. For this purpose, we drew up in line, having altogether about twenty men, and moved on them cautiously. When within a few hundred yards of the bottoms, we were halted by a vidette picket, who from his brogue, proved to be an Irishman. This indicated to our party that the camp was of United States troops, and not Indians.

On arriving in camp, we found Major Van Dorn with a troop of cavalry, on his way from Fort Phantom Hill to Camp Cooper. The major, of course, was glad to have us camp with him. During the night, Mr. Rucker learned that Colonel Patton intended going straight for the settlements, without company except myself. Major Van Dorn sent for Colonel Patton and begged him to go to Camp Cooper with him, where he would no doubt find company from there to Fort Belknap, and then again from Fort Belknap to Weatherford, all of which were dangerous routes for one or two men to travel alone, on account of

Indians, but Colonel Patton wouldn't listen to such advice, claiming the Indians would never bother him and he would have no trouble in getting back to the settlements with me.

The next morning, we struck out in a straight line for the settlements, all alone, without taking any provisions, as the old man was mad with Rucker and would not ask for them, nor accept any when they were offered.

This ride to the settlements proved one of the most trying the old gentleman had ever been subjected to. It was, likewise, for me. We were without water for a day and a half, when we struck running water in the North Fork of Palo Pinto, and the second evening, late, we found a small cornfield, about three or four acres, with a board shed and a pile of ashes, indicating that this corn was made by some parties who had camped there and finally abandoned on account of Indian depredations. We then found a well-beaten path from this, leading in the direction we were traveling.

About six or eight miles from there we found a house, the home of a frontier settler, with a wife and two children. All were much rejoiced at seeing us and insisted on our staying a week, which, of course, we had to decline and left the next morning, on our way home to Waxahachie, which was reached in due time. This ended my frontier visitation, determined never to go outside of the settlements again, which I never did.

Soon after reaching Waxahachie, I was induced to accept a position with a Mr. Leander Cannon at Hempstead, Austin County, who was then conducting the largest mercantile business in that section of the State. After serving about a year in the dry goods and clothing department, I was induced by Mr. Cannon to take charge of his books, which I did for about six or eight months, when he decided to sell out and offered me his business, giving me all the time I needed to pay for it, if I would enter into co-partnership with one J. W. Fosgard, his former bookkeeper, who was an educated, college man, from Sweden. Fosgard was very egotistic and overbearing and I knew we could never get along, therefore, I declined Mr. Cannon's generous offer. He sold out to Fosgard alone.

A short time after, I had an invitation to join R. P. Faddis in the purchase of the business of Young & Bush, who, at the time, had a better stock of goods than Cannon and made us a very attractive offer, giving us all the time we wanted to pay them. This offer we accepted, constituting the firm of Faddis & Graber. Faddis was the bookkeeper of Young & Bush, and was a very popular man with the trade, which was largely composed of the leading and richest planters in that section of the Brazos country, and we soon built up a profitable business, though unfortunately, for us, our country soon became involved in sectional troubles, which prevented our restocking our reduced stock of goods and finally culminated in secession and war.

CHAPTER 4

My First Military Experiences

R. P. Faddis was a native of Minnesota, raised and educated there, and was about nine years my senior. He was more familiar with the true conditions in the North than I was.

When war was threatened, before Sumter was fired on, minute companies were organised in many of the important towns of Texas; forts and arsenals on our frontiers were taken possession of by the State, and the garrisons shipped North. A Captain Stoneman collected about five hundred picked troops at Fort Brown and refused to surrender. Colonel Ford, an old commander of Texas Rangers, collected about three hundred men and demanded the surrender of the fort, which was refused.

An old New Orleans boat, called the *General Rusk*, was dispatched to Galveston for reinforcements. On its arrival there, telegrams were sent to Houston, Hempstead and Navasota, which places had organised companies, for the companies to report by twelve o'clock that night for passage on the *General Rusk*, for Brazos, Santiago. Twelve o'clock that night found four companies aboard of this boat, coasting down the Gulf in a storm, without ballast, rolling and making us all seasick; nearly five hundred men lying on the lower deck.

We finally arrived at Brazos Santiago, where we found some other citizen soldiers in the old army barracks, including the Davis Guards, under command of Captain Odium and Dick Dowling.

After two weeks' camping on Brazos Santiago Island, Captain Stoneman surrendered Fort Brown, and, after disarmament, was sent North with his troops. We then returned home and resumed our civic avocations.

We next organised a cavalry company, commanded by a Captain Alston; Hannibal Boone, First Lieutenant, and W. R. Webb, Second Lieutenant. I was offered the second lieutenancy, but declined, saying

I would only serve in a private capacity. I was not a military man, and never expected to be. In about thirty days we were called to hasten to Indianola on horseback, where they had collected more troops, which had refused to surrender. We immediately started there and, when near Victoria, we got information that these troops had also surrendered, making it unnecessary to go any further, and we again returned home to resume our several pursuits. The company then disbanded and largely merged into a new company, organised for frontier protection against Indians. I remained at home, attending to my business with Faddis.

A couple of young Englishmen had come to Hempstead about a year before and started a foundry and machine shop, the second one in the State. They were both experts in their business and good men, receiving the financial support of the community, and soon owed our firm a large amount of money for advances to their hands and monies loaned.

In July, 1861, the same year, Colonel Frank Terry, a large sugar planter in Fort Bend County, and Thomas Lubbock of Houston, returned from the battle of Manassas, where they had served as volunteer aides on the staff of General Beauregard and through their intrepid daring and valuable services, were commissioned to raise a regiment of Texas Rangers.

Immediately upon their return, they issued a call for volunteers, to serve during the war, in Virginia; the men to furnish their own equipment. The response was prompt; in less than thirty days ten companies of over one thousand men were on their way to Houston to be mustered into the service of the Confederate States Army for the war. The personnel was of the highest order, some of the best families in South Texas were represented, many were college graduates, professional men, merchants, stockmen and planters; all anxious to serve in the ranks as privates; all young, in their teens and early twenties; rank was not considered and when tendered, refused; the main desire was to get into this regiment.

I told Faddis our firm must be represented, on which we agreed, and that I wanted to join, but he insisted that it was his time to go, that I had been out twice, and I finally had to yield him the right. He then subscribed to join. The day he was ordered to Houston to be mustered in, he declined to go and frankly told me that he only signed to keep me from going, and he did his best to persuade me not to go. He said that the South was deceived in the spirit and strength of the North;

that the North had every advantage of us—they had the army and navy, the arsenals, the treasury and large manufactories, as well as five men to our one; the whole world open to them, while we had nothing, our ports would be blockaded and we would be forced to depend upon our own limited resources, and, as to relying upon the justice of our cause, in the language of Abraham Lincoln, "might was right and would surely conquer."

I told him I could not agree with him and was satisfied the war would not last three months. As soon as we could drive these people back into their own territory, they would be willing to let us alone. "I am going to take your place, Faddis." I had about an hour to arrange for board for my young brother and sister and Faddis agreed to look after them and pay their board out of my interest in the business, which he pledged himself to continue for our mutual benefit.

When we parted I expected to return inside of three months; he expected he would never see me again, as I might be killed and, if I should return, that I would be a crippled, subjugated man.

Faddis continued the business as far as he was able and finally, to protect us, had to take over the foundry and machine shop, arranging with our Englishmen to run it for him. He then, to keep out of the army, turned his attention to repairing old guns, making swords and other arms, and finally, on the persuasion of his English friends, cast a nine-inch Armstrong gun, the only one ever successfully made in the Confederacy.

This drew the attention of the Confederate Government, who impressed our property, paid him eighty thousand dollars for it and gave him a permit to stay in Brownsville and run cotton into Mexico, returning with goods.

On my return from the army, after four years, I heard of him through a party who knew him in Brownsville. This party reported that Faddis had more gold than he knew what to do with, and I concluded that I was fixed, too, but I was unable to communicate with him, as we had no mails, and did not hear from him until after two years, when he returned to Hempstead broke. He had lost all in grain speculations in Chicago.

I next proceeded to Houston, where I was mustered in with the balance of the regiment, to serve in Virginia, during the war. While in camp at Houston, we organised our company, electing John A. Wharton of Brazoria County captain of the company; who, on his election, made up a speech, in which he said that he had no ambition to gratify more than to command Company B, that he expected to return captain of Company B and did not want any promotion. He was offered by the balance of the regiment in connection with our company, the office of major.

The balance of the commissioned officers of the company were Clarence McNeil, First Lieutenant and Theodore Bennett, Second Lieutenant; and the non-commissioned officers were distributed among the different sections from which the company was made up; nobody caring for an office of any kind, as a private was generally the equal of any officer in command. All went to do their patriotic duty and contribute their mite for the success of the cause.

We now started on horseback. After reaching Beaumont we returned our horses to Texas, having to take boat to Lake Charles, Louisiana, from whence we were forced to walk to New Iberia, carrying our saddles and other equipment on wagons, across the country. At New Iberia we again took boat for New Orleans; this was the only route open, as our ports had been blockaded for some time, both at Galveston and at the mouth of the Mississippi River.

During our stay in New Orleans for three or four days, we had a good rest and waited for the balance of the companies to catch up. Colonel Terry received a telegram from General Albert Sidney Johnston at Bowling Green, Kentucky, stating that he had been ordered to take command in Kentucky, and requested Colonel Terry to urge the men to come and serve under him and, by way of inducement, authorized him to say that we should be mounted on the best horses that Kentucky afforded and that we should always remain a separate and distinct command, never to be brigaded with any other troops as long as he lived.

General Johnston was well acquainted with the character of Texans, regarding them as fearless and enthusiastic people, proud of their Texas history; and, knowing the young men composing this regiment would endeavour to emulate the example of the heroes of the Alamo, Goliad and San Jacinto, on which point, he was not mistaken. General Johnston had been connected with the army, under General Houston, and had also engaged in sugar planting near the Kyle and Terry plantation in Fort Bend and Brazoria Counties, where a great friendship sprang up between him and Colonel Terry. Colonel Terry's influence with the men of the regiment was unlimited and he had no trouble in persuading the men to accept General Johnston's offer and serve with him in Kentucky.

While in New Orleans Colonel Terry made an official visit to General Twiggs, an officer of the old army, who had resigned, and tendered his services to the Confederacy, and who was then in command at New Orleans and the Southwestern territory. Colonel Terry, while there, asked information on the matter of obtaining cooking utensils and tents. When General Twiggs, who had served many years on the frontier of Texas, laughed him out of countenance, saying, "Who ever heard of a Texas Ranger carrying cooking utensils and sleeping in a tent?" It is needless to say that this matter was not mentioned again by Colonel Terry.

Our company arrived at Nashville, Tennessee, ahead of the balance of the regiment, where we were quartered in the Fair Grounds, there to await the arrival of the rest of the companies. I forgot to mention we started out with the name of the "Texas Rangers," with a reputation we had never earned, but were called on to sustain; how well we did it, we leave history to record our services during the four years we served the Army of the West. While I would not make any invidious distinction as between our regiment and others who served under Forrest, Wheeler and Wharton, I am proud to be able to say that opportunities were afforded us, largely by accident, that demonstrated our ability to meet every expectation of department commanders, as evidenced by the following expressions during the war:

"With a little more drill, you are the equals of the old guard of Napoleon."—General Albert Sidney Johnston. "I always feel safe when the Rangers are in front."—General Wm. J. Hardee. "There is no danger of a surprise when the Rangers are between us and the enemy."—General Braxton Bragg. "The Terry Rangers have done all that could be expected or required of soldiers."—Jefferson Davis.

While camped in the Fair Grounds, the citizens of Nashville, largely ladies, came rolling in, in carriages and buggies; all anxious to see the Texas Rangers, about whom history had written so much about their fearlessness and being great riders. Colonel Terry called on, not a few of our men to ride horses that were taken out of buggies and carriages, for the purpose of showing their horsemanship—the most popular feature being a deposit of gold coins on the ground, the rider to run at full speed, stooping down and picking them up. This extraordinary feat, in connection with their general appearance; being armed with shotguns, six-shooters and Bowie knives, seemed to sustain their idea of the Texas Rangers that fought at the Alamo, Goliad and San Jacinto and served under Jack Hayes, Ben McCollough and other Indian and Mexican fighters.

The regular army equipment for cavalry was the sabre, the carbine and six-shooter. This difference in equipment alone indicated that the Texas Ranger expected and would fight only in close quarters. After a pleasant stay at Nashville of nearly two weeks, we were ordered to go by rail to Bowling Green, Kentucky, where we found an army of infantry and artillery and three regiments of cavalry. Here we drew our horses by lot and it was my good fortune to draw first choice out of about a thousand horses tied to a picket rope. When all were ready to make their selection, I was directed to where these horses were tied and ordered to make my selection, which I was not permitted to do with any degree of deliberation.

Having about a thousand men waiting on me, all anxious to make their selection, a comrade, seeing I was confused and embarrassed, offered to exchange his thirty-second choice for my choice, paying me a liberal bonus. I was glad to accept it, mainly to get time to look around among the rest of the horses, believing I would stand a better chance to get a good mount. I had got short of money by that time, as we paid our own expenses, except transportation, and this comrade was glad to pay me for my first choice. We had no time to take out a horse and try his gaits, and it proved largely guesswork in the selection of the horses. The best gait for cavalry service is a long swinging walk and fox trot; unfortunately, my thirty-second choice proved a pacer.

After drawing our horses and preparing everything ready for active service, the regiment under Colonel Terry was ordered on a scout to Glasgow, Kentucky, where we were kindly received by its citizens and took up our quarters at the Fair Grounds. Here the regiment spent several days pleasantly, feasting on the good things brought in by the ladies of the town.

The second day Colonel Terry ordered Captain Ferrell, with his company and Company B, of which I was a member, to the little town of Edmonton, Kentucky, where it was reported a part of a regiment of Federal cavalry were quartered.

We started at night, which proved to be one of the coldest we had ever been out in, riding all night. When nearly daylight, we reached the suburbs of the town. I was riding a very spirited and nervous horse, which refused to be quieted, while riding in line. In order to keep him quiet, I had loosened the strap on his curb, which proved to be a mistake. Nearing the town, the order came down the line "Silence in ranks," and soon my horse got to prancing. I jerked him by the reins, throwing him on his haunches, when the hammer of my shotgun struck the horn of the saddle and fired off my gun, which raised the alarm in town.

Immediately the order was given "Form fours; Charge!" which excited my horse to such an extent that he broke ranks and flew up the line to the front. Carrying my shotgun in my right hand, I was unable to check him without the curb and he ran away with me, carrying me up into the town on the square, about three hundred yards in advance of my command, where I succeeded in checking him. For this I was reprimanded by Captain Ferrell, who would not receive my explanation that the horse ran away with me and claimed that I was too anxious to get there first.

Had the garrison not received information that we were moving on them for an attack and left during the night for Mumfordsville, instead of occupying the town as we expected, I no doubt would have been killed in this, our first charge.

Captain Ferrell had orders from General Johnston to try to capture a spy by the name of Burrell, who was making this town his headquarters and who always stopped at the hotel. As soon as we entered the square, we were ordered to surround the hotel, which was done promptly. Captain Ferrell then called the proprietor to the door, told him to tell the ladies in the house to rise and dress, as he would have to search the house for Burrell. The hotel man said that Burrell was there the evening before, but left for Mumfordsville and was certainly not in the house. Captain Ferrell told him that it made no difference, but to hurry up, he was going to search the house.

The house was partly a two-storey building, which had been added to the gable end of the one-storey building and the stair landing, built against the gable of a one-storey house, with a solid wood shutter covering, and opening into the attic of the one-storey building. The ladies took their own time about getting ready for our search, perhaps nearly an hour; some of them in the meantime coming to the door and repeating the proprietor's statement—that Burrell had left the evening before. When they announced ready, I being near the door, dashed in ahead of all the rest and up the stairs, when I discovered the wooden shutter, which I jerked open, peering into the dark attic.

Daylight had now fairly lit up the surroundings and I discovered, through the light of the cracked shingles, what I took to be a bundle of clothing at the far end, under the corner of the roof. I cocked both barrels of my gun and called out, "Come out; I see you; I'll shoot if you don't." He answered, "Don't shoot." If he had not answered I, no doubt, would have concluded, and perhaps others that followed me, too, that it was an old bundle of plunder. Proceeding downstairs with the prisoner, Burrell, who proved to be quite an intelligent and good-looking gentleman, I carried him into the parlour, where the ladies had congregated. They were all in tears, with some of our boys laughing at them and telling them they were story tellers.

Captain Ferrell, immediately on entering the square, detailed two men for each road leading into the town, to picket these roads about one-half mile from town. We built log fires on the square to keep us warm during the day until about three o'clock in the evening. A citizen then came in and, in an excited manner, told Captain Ferrell that a large cavalry force was moving in between us and Glasgow, with a view of cutting us off from our main command. The pickets arrested everybody coming into town and by three o'clock we had about fifteen or twenty prisoners, including some four or five Federal soldiers, who rode in on them, thinking the town was still occupied by Federal troops.

On receiving information about this large cavalry force moving on a road between us and Glasgow, Captain Ferrell gave the order to mount and form fours, selecting what prisoners (about seven or eight, including Burrell) and the soldiers, to take with us, and turning the balance of them loose. He then placed me in charge of the prisoners, with four others to help guard them. We then commenced our retreat to Glasgow.

When about three miles from town, another citizen dashed up to Captain Ferrell, who rode in advance of the column, and reported the same large cavalry force occupying our road some few miles ahead of us. Captain Ferrell, who, by the way, was an old frontiersman, Indian and Mexican fighter, dropped back and ordered me to tie Burrell's ankles together, under the horse's body and if we got into a fight and he attempted to escape, to not fail to kill him the first one. I don't think I ever did anything during the war that I hated as bad as I did to tie this man's ankles under the horse, but it was my orders from a man I knew would not permit any plea for its modification, and I had to obey.

After riding about eight or ten miles, in this way, feeling sorry for Burrell in his pitiful plight, I couldn't stand it any longer and told him if he would promise me, he would not make a break when the guns opened, that I would unloose the ropes and free his legs, for which he thanked me. Then I told him to be careful and carry out his promise, for if he did attempt a break, I would surely shoot him.

It seems that the report of these citizens proved only a ruse to induce us to liberate our prisoners, as we were never fired on or again heard of any Federal Cavalry in our front and safely reached Glasgow, where we still found the balance of the regiment in camp.

Colonel Terry sent our prisoners to Bowling Green, highly pleased with the capture of Burrell, for whom he had a special order by General Johnston. I am satisfied Burrell was sent to Richmond, Virginia, and was ultimately exchanged, as I saw the name of a Colonel Burrell, commanding Kentucky troops mentioned in a war history, published in the North some years after the war and on which point, I trust I was not mistaken, and that he is still, (1916), in the land of the living.

CHAPTER 5

Our First Engagement

We now took up our line of march for Ritters, a point on the Louisville & Nashville Pike, between Cave City and Woodsonville, with Hindman's Brigade of infantry and a battery of four pieces, camped at Cave City, a few miles in our rear, and established our permanent camp, for the purpose of scouting and picketing. This camp at Ritters in winter proved to be a very trying one to us, raised in Texas in a mild and genial climate. We had a great deal of snow and rain and the exposure on scouts and picket duty soon developed pneumonia, measles and other troubles, necessitating our patients to abandon camp life. They were sent to the hospital at Nashville, where the ladies of Nashville were daily awaiting trains.

They would not permit patients to be carried to the hospital but would take them to their private homes for personal care and treatment. They showed a partiality for the Texas Rangers, no doubt largely through sympathy, as we had left our distant, comfortable homes, burning all bridges behind us, to fight for them and their country. Our regiment soon dwindled down from a membership of one thousand to not more than about four hundred for duty; many of the sick were permanently rendered unable to return, while a great many died.

After serving nearly a month in the capacity of picket and scouts, General Hindman, anxious to bring on an engagement with the enemy, who were camped on Green River at Woodsonville and Mumfordsville, conceived the idea of moving his camp. Instead of avoiding a collision, as he had orders to do, he moved right toward the enemy's lines, ordering Colonel Terry, with our regiment, to move about a mile in his advance.

I was on picket duty, with part of a company, at Horse Cave, about three miles south of the main pike from Bowling Green to Louisville, when Captain Ferrell of the regiment, with part of his company, came by and took us along, moving towards Woodsonville on a dirt road running parallel with the pike on which were Hindman's Brigade of infantry; with the Louisville & Nashville Railroad running between the two. Just as we came in sight of Rowlett Station, a point on a high ridge this side of Woodsonville, we discovered the regiment, with Colonel Terry and General Hindman about fifty feet in advance, moving in the direction of Rowlett Station. Colonel Terry and General Hindman then discovered a Federal line of infantry lying down behind a rail fence in front of them.

Hindman's infantry were at least a mile behind, coming on, when they discovered the enemy. General Hindman ordered Colonel Terry to withdraw the regiment and let him bring up the artillery and infantry, and dislodge them from their position. In the meantime, Captain Ferrell, in command of the party I was with, had discovered the enemy in our front, which was just across a railroad cut, spanned by the pike bridge. Colonel Terry, in place of obeying the order of General Hindman to withdraw, answered, "General Hindman, this is no place for you; go back to your infantry," and called on Captain Walker, who was in the rear with the balance of the regiment, to come on, form into line and charge.

Simultaneously with his charge on the west side of the railroad, we, under Ferrell, charged the enemy in front of us, behind the rail fence. As soon as we moved forward, other Federals, behind trees and rocks, on small hills on both sides, opened fire on us. Their troops behind the fence held their fire until we got within fifty yards of them, then turned loose. In less time than it takes to tell it, we charged them, delivering our fire of double-barrelled shotguns, breaking down the fence and getting among them with our six-shooters.

In a few minutes we had run over them, although they numbered two to one, and to save themselves many of them "possumed" on us, and feigned being dead, and by that means saved their lives, though the main portion of them fled towards Woodsonville, where, down in the edge of the timber, they were met by heavy reinforcements. In this charge we lost a number of our best men, killed and wounded.

Among the killed was Colonel Terry, which proved an irreparable loss, as no doubt, considering his fearlessness and dash, as also his ability as a commander, he would have proven another Forrest, a Napoleon of cavalry. General Hindman brought up his infantry and artillery, a battery of four pieces, with which be opened on their fort at Mumfordsville, and also on their line of infantry in the woods about a half mile below us.

The fort responded, but largely overshot us and our battery. This proved our first baptism by fire. General Hindman was notified by a scout that the enemy was crossing Green River in very heavy force, near the Mammoth Cave, moving in our rear, which necessitated falling back to Cave City. We brought off the bodies of our dead and wounded, the remains of Colonel Terry being sent to Texas in charge of Captain Walker, who was wounded, and the balance of the wounded were sent to hospitals at Nashville.

The enemy we fought at this point proved to be the Thirty-Second Indiana Regiment, under Colonel Wilich, a German regiment, said to be the best drilled regiment in Rousseau's Army.

We next established our camp at Bell Station, a few miles in advance of Cave City, where we continued scouting and picketing for the army. Both armies now remained quiet for several months, collecting reinforcements for a final clash; the rigors of the winter affecting our army perhaps more than it did the Federal Army, as they were used to a colder climate. Our regiment was especially affected.

While encamped at Bell Station, I had a messmate by the name of McDonald, who was taken sick with pneumonia and was unwilling to be sent to the hospital at Nashville. He insisted on being taken to some good private family in the neighbourhood. I succeeded in finding the family of Isaac Smith, an old gentleman who had six sons in Breckenridge's Brigade of infantry, and living about three miles from our picket stand with his wife and two daughters.

These good people were willing to take McDonald and nurse him, our own surgeon attending him and myself assisting in nursing him, frequently spending the night there. The oldest daughter was also very sick, attended by a citizen doctor in the neighbourhood, who also took a deep interest in McDonald.

One day I received orders to report to the command; that Bowling Green was being evacuated. We were ordered to join the army as quickly as possible, Hindman's Brigade having already arrived at Bowling Green. This information proved to be bad news for McDonald, who was already convalescent, but still very weak. He begged and pleaded to be taken to Bowling Green and Nashville, saying he did not want to be captured. Old Mr. Smith, then perhaps fifty-five years old, decided to hitch up his wagon, as he had no buggy or hack, and haul McDonald to Bowling Green in a wagon, as he wanted to refugee and stay with his boys in the army; he feared to stay at home, surrounded by ugly Union neighbours.

We now put a mattress in the wagon, with plenty of bedclothing. We put McDonald in the wagon, well protected from the cold, and, after a sad parting with the family, proceeded to the Bowling Green pike, the old man driving the wagon and I following on my horse. We reached Bowling Green near night, just in time to witness the last cannon shot striking one of the main pillars of the railroad bridge, which was an iron extension, and saw it drop into the river. We crossed on a covered wooden pike bridge.

On our arrival in town, we inquired for a good place to leave McDonald for the night, which we were unable to find, but were recommended to go out about two miles to a Mr. Roe's, who had a large flouring mill. This we did, and found excellent quarters for McDonald and myself for the night; old Mr. Smith driving back to town and taking the Nashville pike to try to find Breckenridge's Brigade of Infantry, with which his sons were connected.

During the night we had a very heavy snow. Mr. Roe had his buggy hitched up and drove McDonald to the railroad station in town, myself following. Roe was unable to remain with us, as we were expecting the enemy to cross the river any moment and enter the town, hence left us by the side of the track and returned home.

After a while, Colonel Wharton, with about fifteen or twenty men out of our regiment, was ordered to destroy the depot and proceeded to fire it. A train with a few passenger coaches and an engine to pull it, was standing on the track on the outside, waiting for orders to move. A good many convalescent soldiers from the hospital, including my friend McDonald, squatted down by the roadside, waiting for the coaches to be opened. As soon as the fire started in the station, the enemy opened a battery on the place, using shells, which exploded all around us. The engineer got scared, uncoupled his engine and pulled out, leaving our train at the mercy of the artillery fire.

Looking around for some kind of a vehicle to take McDonald out of there, as he was too feeble to attempt to ride my horse, I rode up town and found a two-horse wagon, loaded with hams, flush to the top of the bed, which the driver had taken from our commissary building and was hauling home. I stopped and told him that I had a sick friend down at the station; that I wanted him to go down there and haul my friend away. He said he wouldn't go down there for anything in the world. I pulled out my gun and told him to go; and he went.

Arriving at the place, we cut open some infantry baggage that had blankets tied to the knapsacks and put about a half dozen blankets on top of the hams, lifting McDonald and laying him on top, covering him with more blankets. In the meantime, the station was about consumed and the artillery had ceased firing. After getting up on the square and finding our troops had all left, I told this man that he would have to drive on the Nashville Pike until we could catch up with our command, which he did most reluctantly and only under the persuasion of my gun.

About a mile and a half below town we found our regiment drawn up in line of battle. I sent for our surgeon, who examined McDonald and said to the driver, "You will have to drive on down the road until we catch up with my ambulances." The driver said that he wouldn't go any further; said I, "If you don't, we will have to hold on to this team until we unload; I am going to save these hams for our regiment." They were meat that belonged to our commissary. He said that he wouldn't go any further, that we could take his team and wagon and go to —— with it. The fellow was evidently afraid that we would force him into the army; he thereby lost his team and wagon, which we had no idea of taking, and he could have saved them by continuing with us.

Our army now took up its long line of retreat for Nashville; our regiment covering the rear without any engagements, or the firing of a single gun. On reaching Nashville, crossing the Cumberland River on the suspension bridge about midnight, we got information that Fort Donaldson had surrendered, which made it necessary for our troops to leave Nashville in great haste, which they did; protected in the rear by our regiment. The army continued to Shelbyville, while we were ordered to Fort Donaldson, to cover the escape of many men of the Fort Donaldson army, whom we met scattered all along the road. The weather was most severe.

The winding up of this winter I had a sad experience. About midnight, the second night out, we pulled into a cedar grove by the side of the road, the ground of which was soft and muddy. We tied our horses to the trees around us, and arranged as best we could, to get a little rest and sleep, putting down our oilcloths next to the mud, then our saddle blankets and each having a good blanket and overcoat for cover. My messmate, John Cochran, laid by me, and we soon dropped into a sound sleep, being tired and worn out, and without having had a bite of anything to eat that day and no forage for our horses.

Waking up some time during the night, I felt a curious feeling about my head. Putting my hand to my head I found my hair clotted with blood. I woke up Cochran, my companion, and told him that someone had struck me over the head with a gun, which proved a mistake. Our horses being tied in the cold, without any feed, had pulled the length of the rope and commenced pawing, when one of them pawed me on the head with a sharp shoe, which caused a deep cut of my scalp. We then decided we would move through the woods until we could strike some house, and soon struck a country road. After traveling perhaps, a mile, we discovered a little log house by the side of the road and through the cracks of the batten door, we saw a bright fire burning on the inside.

We knocked on the door, which was answered by a very old gentleman, whom we told that we wanted to come in and dress my wounds. He asked who we were. We told him we were Confederate soldiers, camped near there and the cause of my hurt. He received us very kindly, invited us into his main room, which contained a double bed where his old wife was sleeping. As soon as she saw my bloody condition, she jumped up, dressed, heated some water and with nice clean towels, commenced bathing my head and dressing my wounds. She then went to work, put some clean sheets and pillowcases on the bed and insisted on our lying down and taking a good nap, while she prepared breakfast for us.

While we told them that it was dangerous for us to sleep in a bed, as we were not used to it and it would give us a cold, we were compelled to take the bed on their refusal to listen to anything else.

When we awoke next morning after daylight, the old lady had a splendid breakfast of fried chicken prepared for us, fine biscuit and good Confederate coffee—made of rye and parched sweet potatoes; everything on the table was neat and spotlessly clean and I do not think we ever enjoyed a meal during the whole war better than we did this.

When we prepared to leave, we asked the old gentleman for our bill; he seemed to feel hurt, and said, "The idea of charging a Confederate soldier for anything he had!" This was out of the question with him; all he asked, if we ever happened in that neighbourhood, in twenty miles of him, to be sure to make him another visit, for he hoped to meet us again. Thanking them for their exceeding kindness, we then walked back to camp, where we found many of our comrades still in deep sleep, with no forage for the horses.

In the course of a few hours the bugle called to saddle up, and we resumed our march to Shelbyville, and caught up with a good many of our retreating infantry. Here we spent two days and had our first taste of an attempt at discipline by Major Harrison, who was then in command; Colonel Wharton being sick somewhere on the line of our retreat.

It seems that Major Harrison met a couple of our men in town without permission and ordered them to return to camp immediately, which they refused to do. When he returned to camp, he ordered these men arrested by the camp guards and placed on the pike, marking time. A Mr. Sam Ash of Company B (now still living in Houston—1916) went to these men and led them back to camp, telling them that no such disgraceful punishment should be inaugurated in the regiment. The infantry were passing frequently and we considered it a disgrace to the Texas Ranger to submit to such punishment. Major Harrison finally yielded and passed the incident, but to a great extent, lost the respect of the command.

The army now continued its retreat through Shelbyville, Huntsville, Decatur to Corinth, Mississippi, without incidents of note, except the burning of bridges behind us. We also destroyed the magnificent bridge across the Tennessee River at Decatur.

It may be not out of place, before going further, and to give the reader a better idea of the character of the Texas Rangers, to mention an expression of Hardee's. While passing through Huntsville, Alabama, some ladies, in company with General Hardee, were standing on the sidewalk, watching us pass, cheering and waving their handkerchiefs at us, when one of them remarked to General Hardee, saying "General, the Rangers are the best soldiers you have; are they not?" He told them no, he was not stuck on them, saying that they would not submit to any discipline or drill; but he was willing to say that in a battle, or when called on to meet a forlorn hope, the Rangers always responded. General Hardee was one of the strictest disciplinarians in our army and wrote the military tactics that were used by both sides.

We soon arrived at Corinth, where we were assigned a camp ground about two miles from the place, near a spring and we here witnessed new additions to the main army. Occasionally scouting parties from the regiment were sent out in different directions towards the Tennessee River, which duties were always performed to the satisfaction of the commanding officers.

CHAPTER 6

An Accidental Injury—Shiloh

Our regiment, one night, was ordered out to report at daylight to some point up the Tennessee River, the night being very dark—one of the darkest nights we ever travelled in—and branches and small streams very boggy. Colonel Wharton, at the head of the regiment, was riding a very fast walking horse. We struck many places in these branches where it was only possible for one horse to cross at a time, and Wharton, as soon as across, would strike out in his fast walk, leaving the rest of his command to come on as best they could. This threw the rear end of the regiment considerably behind and we had to lope at full speed to catch up with our file leaders after crossing these bad places.

In one of these races to catch up, my horse stumbled and fell, pitching me over his head, with my left arm extended, and I sustained a dislocation of my left arm. Considerably stunned by the fall, and suffering great pain from this dislocation, a comrade was sent back with me to Corinth, where I had a surgeon to replace my arm, with instructions to carry it in a sling until it got well. Our regiment returned the next night without having discovered any of the enemy and was then ordered to prepare three days' rations, as was also the rest of the army.

In the meantime, the enemy had landed a large force, under General Grant, at Pittsburg Landing. Our regiment was ordered out with no one knowing where they were going, until they moved in the direction of Pittsburg Landing. They were immediately followed by the whole army, and on the fifth of April, they engaged the enemy and fought the Battle of Shiloh; our regiment was moved about on the field from right to left.

As the dense woods did not afford an opportunity for mounted cavalry, they were unable to do much fighting, except, about ten o'clock the first day, they were dismounted and ordered to charge through a thicket at Owl Creek, which they had to do single file, and were shot down by a large infantry force as fast as the men made their appearance in the open. Soon realising that it was impossible to dislodge the enemy from their position with this handful of men, they were immediately ordered to fall back. This proved the extent of their active engagement, but they served as a corps of observation on both flanks until Tuesday evening.

After the second day's engagement, Grant's army having been reinforced on Sunday night by the whole of Buell's army (as large as our army originally), our army was compelled to retreat, which was done in a heavy rain, rendering the road to Corinth almost impassable for artillery and ambulances. Realising that our army was in great danger of being annihilated, General Beauregard sent for General Breckenridge, who was on the field with his Kentucky Brigade, ordering him to cover the retreat and try to save the army. General Breckenridge responded that he would protect the army if it cost the last man he had.

This occurred on Tuesday after the battle. Our regiment, what was left of it, and Colonel Forrest, with about fifty men, were ordered to support General Breckenridge. Breckenridge's Brigade was drawn up near the old battlefield. In their front, about a quarter of a mile away, two lines of battle of the enemy were seen to form with a brigade of cavalry, mounted, in their front, covering their movement, Breckenridge's Brigade was then moved to the rear a short distance, to a position where they were hid by lying down. Our regiment, in command of Major Harrison, and Colonel Forrest with his fifty men, soon formed in front of Breckenridge, preparing to charge the enemy.

As heretofore stated, Colonel Harrison, up to this time, on our retreat, did not have the confidence or respect of the men on account of a blunder he committed at the small town of Jimtown in Kentucky, which caused him to be dubbed the "Jimtown Major;" then again, on account of his ordering some boys to mark time on the Shelbyville Pike, was dubbed the "Mark-time Major."

A large number of the regiment had been congregated on the pike, at the point from which Ash had led the prisoners, and when Major Harrison reached the spot, after hearing what had been done, he was met by angry glances on every hand for presuming to treat two gentlemen so inconsiderately. Disregarding their menacing looks Major Harrison called out, "Is there an officer of my regiment present who will execute my orders?" when Pat Christian (then a lieutenant in Company K) stepped to the front, with a salute, and said, "Major, I will." Then Major Harris ordered him to get a file of men and bring the two prisoners back to complete their sentence, and to inform him instantly if interfered with.

It was here that Christian, afterwards captain of his company, and then major and later lieutenant colonel, first attracted the attention of the regiment, afterwards so devoted to him, for his gallantry and his good traits of character, and here that the regiment had its first lesson in military discipline, under an officer temporarily unpopular, who afterwards won their high respect.

For the first time since our retreat, he was in command of the regiment, Colonel Wharton having been wounded, and very soon the enemy commenced a scattering fire, while the regiment was forming, occasionally striking a man or a horse. The men became restive and wanted to charge, but Major Harrison rode down the line saying to them, "Be quiet, boys, 'till your 'Jimtown Mark-time Major' gets ready for you," in a very cool and deliberate manner, and finally in ordering the charge said, "Now, follow your Jimtown Major." He led them on to the cavalry, which, in an impetuous charge, they drove right in among their infantry, and, on account of their being confused in the mix-up, the enemy fell back a short distance, and the regiment brought out a number of prisoners. While this charge proved a success, we lost a number of valuable men in killed and wounded. This was the last fighting on the battlefield of Shiloh.

I have not entered into any details of the battle, as history gives such a complete account, written by both sides, that its details are well known, and as the purpose of this writing is to recount my own personal history and because I was not actively engaged with the regiment during the battle, I find it unnecessary to give the details.

As heretofore stated, I was suffering with a dislocated arm, the effects of my fall, and did not move out with the regiment when they started on this trip; but on Sunday morning, hearing the guns of Shiloh in our camp at Corinth, I mounted my horse and struck out for the field. Unable to learn where our regiment was posted, I remained with an infantry command, offering my services to the extent of what I was able to do, but I was not called on during the several days' battle, except to carry a few orders from place to place.

I reached Corinth, Mississippi, where our camp was located, on Thursday, aiding and assisting about a half dozen wounded men of the Second Texas, allowing them to ride my horse when they were able. These men were completely exhausted, as they did nothing else but stand in line all day Sunday 'till four o'clock in the evening, firing their guns, and again on Monday, opposed to Buell's fresh army, which proved the hardest fighting during the battle. "All honour to the Second Texas."

Recalling General Albert Sidney Johnston's promise in a telegram to Colonel Terry at New Orleans, that we should never be brigaded as long as he lived; his death at four o'clock on Sunday evening cancelled this promise. General Beauregard then took command of the army.

A few days after the Battle of Shiloh, having recuperated our horses, as well as the men, Colonel Wharton was ordered to report to a General Adams, who had a Kentucky regiment, and General Adams, with this regiment and the Eighth Texas, was ordered on a raid into Middle Tennessee, with instructions to capture and destroy everything of the enemy he could meet up with and was able to handle.

We crossed the Tennessee River at Lamb's Ferry, the ferry boat being propelled by a paddle wheel, driven by a horse-tread power. Here we left our wagons and all our extra luggage, as well as cooking utensils, awaiting our return, but the Federal cavalry a few days after, crossed the river, captured our entire storage and we never saw cooking utensils or tents afterwards, and were thereby reduced to the condition of the real Texas Ranger as on the frontiers of Texas.

Immediately after crossing the Tennessee River, we struck a considerable infantry force, with artillery. General Adams, in place of attacking them, moved us around them in great haste, thereby avoiding a collision and getting away, leaving them shelling the woods for several hours, while we were making distance. We next struck the Pulaski Pike, finding about two hundred wagons, loaded with two bales of cotton on each and a guard of two men with each wagon. General Adams drew us out of sight and hearing and would not allow Colonel Wharton to capture this train, which could have been done without the loss of a man. But no doubt as General Adams suggested, in doing this we would stir up a hornet's nest and get the whole Yankee Army in pursuit of us. Wharton was powerless to do anything, held back by General Adams.

When near the town of Fayetteville, Lincoln County, Tennessee, a citizen sent out by the garrison of the town, numbering about five hundred cavalry, told us to come in; they wanted to surrender; they were tired of the war and wanted to go home. General Adams conceived this to be a trick of theirs and declined their invitation, moving us around the town in the night by a path in the woods, guided by a citizen, thereby losing a splendid opportunity of capturing this garrison.

The second night after this, we camped at the town of Salem, about ten miles south of Winchester, and at Winchester the next night, where information reached us that about two thousand infantry, moving in wagons, and a battery of artillery, had been in pursuit of us and had been camped at Salem the next night after we were there, and was expected to follow us to Winchester. The road from Salem to Winchester was a straight lane with high rail fences on each side. At a point about equal distance between Salem and Winchester, was a large woods lot, running up to the lane, as noticed by Colonel Wharton. He suggested to General Adams that we go back, remain concealed in these woods, close to the road and when the enemy came along, riding in wagons, that we charge them and force them to surrender. This seemed good to General Adams and an opportunity he was willing to risk.

We moved around to this woods lot, remaining there until about daylight, when information reached us that the Yankees had already passed and were then occupying Winchester. We immediately returned to Winchester and found them drawn up behind a railroad cut, with a commanding position for their battery. They opened this battery on us, using shells, as soon as we came in sight. Then Colonel Wharton, riding 'round hunting a place to charge them, decided this could not be done without the loss of a great many men and a charge might result in failure; we, therefore, moved around Winchester, passing through Decherd's depot and pitched camp in Hawkins Cove, perhaps twenty miles distant from Winchester.

The second day in camp in Hawkins Cove, a citizen came and reported to General Adams that the Yankees were at his house with a couple of wagons, loading his meat, and begging him to send a small force to drive them away. A company of the Kentucky regiment and Company B of the Rangers, which was the company to which I belonged, were detailed for this service. When we reached this man's house they had already left with his meat and were driving fast, back into town. We struck a lope, endeavouring to catch up with them, but failed. The Kentucky captain, being the ranking officer, was in command; riding at the head of the column and running over the pickets on a bridge near town, he carried us right into the town, up to the courthouse square.

This charge proved a complete surprise. We found the enemy scattered all over town and a large party of them in the courthouse, being the only parties we felt free to fire on, as there were no women and children about. We heard the artillery bugle and concluded to get out of there, which we did very promptly and in such good time the artillery never had a chance to fire a shot at us.

Some years after the war, a Winchester paper was sent me, giving an account of fifty Texas Rangers attacking two thousand infantry and artillery in their town, with a loss of only one man, who had his arm broken by an explosive ball.

We returned to our camp in Hawkins Cove. On that night General Adams came down to Colonel Wharton's camp fire and announced that he would start across the mountain, for Chattanooga, the next morning, and secure artillery, that he could not undertake to remain in Middle Tennessee without it. Colonel Wharton had become exasperated at General Adams' conduct the entire trip and told him to take his Kentucky regiment and go to Halifax with it, if he wanted to—that he intended remaining in Middle Tennessee and doing what he could to carry out the original order of General Beauregard.

After a few days' rest in Hawkins Cove, where the enemy did not attempt to molest us, a messenger reached us, with orders from General Kirby Smith at Knoxville, to report to Colonel Forrest at McMinnville, which Wharton did, as soon as we reached there. After a day's rest Colonel Forrest (who had the First and Second Georgia and a Tennessee battalion, all cavalry) in conjunction with our regiment, started, late evening, for Murfreesboro, which was then the headquarters for Tennessee, of the Federal Army, with Major General Crittenden in command. Murfreesboro's garrison consisted of the Ninth Michigan Infantry, a part of a regiment of cavalry located in their camp to the right of town, the Third Minnesota and a battery of artillery on the northwest of town. They had about one hundred prisoners in the courthouse, upstairs, with a strong guard downstairs.

Greatly outnumbering us, our success depended on a surprise. When near their advance picket on the pike, Colonel Forrest asked for some Rangers to capture this picket without the fire of a gun, which was done in very short order. He then had a consultation with the commanders of the different regiments, and it was decided that Colonel Wharton, with our regiment in advance and the Second Georgia next in column, attack the Ninth Michigan and the cavalry camp on the right. To reach them he had to turn into a side street about two or three blocks from the courthouse, where Colonel Forrest halted, awaiting for his part of the command to come up to take them through town to the Third Minnesota and battery camp, ignoring the courthouse as much as possible.

After our regiment had passed into the side street, following Wharton, Forrest discovered that the Georgians and Tennesseans had failed to come up and immediately decided to take what was left of our regiment and lead them to the attack on the Third Minnesota and the battery north of the town. This gave him a force of only about fifty or sixty men. By this action he cut our company about half in two, which threw me into the first set of fours at the head of the column, with Forrest riding by my side, on my right. Nearing the courthouse, a couple of Federals up in the second story door, dropped down on their knees and raised their guns to fire, but Forrest and I fired ahead of them. When Forrest fired his pistol, his horse dodged almost in front of me, just as I fired, very nearly shooting Forrest through the head. I have often thought what a misfortune this would have been, as I came very near killing a man who turned out to be the Napoleon of cavalry.

In the upper storey of the courthouse were confined about one hundred prisoners, some of Morgan's men, but mostly civilians, and the courthouse was guarded by about one hundred men, who fired on us through doors and windows. We moved around the courthouse, some to the left and some to the right, as the courthouse was standing in the middle of the square immediately fronting the centre of the street we came up on. About the time we reached the courthouse, Wharton, with the balance of the regiment, had charged the Michigan camp, many of whom were asleep in their tents, and the noise of the battle reached us about the time we fired into the courthouse.

As stated, Forrest with about fifty men in columns of fours, except a few that were left on the courthouse square, shot down by courthouse guards, moved on to the north of town, where he lost his bearings and was compelled to get a citizen out of his house, to pilot us to the Minnesota camp and battery. When we reached there we found the men up and dressed and the battery opened on us, throwing a few shells among us, which scattered us and caused the disappearance of Forrest. We were in an old field, and on leaving, I was called by a Kentuckian, who had volunteered to go with us into the fight and had his arm shattered by a piece of shell, begging me to not go off and leave him. He was hardly able to sit on his horse.

I rode up, taking his horse by the bridle, leading him up to a fence in the edge of the timber, with a scattering fire directed on us. I dismounted and let down the fence, leading his horse over it. While doing this, noticing I was trying to get off a wounded comrade, they gallantly ceased firing on us. I now led my wounded friend through the woods, until we reached a house, about a mile from there, when the gentleman at the house hitched up his buggy, and, placing my friend in the buggy, he drove around the town, with myself following, leading the wounded man's horse, until we reached a point about a mile below town, where we found the Rangers collecting what was left of them, out of the Michigan camp fight and also the few men who were with Forrest in the old sedge field when fired on by the Third Minnesota and battery.

The regiment formed and gathered at this point about a mile below town, awaiting further orders, with Wharton, wounded again, directing the formation, when a messenger came from Forrest, who was then up town with his Georgia and Tennessee battalions, ordering us back up into town. After joining the Georgians and having displayed about three times as many men as he really had, by moving them around a block, in sight of the enemy (who had gathered and formed, in a splendid position, supported by their battery) Forrest went in, under a flag of truce and demanded their immediate surrender, telling them that he had five men to their one and was determined to take them; that if he had to make another charge on them, on their own heads be the responsibility; that the little fight had, was only with his advance guard, that he had five hundred Texas Rangers he couldn't control in a fight, and the responsibility was with them.

After deliberating on the matter for a few minutes, they raised the white flag and surrendered. The result of this surrender was a parole of eighteen hundred and sixteen privates at McMinnville, the further capture of forty-seven commissioned officers, including Major General Crittenden, with Colonel Duffield of the Ninth Michigan badly wounded in the Michigan camp; thirty-eight wagonloads of valuable stores; a magnificent battery of four pieces of artillery and several million dollars' worth of commissary and quartermaster's stores, destroyed by fire.

I would also mention the release of two citizen prisoners confined in the jail, who were condemned to be hung the next day, as spies. The wife of one of these men, with many other ladies, witnessed our passing through Woodbury. Learning that we were going to Murfreesboro, she wrung her hands and begged and plead with us to bring her husband back. Some of the men who heard her, answered that we would surely bring her husband back, which we did the next day.

A dastardly act I will recount here—of one of the Federal guards stationed at the jail. When he found we were about to capture the town, he set fire to the jail, which no doubt would have burned the poor prisoners, but the fire was promptly extinguished by several of our men, who succeeded in capturing the fellow who started the fire and in taking him before General Forrest. Forrest pulled out his pistol and killed him on the spot, a well-deserved punishment.

On marching our prisoners to McMinnville, the commissioned officers who had been captured, were given the privilege of the pike, they taking a parole not to attempt to make their escape. When this high privilege was offered Major General Crittenden, he refused the courtesy, telling Forrest that he could not accept, as his government didn't recognise him as a regular Confederate soldier and only knew him as a guerilla.

Forrest told him that it made no difference with him and he furnished him with a guard of two Texas Rangers, dressed in buckskin, wearing Mexican *sombreros*. These men were somewhat wild in appearance, no doubt, to General Crittenden. After riding along with his guards for an hour or two, one man on each side of him, occasionally nodding at each other, the general concluded that perhaps they were planning to kill him, and had them take him up to Colonel Forrest, when he asked Forrest to parole him and give him the privilege of the pike, like the rest; saying he verily believed that these men would kill him.

After paroling the privates at McMinnville, permitting them all to retain their private property, which included a magnificent set of silver band instruments, Forrest told the officers that they would have to be taken to Knoxville to General Smith's headquarters and directed Colonel Wharton, who was wounded, with Company B, his old company, to take charge of them, the battery and thirty-eight wagonloads of valuable stores. He requested Colonel Wharton, when he got safely up on top of the mountain, by way of Sparta, to send back a messenger, reporting that fact, and I was sent back with this message to Colonel Forrest.

Reaching Sparta about daylight, I could not find anyone who could tell me the whereabouts of Forrest's command, and struck out, back in the direction of McMinnville, when incidentally I met a citizen, who reported that they were camped at a certain place in the woods between Sparta and Lebanon, which I succeeded in finding about noon. Reporting to Colonel Forrest that Wharton had got up on top of the mountain safely with his prisoners, artillery and wagons, I told him that I didn't feel like going back to catch up with my company, going to Knoxville, lying around in camp and that I wanted to remain with the regiment and asked his permission to do so. He kindly consented and told me to report to the regiment and stay with them.

CHAPTER 7

I am Wounded and Captured

The Rangers now felt that they were commanded by somebody who meant business and that there was plenty of work in store for them. After remaining in this camp another day, we started for Lebanon, in the night, where it was understood a considerable cavalry force of the enemy were camped. Reaching the town about daylight, we formed fours and charged in, being greeted by ladies, through their windows, waving handkerchiefs and cheering, with no Federal cavalry in town, they having moved to Murfreesboro during the night, in great haste, learning we were on the way.

Here at Lebanon, we found, as in nearly every town we had been in in Middle Tennessee, a strong Southern people, who, while we were camped there for two days, gave us a great feast of everything that was good, which was heartily enjoyed by the whole command. Forrest, on being interviewed as to what was next on docket, said that he was going to take Nashville, though strongly fortified, and garrisoned by an infantry force of not less than ten thousand men under General Nelson.

On the early morning of the third day, we started out on the main Nashville pike, moving along at an ordinary gait, occasionally meeting citizens, out from Nashville, saying there was great excitement among the Yankees, and they were digging additional pits and preparing a strong defence. When we reached within twelve miles of Nashville, we struck a road leading through the cedars, to LaVergne, a station between Murfreesboro and Nashville. Before reaching La Vergne, General Forrest detailed about two hundred Rangers, under Captain Ferrell, to meet and capture a train from Murfreesboro, at La Vergne, which they succeeded in doing, capturing a large number of commissioned officers, who were on their way home on furlough, and capturing also the mails and express freight. Among these prisoners I will mention the kind-hearted and excellent business man among us today, a Mr. Fordyce, of the Pierce-Fordyce Oil Association, one of the largest oil concerns doing business in Texas.

Forrest, with the balance of the command, went to work tearing up the railroad between La Vergne and Nashville, burning trestles and bridges and tearing up the track. We then again retired to McMinnville. Before leaving in front of Nashville, Colonel Forrest asked for a detail of about fifteen or twenty men, who were selected from the Rangers and joined by four or five of Morgan's men, who happened to be along. I was one of this party, and we were all under the command of a Captain Gordon, who proved to be a reckless fellow, unfit to command such a party successfully.

We crossed Cumberland River near Lebanon, in a bend called Little Dixie. Little Dixie was settled with some of the strongest Southern and most liberal people in the State, and regarded as a safe haven for the wounded Confederate soldiers, whom these good people would nourish and care for, to the extent of any character of risk. While crossing there, we promised the ladies if any of us were wounded, we would not fail to make our way back, so they could take care of us until able to join our command. Our orders from Colonel Forrest for the expedition were to collect information on the disposition of the Federal forces, preparatory to a general raid of our cavalry.

After crossing the river, we moved up towards the Louisville & Nashville Railroad, circulating through that section quite extensively, gathering information, and, on our return, we decided to capture a railroad train, with the mails from the army, which always proved very valuable, as the soldiers were always writing home on the movements of their army, which proved most valuable information for our headquarters.

In accordance with our plans, we struck the Louisville & Nashville Railroad between Woodburn and Franklin, at a point about equidistant between the two places; watering our horses at a branch within hearing of a Union man's house, who was awakened and decided that we had about three hundred men, supposing us to be of Morgan's command. Riding around in the branch, as we did, led him to the conclusion that we had about three hundred men. We struck the railroad about daylight, when we removed a few spikes, spreading the track, for the purpose of stopping the train and, being in thick woods out of hearing, with no settlement near, we all laid down for a short nap. The mail train from the army was due at this point about eleven-thirty; another mail train from above was due about twelve o'clock, with numerous freight trains, carrying troops and war material, due throughout the day, also trains returning with wounded and discharged soldiers.

We heard the mail train whistle, from below, when it reached Franklin, and nothing of any other train, waiting until between three and four o'clock in the evening. I became satisfied that we were going to be caught in a trap and so told Gordon, insisting on leaving there, but Gordon refused to listen; he had just about sense enough to lose what he had. Finally, between three and four o'clock we heard the train, and immediately took position by the side of the track, having nineteen men for the fight, two of the men remaining with our horses, in the rear.

All that could get trees for shelter, within twenty feet of the track took position behind trees, while eight of us, unable to find trees convenient, laid down flat on the ground. Very soon the train came up, turning a bend in the road about a half mile below us. The engineer, to fool us, put on more steam, making us think that they were entirely ignorant of our presence, and stopped right at the place we had shifted the rail. Soon they were right on us and began firing with about three hundred muskets, killing seven of our party, who were lying on the ground and jumped up, and badly wounding me, but the balance of our party, eleven strong, behind trees, with six-shooters, drove those fellows off the train on to the other side of the track.

There the commanding officer, Lieutenant-Colonel (Blank), succeeded in forming about a hundred men in line in about twenty minutes, so he stated to me at the hospital at Bowling Green, where he made me a visit about a week after, furthermore stating that, he believed if we had had about twenty-five more men we would have gotten his train. It seems that this was the first time these people were ever under fire and when under the impression that we had three hundred of Morgan's men, they were no doubt demoralized at the noise of their own guns.

The citizen at whose house we watered our horses at the branch had spied out our exact location on the railroad, a desolate place, where Morgan's cavalry had captured a train before. He went to Franklin, where he met the train from the army, reported three hundred of Morgan's men, when they ran the train back to Gallatin, Tennessee, unloaded the mails and express freight and took this regiment aboard, also notifying other trains that we were on the road, which caused their delay.

While the Federals were jumping off the train on the other side, we fell back to our horses, mounting, leaving the horses belonging to the men that were killed; not knowing at the time just who was left behind. I was able to run back and mount my own horse, with the assistance of a comrade. We hurried out of there, taking the road by which we had come, by this Union man's house, where I stopped to get me a drink of water. I had just been relieved of my pistol belt, and had grown very weak and faint from the loss of blood, which had collected in my boots, and was about to fall from the horse when I was caught by a comrade.

Someone called out, "Here they come!" This aroused me. I made them hand me my pistols. We drew up in line in the lane and saw a party in the edge of the timber. Drawing our pistols we waved them at them and urged them to come on, which they didn't do. We soon discovered that they were only parties from the train who had found our dead men's horses and were afraid to come forward.

We now continued our march on this country road about eight or ten miles. I became too weak to travel and, satisfied that being encumbered with me would cause them all to get captured or killed, I insisted on their leaving me, believing that I was done for, anyway.

We soon reached a Mr. White's (a humble log house) who had two sons in Breckenridge's Brigade, and had with him his wife and daughter. He was an ardent Southern man and promised my comrades that I should have every attention, if left with them. Before leaving, I begged them to let me keep my pistols, which they failed to do, thinking it was best to leave me disarmed, as it proved to be.

My comrades then proceeded in haste to get out of that neighbourhood and made for the Cumberland River, our main army then being near Chattanooga. In about an hour a citizen doctor came to see me and filled my wound full of cotton, in order to check the bleeding, saying that this was all that he could do for me; he had to hurry back home, lest he was caught giving me his attention, believing his neighbours would hang him and burn his family out of house and home, as this section of the country was inhabited by a desperate, vindictive Union people.

During the evening a young man called and claimed to be a good Rebel, saying that he had an uncle, who was also a good friend of the South, living up in the mountains, and if he could succeed in taking me there, that I would be perfectly safe. He arranged with me to come that night, with a hack, and take me to his uncle's, which he failed to do.

Mr. White's house was a double log house, a room at each end, with about a ten-foot hall in between, but no porch in front, a step at each room, leading out into the yard and heavy batten doors covering the door opening. Old Mr. White occupied a bed in the room with me, while his wife and daughter occupied a room at the other end. They had improvised a cot for me, in the middle of the room, so they could get around it. They used wick and tallow lamps for lights, which created a bad smell in the room and annoyed me a great deal, as I had considerable fever.

Sometime after midnight I begged the old man to extinguish his lamp, and very soon thereafter, I heard voices in the yard and immediately a pounding on the door with the butt end of a gun. The reader can imagine my feelings; I was satisfied they were Tories and my time had come. I would then have given a kingdom for my pistols and, no doubt, would have opened on them as they came in. They called and demanded of the old man to open the door quick. He told them to wait until he could strike a light, which he did. I was in position, from where I lay, to notice them coming in and to my great relief, saw a lieutenant and ten men in uniform, passing around me.

Here was one time I was glad to see the Federal uniform. When they got up to my bunk, I feigned sleep and listened to what they had to say. The lieutenant asked the old man if I was badly hurt. He told him to turn down the sheet and he could judge for himself, when the lieutenant expressed his surprise and said, "I'm afraid we won't be able to move him." Now I concluded it was my time to say something. I opened my eyes and feigned bewilderment, looking up at them. The lieutenant asked, "Are you hurt much, sir?" I told them no, I did not think I was, and couldn't understand why I had been left there.

The lieutenant asked if I thought that I could stand to be hauled to Woodburn, a station about five miles from there and the first station this side of Bowling Green. I told him I was satisfied I could stand it all right. He then ordered the old gentleman to direct him where he could find feed for his horses, also to have breakfast for his men by daylight and have his own team and wagon ready to haul me to their camp at a church about four miles from there, where the balance of his regiment, the Eleventh Kentucky Mounted Infantry, were camped.

About daylight they started for their camp, with me lying on a mattress in the wagon. We reached camp in due time. The lieutenant-colonel commanding the regiment, which had been started in pursuit of our party, then stood up on the wagon wheel and questioned me as to where the balance of our party had gone. I told him they had gone up on the railroad towards Louisville, where they expected to capture a train before they returned to the army, thus directing him off their trail, as they were making great haste to cross the Cumberland River and were avoiding pursuit.

When this officer called to see me at the hospital at Bowling Green, he referred to my throwing him off my comrades' trail, saying that he couldn't account for accepting my statement, as he did, but "you seemed so honest in your statement, that I believed you, and committed one of the greatest blunders I was ever guilty of."

After questioning me at this camp, he sent a sergeant and two men, with a wagon, to haul me to Woodburn, the first station, where I was lifted into a boxcar on a train for Bowling Green.

Arriving at Bowling Green I was taken up to General Judah's headquarters, laid down on the floor of his room, surrounded by some soldiers, and he questioned me on the number of our party, what command we belonged to; he also asked if we had ever been engaged in that kind of warfare before. I told him that it had been the business of our regiment to destroy their line of communication, capture trains and everything else we were able to do to annoy the enemy, when he said, "Young man, you will never fire into another train."

I told him that I expected to fire into many a one, that this little scratch would soon get well and I would be ready for service again. He said, "Young man, we've got a rope for all such fellows as you." I told him there was a higher authority than he, that would have my disposition. He said, "Who?" I told him, "President Davis." He laughed and said, "Jeff Davis has no authority here."

I told him that I hoped it wouldn't be long before he would have. Feeling very irritable, with a hot fever on me, I was able to resent his threat in the manner I did and felt able to talk to him, although an officer of a high rank, in resentment of his threat.

I was then taken to their regular hospital, located on Barren River, about a mile and a half from town, where I was very kindly received by the surgeon in charge, who turned out to be a very sympathetic, kind-hearted man. I was furnished a cot, the same as their other sick, in the principal ward, and had a guard detailed to stay with me all the time. This guard consisted of two men, who were on duty every alternate six hours.

Under the care of this doctor and good nurses, I soon began to recover my strength and began to hope that I would be permitted to stay there until able to travel on foot, having no doubt I could make my escape out of there, when ready.

Unfortunately, the Rebel ladies of Bowling Green, learning there was a wounded Texas Ranger at the hospital, would get permission from the provost marshal to visit the sick, he supposing that they meant the Federal sick. When admitted to the wards they would come directly to my cot and deposit flowers, fruit and cake, and encourage me in the belief that I would soon get well again.

My generous, kind-hearted surgeon would sometimes send and get fish or oysters for me, evidently in the belief that he was doing a last kind act for me, as he expected me to be court martialled and sentenced to death, having frankly told me so, trying to persuade me to take the oath, which I refused to do.

As soon as I was able to sit up and talk without effort and overtaxing my strength, we had several discussions about the conduct of the war and the merits of the two armies. On one occasion I said to him, "I'm going to make an assertion, Doctor, and before I make it, I want to qualify it by stating that you have many good, patriotic men in your army and you are one of them; but, taking your army as a whole, they are an army of hirelings, fighting for their bounties and their pay, and would not hold together thirty days if their pay was stopped."

He spurned the idea, telling me that I was sadly mistaken, while there might be a few men that could be classed as hirelings, the bulk of their army were prompted only by patriotic motives and were not considering gain or pay. I said, "Doctor, I will prove my assertion right here in your presence," and called up some convalescents.

Addressing one, I asked him, "What induced you to join the army and what are you fighting for?"

He said, "I am fighting for the flag and the Union," but I said, "As a matter of fact, were you not paid a bounty?" He admitted that he had been paid six hundred dollars by his State.

Then again, "What pay do you receive?"

He said, "Twelve dollars per month."

"What do you do with your money?"

He said, "I send it home, for safety."

"Why don't you spend it?"

"I have nothing to spend it for."

"Does your government furnish you everything you need?"

"Everything," he said.

I interrogated a second one, whose answers were about the same. I then detailed the treatment our government had been forced to accord our army, who were frequently without pay, often without rations or clothing, especially without shoes, sometimes forced them to go barefooted, leaving their bloody tracks on the road. "Now, boys, if your government treated you in such manner, what would you do?"

They replied, "We wouldn't fight for any such d—— government; we would go home and stay there."

I said to the doctor, "Withdraw your pay and rations from your army and you wouldn't hold them together for sixty days," on which point we could not agree and he said, "Graber, you are too good a man to be engaged in such a cause."

I replied, "Doctor, that is just my opinion of you; you ought to wear the gray in place of the blue,"' all of which he took in the kindliest spirit. I frequently conversed with the ward master and some of the nurses, who seemed to have taken a great fancy for me on account of my bold, outspoken sentiments, and they sympathized with me in my helpless condition.

I had concluded to try to make my escape as soon as I got strong enough to undertake walking through the woods, over a rough country across the river. There were always a number of boats tied to the river bank. I would have had no difficulty in crossing Barren River. One night a guard on duty with me was sound asleep, snoring, with his head resting on the foot of my cot and I was wide awake. The nurse on duty went over to the ward master's bed, not far from my cot, and woke him up. He aroused himself, and the nurse in a low voice told him, "The guard is asleep; let us tell Texas to get away."

The ward master said, "No, don't do that; you had better wake up the guard," which he did. A little pleading on my part then would, no doubt, have had their consent, but I was still too feeble to undertake the hazard.

After spending about a month at this hospital, the provost marshal had heard of the ladies abusing his confidence and calling at my berth only, and rarely ever having a kind word for the Federal sick, so he had me moved to the prison, where I found about twenty-five or thirty men confined, most of them Morgan's men and a few highway robbers, who sought the protection of the Confederate Government by claiming to belong to certain Confederate commands, which I was satisfied was not the case. Kentucky afforded a good territory for these highwaymen to operate, on account of this condition.

Arriving at this prison proved the commencement of my suffering and trouble, as the surgeon in charge was a brute. He came in and threw some soap and bandages at my feet and I never saw him anymore.

The prison was a two-storey stone building with a brick gable, with the side fronting the street; it had been a two-storey residence, converted into a jail by attaching iron gratings in the large windows; it had only four rooms, two upstairs, occupied by the prisoners, and two downstairs, occupied by about twenty guards on active duty. There was also a room for the lieutenant commanding. There was a stairway, leading down into one of the rooms below, with a door at the foot of the steps. About two companies of infantry camped in the back yard, which was surrounded by a high board fence, and there was a sink in the back end of the yard. These troops were quartered in tents. The building was located diagonally across the street from a big hotel, which was occupied by the commanding officers, as headquarters.

Here I made the acquaintance of a Lieutenant Clark of Morgan's command, whose home was Bowling Green, where he was teaching before the war. Lieutenant Clark was a brother-in-law of Captain Tom Hines, one of Morgan's trusted lieutenants and the man that planned Morgan's escape out of the Ohio penitentiary. Lieutenant Clark and I were both held under the same charges for court martial, Morgan's command raiding Kentucky, destroying their line of communications and Forrest in charge of Middle Tennessee; it is hardly necessary to say that we became fast friends and plotted and planned escape, the only chance for which was frustrated.

Colonel Clarence Prentice, in conjunction with Major Kit Ousley, also of Morgan's command, was sent into Kentucky by our War Department to recruit a regiment for the Confederate Army.

Colonel Clarence Prentice was the son of the publisher of the Louisville Courier, which was largely responsible for retaining Kentucky in the Union. The family were divided in sentiment; the father was a great Union man and particular friend of Abraham Lincoln, while Mrs. Prentice and the two sons were strongly Southern in sentiment, the sons joining the Confederate Army.

Colonel Prentice, immediately on his arrival at his home, was captured and through the influence of his father, was sent around for exchange. Major Kit Ousley was captured near Bowling Green, in citizen's clothes, therefore treated as a spy and placed in prison with us, awaiting court martial. When Ousley was captured, they found a letter on his person from Fountain Fox, whose home was in Elizabethtown, this letter stating that Fox had succeeded in raising a company of one hundred and four of the best young men of his neighbourhood, ready to move at a moment's warning. They immediately sent up and arrested Fountain Fox and placed him in prison with us.

Fountain Fox's father also was an influential Union man, and the Fox family was divided like the Prentice family, Mrs. Fox and sons strong Southern sympathizers, and Mr. Fox a personal friend of Abraham Lincoln. When Lincoln commenced making his appointments abroad, he appointed Fountain Fox, Consul to Madrid, Spain. Consulting with his mother about the appointment, she advised him not to accept, telling him he would see the time very soon when he would blush to represent the American Government abroad. Taking his mother's advice, he declined the appointment.

After a short time, to appease his father's anger, he accepted a captaincy in the Home Guards, in which capacity he served about a year. On the reorganisation of the regiment, he was appointed major, serving in this capacity about three or four months longer, when they were ordered to Franklin, Tennessee, to the front. He said, "Considering that all of his youth's companions and nearly all of his schoolmates were in the Southern Army, he could not go down there and fight them" and made haste to resign.

Some sixty days after his resignation he met Major Ousley some distance from Elizabethtown, out in the country. Being well acquainted with him Ousley gave Fox a commission to raise a company for the Confederate Army, and he soon wrote Ousley the letter that was found on Ousley's person when he was captured, and which caused Fox's arrest.

His father immediately went to see the President and secured an order for his release, provided he would take the oath of allegiance to the United States and remain north of the Mason and Dixon's line during the war, also giving a bond of fifty thousand dollars, all of which he did, remaining in prison with us perhaps only two or three weeks. This prison was directly in charge of Major Erastus Motley, provost marshal, an old friend of Clark's before the war and a schoolmate of Captain Hines. He, like many Kentucky officers in such position, had made himself very obnoxious by his tyrannical treatment of the families of Confederate soldiers and seemed greatly prejudiced against Clark and myself.

CHAPTER 8

The Escape of Major Ousley

A court martial to try Major Kit Ousley was soon organised and his trial resulted easily in conviction, as he occupied the position of a spy, being captured in citizen's clothes. Very soon his sentence was returned from General Burnside, and approved by him, General Burnside being in command of Kentucky and Ohio, with his headquarters at Cincinnati.

Major Ousley, while recruiting up in the Blue Grass region near Lexington, married a very wealthy and beautiful young lady, who as soon as she heard of his capture and imprisonment at Bowling Green, came down to render what assistance she could, and succeeded in bribing a lieutenant, who had an office in town, paying him eight thousand dollars for his assistance. This officer kept her posted and gave her the information about the return that evening of the verdict of the court martial, approved by General Burnside, which was his conviction as a spy and his punishment death by hanging. He was to be placed over in the courthouse in irons under a special guard until the day of his execution, which was fixed for the 29th of May, while this information was imparted on the 14th of May.

Major Ousley asked permission that evening to go to a barber shop, which permission was granted by sending a special guard with him. At this barber shop he met his wife, who succeeded in obtaining a private interview with him, when she imparted the information about having bribed this lieutenant and the location of his office, which Ousley understood, as he was well acquainted in Bowling Green. She had also received from the lieutenant a pair of surgeon's shoulder straps and the password for that night, which was "Columbia," and which was imparted to Lieutenant Clark and myself by Ousley, after he returned to the prison.

Major Ousley had a visit that evening from several officers of the court martial, who seemed to be old acquaintances of his and had quite a long chat with them, with a good deal of levity, which of course was a matter of surprise to Clark and myself, as he seemed to be completely at ease. Considering his condition with his doom already sealed, we thought he displayed more nerve than any man we ever saw.

Major Ousley requested his officer friends, before they left him, to send him a bottle of brandy, which they did and which he distributed freely among the guards on duty in the lower room, hoping to load them up, and in doing this we were afraid he imbibed a little too much himself.

Now, it was imperative for him to make his escape that night, for, as stated, he was to be placed in irons the next day and kept in the courthouse under special guard. With Clark and myself, and other trusted friends in the prison, we planned that the only means of his escape would be to cut a hole through the plastering overhead large enough to admit a man into the attic; then take a sufficient number of bricks out of the gable end which connected with the roof of a single-story house adjoining, all of which was done by the willing hands of our comrades; but a mistake was made in the location of the hole through the brick wall. This hole opened on top of a roof, on the side facing the street in full view of the headquarters on the other side. Major Ousley imparted the countersign to Clark and myself with an injunction and earnest request not to attempt to get out until after giving him four hours the start, as his case was the most desperate one and we had not been tried by the court martial. This promise we fully kept.

When Major Ousley passed through the hole in the brick wall on to the roof of the other house, it was drizzling rain and the night was very dark, so the hole could not be discovered on the other side of the street. He laid flat on the roof for a few minutes, then quietly crawled over the comb of the house, on the other side, out of sight of the street, then to the far end of the roof away from the prison and dropped down into the yard of a private residence when a large dog got after him, giving one bark and no more.

Ousley told me afterwards that he hit this dog with his fist and said, "I reckon I killed him!" Some of the guards in our prison yard rushed to the fence and asked a lady who came to the door, what was the matter; she said, "Nothing that I know of, everything is all right over here," which seemed to quiet their suspicion, so they went back to their tents.

Major Ousley soon was heard to come down the walk in front of our prison. He was halted by the guard, asking, "Who comes there?"

"A friend with the countersign."

"Advance, friend, and give the countersign."

He gave the countersign and passed on down the street and found the lieutenant's room. The lieutenant told him it would not be safe for him to attempt to go out that night, but to go down into the river bottoms, stay there all next day, then return to his office, when he would have a horse and side arms for him and give him the new countersign for that night. Ousley went down to the river bottoms and spent the day until very near night. Then, being very hungry, he decided to go to a friend's house, who lived away out in the suburbs and get something to eat. Just before reaching his friend's house, he struck the big road and immediately heard the running of a horse behind him, which proved to be a man on horseback loping towards town. Though he did not suspect any such thing, the man evidently went to town and raised the alarm.

On entering the house his friend's wife met him. She was well acquainted with Ousley, but her husband was not at home, and she, of course, was surprised and alarmed, as she knew that he was a prisoner. When he made known his wants, she rushed in and prepared a lunch, while he stood at the front door, watching. As soon as the lunch was ready, she invited him into the dining-room and took his place watching. Before he finished his lunch she rushed into the dining-room, saying, "My God, Major Ousley, you are lost, you are lost."

He told her to keep perfectly quiet. "The safest place is among the enemy," he said, and grabbed a couple of biscuits, stuck them into his coat pocket, and started out of the front door when a couple of guards behind a rosebush, jumped up, threw their guns down on him and told him to halt. He cursed them and told them to get behind that bush, Major Ousley would see them, making them believe that he was one of their own officers.

I forgot to mention that he had the surgeon's shoulder straps sewed on to his coat at the shoulders, the same as was the custom in the Federal Army. As already stated, when captured, he had on a splendid double-breasted frock coat and black pants, all of which in the dark could easily be mistaken for a Federal uniform, hence on the spur of the moment, he made the two guards believe that he was one of their own officers. He walked to the gate and passing outside, walked very fast up the fence, and when about a hundred yards these men began to call, "Halt," when he broke into a run and left them firing after him, not receiving a scratch. While, of course, they ran after him I imagine they didn't try very hard to catch him, fearing perhaps that he had accomplices, prepared to defend him.

Major Ousley next circled around the town and again made his way to the lieutenant's room, who had a horse ready for him, gave him a couple of six-shooters and the countersign for that night. He boldly rode down the main street leading to Barren River bridge, where he gave the countersign to the guards, then up the pike towards Louisville.

After an all-night's ride he pulled up at a friend's house, where he decided to stay until Morgan's command came in there and go with them back to our main army, telling his friend his purpose. His friend said, "Major, you can't stay here; there is a brigade of Yankees camped at a spring about a mile from here and Colonel Gross, the commander, comes over occasionally and has a game of poker with me." Ousley told him that would not make any difference, he was going to stay anyway and take a hand with him at poker.

He then proceeded to disguise; cut off a heavy moustache, and also cut his hair short, which made him look like a different man; and he actually stayed at this friend's house for nearly three weeks, joining his friend and Colonel Gross in several games of poker. He finally heard of Morgan's command in the blue grass region, mounted his horse to try to find them and telling his friend goodbye and to give him a half hour's start, and then to tell Colonel Gross who he was and tell him the next time they met pistols would be trumps. His friend said that he wouldn't do such a thing for anything in the world; he said, "Colonel Gross never will find out through me or mine who you were."

Major Ousley succeeded in finding Morgan's command and went out of the State with them, reporting to the War Department at Richmond, and was given a job in the department and an order forbidding him to re-enter the army. I met him again at Richmond, where he detailed all of the features and incidents of his escape from the time he dropped into the adjoining yard and knocked over the dog.

CHAPTER 9

In Prison at Louisville, Where I was Honoured with Handcuffs

Referring to Bowling Green prison, where Major Ousley had left us: Four hours after Ousley's escape, our friends in the prison boosted Clark and me up into the attic, when we found out to our dismay that the weather had cleared and the moon had risen sufficiently high to light up the front of our building, disclosing the hole in the gable. The general's headquarters being diagonally across the street with a guard's beat immediately in front, I whispered to Clark, "We had better wait until the corporal comes with his relief guard in front of the headquarters and watch their actions."

Waiting about thirty minutes, a corporal with a relief appeared on the beat and the three stood for some time talking and looking up at our prison wall, which satisfied us that they had made the discovery of the hole and were only waiting for some of us to crawl out on the roof, when they would have shot us. We, therefore, decided it would be folly to attempt our escape that night, which proved a wise decision.

The next morning at roll call, the discovery was made that Major Ousley was missing, which caused the greatest excitement; and immediately scouting parties of eight or ten men dashed up to the headquarters across the street for orders, and started out in a lope. All that day these parties called for orders and came back and reported at headquarters. Major Motley came up and saw the manner of Ousley's escape, and asked the prisoners who made those holes and assisted Ousley. None of us vouchsafed any information.

He then sent for the most desperate prisoners, some that were not Confederates, as heretofore stated, and told them that their cases were bad, but if they would tell who assisted Ousley in making his escape, and tried to make their escape with him, he would do all he could to let them off as easy as possible.

This we learned through two most excellent citizens, who were in the prison with us, and who were also taken out and offered their liberty if they would disclose Ousley's accomplices. One of these was a Colonel Lewis, living near Franklin; the other a Doctor Vertriece, a neighbour of Colonel Lewis. These men were imprisoned because of our raid on the railroad, which the reader will remember occurred between Franklin and Woodburn. It was the custom of the Federal commander, whenever Morgan, or any other troops, made a raid on the railroad, to arrest the most prominent citizens in the neighbourhoods.

After several days of questioning these prisoners, Major Motley came up; my friend Clark was asleep on a mattress the lieutenant of the guard had favoured me with, on account of my being wounded. He was lying with his face to the wall. I was sitting on the window sill, looking out into the street when Major Motley walked up to where Clark was asleep and gave him a kick in the back, thereby waking him. Clark raised up and asked, "What do you want, Ras'?" when Motley produced a pair of handcuffs, he had held behind him and put them on him.

Turning around to me, he said, "I will have a pair here for you in a few minutes," but as it turned out fortunately there was not another pair of handcuffs in Bowling Green, and he had to send to Louisville after them. After he left the prison Doctor Vertriece suggested to me that I write a letter to Colonel Hawkins, who was then in command of the post, telling him that I was a wounded Confederate soldier, and that Major Motley had threatened to put handcuffs on me. I stated in this letter that our command had captured thousands of their men and had always treated them humanely and kindly, notably the Ninth Michigan and Third Minnesota, who, after we had paroled them and when parting with us, said, "If any of you Texas Rangers are captured, call for the Ninth Michigan and Third Minnesota, and we will see that you are well treated." In winding up my letter to Colonel Hawkins, I called on him as a gentleman and a soldier not to permit such an outrage perpetrated as that of placing irons on a wounded prisoner.

This letter Doctor Vertriece succeeded in smuggling around Major Motley, bribing a guard to take it directly to Colonel Hawkins without Motley's knowledge, and we soon had an answer returned in the same manner from Colonel Hawkins, expressing his regret at our condition, praising Major Motley as a very kind-hearted and good man, and stating that he was satisfied he would do all in his power to alleviate our condition and suffering, and trusting that we would be able to bear up with our condition.

When I read the letter I threw it on the floor, and told Doctor Vertriece he was mistaken in his man; that Colonel Hawkins was no better than the rest of them. He picked up the letter, read it and told me that I was doing a great injustice to Colonel Hawkins, that I was simply misconstruing his position, that he could not have said anything more to me, a prisoner belonging to the army of his enemy, and could certainly not censure Major Motley, an officer of his own army, for his treatment of us, and furthermore suggested that if I would just wait, he was satisfied that the handcuffs would not be put on me.

The next day Major Motley again visited our prison, walked up to Lieutenant Clark and took off his handcuffs, hardly able to look into his face. Turning around, he walked up and down the cell a few times in study, and finally stopped in front of me, saying, "Graber, I want you and Clark to understand that I have no personal feeling in this matter; you are prisoners, have been placed in my charge and keeping; you have tried to make your escape with Major Ousley, and, I am going to keep you here, if I have to chain you to this floor."

I frequently told Major Motley that if they were holding me for court martial, to bring my charges and specifications, to which he replied that I needn't be in a hurry, I would receive them sooner than I wanted to, perhaps, and, when finally brought, the charge was being a guerilla; specifications, my own statement admitting to General Judah that we had been engaged in raiding their lines of communications and destroying them ever since we had been in the army. I concluded they need not resort to any trial, as I was prepared to admit the specifications. In this charge they gave my name, company and regiment, C. S. A. (so-called), which was virtually an admission that I was not a guerilla, but by an order, No. 38, of General Burnside, all recruiting officers captured within his department should be treated as spies, and all raiding parties, not under a general officer, as guerillas.

Finally, one day Major Motley came in about ten o'clock in the morning and ordered me to prepare to leave on the eleven o'clock train for Louisville. I asked him, "What for? Are you sending me up there for safe keeping, or to be treated as a prisoner of war?"

He said, "Never mind about that; you will learn soon enough."

When I reached Louisville I was taken to the general prison and there treated as a prisoner of war.

I found the Louisville prison a most excellent one; two barracks running parallel, with bunks on each side and a brick-paved yard in the centre, with a splendid waterworks. At one end were the offices occupied by clerks and an officer who kept the roll; at the other end was the kitchen, connected on one side with a barrack, and on the other side having a passageway of about three feet, leading into the backyard in the rear of the kitchen, where they had the sinks, and this backyard was kept in a very filthy condition. We had three rations a day, with coffee in the mornings, the rations consisting of a chunk of light bread and a piece of pickled pork, already cut in proper size for each man, in tubs, on each side of the door. On the inside of the kitchen stood a tub, presided over by negro wenches who would shove these rations to us as we passed through, single file, into the backyard.

A negro official, called "Captain Black" by the prisoners, frequently stood on the outside of the door as the prisoners passed in to draw their rations. When some poor, emaciated prisoner, reduced by confinement, barely able to drag his feet, came along, he would curse, tell him to "Hike out, you d—m Rebel," and sometimes push them along. This made me fear this negro to the extent that I always avoided him and always moved quickly in his presence, determined never to give him an opportunity to insult me.

One day I was lying on my bunk, the second from the floor, about five feet high, which was the end of the bunks next to the door. I was feeling bad and having considerable fever, and was still suffering from my wounds, so I decided not to go out and get my dinner rations. All that were able had gone out, a few sick remaining in the barracks at different places. A little negro boy came to the door and looking up at me, asked if I was sick and didn't I want a cup of coffee. I told him yes, to bring me a cup and I would pay him for it. He brought me a small tin cup full of fine coffee, for which I gave him a twenty-five-cent bill.

While lying sipping my coffee, resting on my right elbow, "Captain Black" stepped into the door, and, on discovering me said, "What are you doing here, sir?" I said I was sick and didn't want my rations. He raised up on his toes and said, "Sick?" "Yes, I am sick, too," and he started to order me out when I lost all control of myself and, from my bunk, fell right over on him, grabbing at his pistol. I got my hand on it, but he jerked away before I could clinch it, but he thought I had it, saying, "Foh Gawd, Massa; don't, Massa!" then broke for the gate. Some of the prisoners witnessed the trouble and told the others when they came in from drawing their rations, which created considerable excitement and considerable sympathy for me, for it was believed that

I would be placed in irons and in a dungeon.

In about half an hour after the prisoners returned from drawing their rations, one of them rushed up to me and suggested that I hide. He said, "That negro, with a big sergeant, is in the yard hunting you." I told him that I would not hide, but would go and meet them, walking out into the yard. The negro pointed me out to the sergeant, when he walked up to me and told me to hold up my hands. I asked him, "What for?"

He said, "To put these things on you," producing a pair of handcuffs, which he had held behind him. I asked who ordered it done? He stated, Colonel Orcutt.

I asked, "Who is Colonel Orcutt?"

He said, "Commander of this prison."

I told him, "All right; put them on; they are Yankee bracelets, and I consider it an honour to wear them."

After wearing these irons two or three days and nights, an officer in fatigue uniform, whom I took to be Colonel Orcutt, stepped up to me and told me to hold up my hands. I asked him what for? He said, "To take those things off." I told him he needn't be in a hurry, I had got used to them and considered it an honour to wear them. By this time, he had unlocked them and taken them off. When I turned my back on him and mingled with the crowd, some of the prisoners told me that he started to strike me with them, which I hardly believe.

"Captain Black" very soon came to me and apologised, saying that he was very sorry for what he had done, and that he would never mistreat a prisoner again, that "Dese soldiers had put him up to it." I told him I would give him five dollars if he would steal those handcuffs for me. He said that he would be glad to do that, and would not charge me anything, and he soon reported that they had not been replaced in the office, where they used to hang, and that he couldn't find out where they were kept.

Chapter 10

I Change My Name for the First Time and am Finally Exchanged

After remaining in this prison about a month, a roll was called and the prisoners whose names were called, were ordered to get ready for exchange. We started next morning for City Point, as we were told, but when we reached Columbus, Ohio, we were ordered to march to Camp Chase, where we were quartered in barracks, partitioned into mess rooms of twenty-four in a mess. While here I was very uneasy, expecting to be called for at any time, to be returned to Louisville, as several of the prisoners had been so returned, to meet charges against them, hence concluded perhaps my name appeared on the roll through mistake, but I was fortunate enough to escape this fate and got along fine until I was taken sick with flux.

While confined in this prison I was furnished a New York paper, I think it was the *Tribune*, giving an account of the hanging of one of our comrades of the regiment by the name of Dodd, who was captured near Knoxville, Tennessee, having had his horse killed in an engagement near there, and was ordered to make his way out as best he could. He was raised in Sevier County, and decided to visit his home, while there, and when captured, was taken to Knoxville, there tried as a spy by a court martial, convicted and sentenced to be hung. His conviction was secured on a pocket diary, which he had kept, recording his every-day work.

A correspondent of the *New York Tribune*, who visited him in the jail just before his execution, claimed he found him a very intelligent, educated gentleman, in fact, believed him to be a grand character, and his execution, which he witnessed, proved such a horrible affair that it elicited the following expression from him:

"In the name of humanity and all that is decent, if the terrible exigencies of war require the deliberate taking of human life, let the prisoner be shot or give us the merciful guillotine."

Satisfied if the members of the regiment heard of Dodd's execution they would certainly retaliate, and in return the Federal Army would also retaliate, and as I was the only member of the Eighth Texas, their prisoner, they would certainly call for me for such purpose.

After remaining in this prison for a month I agreed with one of Morgan's men to tunnel out under the fence, and prepared to go to work that night. The fence was only about twenty yards from our mess room, the identical place where one of Morgan's officers had dug out a few months before and effected his escape. During this day we were suddenly called on to move and were again promised that we should be sent to City Point for exchange. All the sick in the hospital were furnished conveyances to carry them to Columbus, where we took train.

As stated heretofore, I had a severe case of flux, which weakened me a great deal, and I was rendered unable to walk soon after we started on our march to Columbus, a distance of about four miles. We were marched by fours with a heavy advance and rear guard and a single file guard on each side of our column. After having marched about a mile, I gave out completely, and my comrades reported my case to a lieutenant, marching by the side of us, who instructed me to sit down by the roadside and wait until the rear guard came up; then to tell them to make a detail to stay with me until I reached Columbus.

Very soon after the main body had passed, one of the rear guards called out: "Hike out, you d—— Rebel," which, of course, made me resentful and I refused to hike out, telling him that I had orders to stop and tell some of the rear guard to bring me up to Columbus. By this time, he had got pretty close to me and I happening to look around found him charging on me with a bayonet, which made me jump, and proved the best medicine I could have taken for flux. It simply infused new strength and enabled me to hike to Columbus.

At Erie, Pennsylvania, we were put in coal cars with the bottoms pretty thickly covered with coal dust, in which we were carried to Philadelphia, being marched through Chestnut Street to a boat landing.

Their object in moving us in these coal cars we construed to be a policy to make us look as dirty as possible. Many of our men, of course, were somewhat ragged, and, altogether, we appeared a motley crowd, in striking contrast to the heroes that had been cherished by our Northern sympathizers, called "copper-heads" by the fanatics of the North. In our march to the boat landing, we were greeted by many intelligent ladies, who were standing on the streets watching our passing, and quite a number of them had their hands full of postage money, which was bills of denominations of less than a dollar, which they threw and scattered among us.

After we reached the boat, on which we were ordered up on the second deck, a dray-load of cheese and crackers was sent down to us by some of the ladies, but the guards on the lower deck appropriated it, and, after eating as much as they wanted, sold the balance of it to all that had money. Then, adding insult to injury, they sent word to the ladies to send more—to be treated in the same manner. The boat then moved out down the river where our journey to City Point for exchange terminated at Fort Delaware, where we were unloaded and were roughly treated.

Fort Delaware proved to be the worst prison we had been in; dirty, with no water fit to drink. Our drinking water had to be taken from the canal inside of the levee, which had a green scum floating on top, and, on the lower part of the island, was used for bathing. After about two or three weeks, an arrangement was made with a boat called the *Osceola* to bring us water from the Brandy wine River, which proved to be palatable and a great treat.

On our arrival at Fort Delaware, we found about twenty thousand prisoners, a large part of them captured at the Battle of Gettysburg; among whom were four or five hundred of Hood's Brigade, and also some from Granbury's Brigade, who were captured at Vicksburg. This created a sad impression on me and made me wish I was back in the saddle again more than I ever did, but there was nothing to do but submit.

While here we also heard of the battle of Chickamauga, the first report of which was most encouraging, as it stated their army was annihilated and Thomas had fled to the mountains. This started the Rebel yell in the prison, and made us feel that we would soon be exchanged, but the next day's report put a damper on our enthusiasm, and made us feel sad indeed, as the report in this New York paper was that their army had rallied and were holding on to Chattanooga, with our army retreating, and, while their loss was very heavy in killed and wounded, ours was double. It made us realise that fate was against us, and we would never be able to gain a decisive victory, which would unquestionably secure our recognition by foreign governments.

As already stated, Fort Delaware proved the worst prison we had been in; smallpox broke out among us and nearly every other disease known. A large number died. Every morning they called at the big gate, "Bring out your dead!" and the dead were buried on the Jersey shore by a detail of prisoners.

Among one of these details one morning was a gentleman by the name of Simpson, from Houston, Texas, who belonged to Hood's Brigade. This man was born and raised in New York State and had lived in Houston only a couple of years, engaging in business and had become thoroughly acquainted with the character of our people, and especially the institution of slavery. In this short time, he became one of the South's strongest friends, ready to give his life for her cause, as demonstrated by his joining the first troops Texas sent to Virginia.

Slipping away from the guards, he made his way to his old home, told his people who had heard that he was in the Rebel Army that he had recanted and taken the oath of allegiance to the United States Government, thereby reinstating him with his family, who lavished money and all else on him until he was fully recuperated from the effects of his prison experience, when he again shipped on board a steamer for Nassau, where he took a Confederate blockade runner and came South, to fight it out to the end.

After the war he entered into co-partnership with a man by the name of Wiggins, constituting the firm of Wiggins & Simpson, which built a large foundry and machine shop. This they conducted for many years, and, at the time of his death, Simpson was wealthy and one of the most honoured and esteemed citizens of Houston, never having expressed a word of regret over his conduct during the war.

It might not be out of place here to say that nearly all Northern-raised men among us within my knowledge pursued the same course. They invariably proved gallant soldiers and did their duty for the South to the limit of their ability, returning South after the war and spending the balance of their lives as our most honoured citizens. We had twenty-six generals of Northern birth in the Confederate Army, twelve of whom were graduates of West Point, and were offered high rank in the Federal Army. This, no doubt, proved a hard problem for the North to understand, and only emphasizes the justice of our cause, because these men were prompted only by a conscientious motive, and faced suffering, death and disgrace in the eyes of their Northern friends by such a course.

While on this subject I would mention the case of General Pemberton, the gallant soldier who commanded at Vicksburg, and directed its defence to the last ditch. He was the son of wealthy parents in Philadelphia, who threatened to disinherit him if he didn't resign his commission in the Southern Army and come North, but he ignored their threat and continued in the Southern Army to the end.

Our suffering at Fort Delaware was almost unbearable. We were crowded into these barracks as thick as we could lie, with all character of sickness and disease among us, receiving additional prisoners occasionally to keep the barracks filled, with only two meals a day of three small crackers and an inch of meat. Many prisoners got desperate and attempted to swim the Delaware River to effect their escape, only to have their dead bodies found washed ashore on the Delaware or Jersey side of the river the next day.

A number of our men were shot without cause by the guard, who, we understood, were promoted for such act; still a few of the men made their escape by swimming the river, among whom I might mention Jim Loggins, a boy about eighteen years old, who belonged to Hood's Brigade. He is now a practicing physician of Ennis, Texas, a father of a large family of children, all highly regarded and respected citizens of their home town.

Prisoners seeking their escape would take canteens, tightly corked, and use them as life preservers. Referring back to the case of Jim Loggins: When he got into the river with others, the tide was running in fast, and the tide took him about five or six miles up the river before he reached a landing on the Delaware side. He then, with one companion, made his way through the State of Delaware into Maryland, crossing the Potomac, then through Northern Virginia, occupied by the Federal Army, back to Richmond, where he rejoined Hood's Brigade, and was in every important battle until the end of the war, surrendering at Appomattox.

Among our prisoners at Fort Delaware were the First Maryland Cavalry, captured at South Mountain, before the battle of Gettysburg. These Maryland men were the sons of leading families, largely men of great wealth in the State of Maryland. Their friends and families at home petitioned Governor Swann, of Maryland, to intercede for them with the Federal War Department, and permit them to take a parole to go home, and stay at their homes, until regularly exchanged, and it was generally believed success would crown their efforts. These men received clothing and money in the greatest abundance from their families at home, and were about the most genteel looking men we had in prison.

In connection with this, I would mention the escape of one of their parties, who, being well dressed and clean shaven, wearing a white shirt and fresh collar, was watching the *Osceola* at the landing about ready to depart, and boldly slipped up on the levee, walked down to the guard, passing him while the guard saluted, mistaking him for a citizen visitor from Delaware City, who came over quite often, then passed on to the boat, walked up on its cabin deck, took a seat in front, with his feet cocked up on the guards, smoking a cigar, when the boat pushed off with him and he was never heard of by us any more, no doubt making good his escape.

Many incidents of interest I might mention, showing the loyalty of the Southern soldier under this most terrible condition, facing death daily, seeing his comrades carried out by the dozen for burial daily, with no prospect for exchange. Certainly, history does not record such remarkable devotion to a country and cause.

In line with this, I might mention the effort of General Schoepf, commander of the fort and prison. He one day conceived the idea of creating a stampede among us, for which purpose he ordered out about three hundred East Tennesseans, formed them in line and made a strong speech to them, telling them of the North's vast resources for the conduct of the war, and our diminishing, limited means for holding on; showing them the impossibility for our ever succeeding, with no prospect of exchange. Then he told them of the great prosperity of the North, where labour was in demand and wages high, of which they could take the benefit by taking the oath of allegiance and thus save their lives, recover their health and strength, live in peace and happiness the balance of the war, and, finally, he called on them, saying, "Now, all of you that are ready and willing to take the oath of allegiance, step three paces to the front." Only one man responded.

General Schoepf evidently thought that East Tennessee, as a section of country in the South, was the most disloyal to our cause, its citizens being largely Union people, and that these East Tennesseans would certainly accept his liberal offer, and, by that means, make a break in our ranks. It is hardly necessary to say that he gave it up as a bad job, and did not attempt another such experiment. In connection with this, however, I regret to have to say that a few weak brothers were found in our ranks, who took the oath of allegiance and were then separated from the rest of the prisoners, in a special camp about a half mile distant, where they were designated by us as "Galvanized Yankees."

After spending a part of the winter at Fort Delaware, one morning there appeared a notice at what we called a post-office, inside of the big gate, calling upon all Marylanders, prisoners of war, to appear at the gate with their baggage; which, of course, was construed to mean that Governor Swann had succeeded in his effort to secure a parole for these Marylanders, and that they would be taken to Washington for the purpose of being paroled and permitted to go home to remain until properly exchanged. This, of course, created considerable excitement and rejoicing among the Marylanders, which was shared largely by the rest of the prisoners, although they could not hope to ever be favoured in the same manner. It was a source of comfort and gratification to us to know that some of our friends, at least, would be saved the sufferings and almost certain death, even if we could not share it with them.

While they were forming in line, by fours, headed for the big gate, an acquaintance belonging to Hood's Brigade, whose name was Robert Brantley, of Navasota, called to me and said, "Goodbye, Henry." I said, "Where are you going, Bob?"

He said, "I am going to try to get out with these men."

I said, "How are you going to try to do that?"

He said, "I have two names and am going to answer to one of them at roll call."

I said, "Bob, you do not want two names; you can't answer to both. If you will give me one of them, I will try to go out with you."

He said, "All right, come on."

I had time enough to go into the barracks and get an oilcloth satchel, which had been given me at Bowling Green; then I had a magnificent cape overcoat, left me by Major Ousley in Bowling Green prison; with this coat on and this citizen's new satchel, the coat extending over the top of my boots, hiding partly worn butternut pants. I passed for a Marylander pretty well, seemingly as well dressed as they were, while Bob looked ragged, like one of these Hood Brigade men that had not had any clothing furnished them in some time, and appeared rather suspicious among this well-dressed crowd.

In giving me the name, he retained the name of Charles Erbert, who belonged to the First Maryland Cavalry, and who had died in prison. The name of Charles Stanley, which he gave me to use, was the name of a son of a preacher Charles Stanley was sick in the hospital, and his father, ostensibly to preach to the troops at the fort, was permitted the privilege of a visit, mainly for the purpose of being with his son in the hospital.

The keeper of the prison roll was a Lieutenant Wolff, a renegade Virginian, who was also a "Galvanized Yankee." Wolff was also acquainted with many of the Marylanders, and particularly with Charles Stanley, on account of his father visiting there. Wolff's acquaintance with the Marylanders was through their clothing and money sent them, which passed through his hands.

We were soon marched out to the wharf, where the *Osceola* was awaiting us to carry us to the flag of truce boat, *New York*, anchored in midstream, as the water was too shallow for her to come up to the wharf. We were held on the wharf for nearly an hour before a roll call commenced, during which time I suggested to Bob to separate, for him to take the opposite edge of the party to the edge that I would take, then to post himself on the circumstances of his man's capture and the location of his home in Maryland, telling him that we might be questioned, and, if posted, we could have a ready answer, thereby keeping down suspicion. Bob said he did not think there was any danger in that; his greatest apprehension was that he would be personally recognised by some of the Yankees, as he had been at work in the cook house, where he made the acquaintance of quite a number, and he thought perhaps Lieutenant Wolff might recognise him, while I had no fear of anything of that kind.

Finally, a major, with several other officers, appeared. Lieutenant Wolff was already there. The major began calling the roll alphabetically. When he called the name of Charles Erbert, Bob failed to answer. I decided if he called it the second time that I would answer to the dead man's name, believing that Bob had lost his nerve and would not answer at all. When he called the name the second time, we both answered, but I kept down, while he jumped up quickly. This drew the major's attention to him, and he never knew who it was that answered over on my side of the crowd. I forgot to mention that we were all squatted down on the wharf. When Bob walked out boldly, attempting to pass the major, on his way to the boat, the major stopped him. "What is your name, sir?"

"My name is Charles Erbert."

The major, without any further questioning, told him to take a seat and called up a guard to take charge of him. This sudden decision of the major that there was fraud was no doubt prompted by both of us answering to the same name, yet it created a suspicion with me that perhaps we had been betrayed, as they kept a lot of spies in the prison all the time. As considerable time was consumed in calling the names, down to the letter S, I had ample time to prepare for the issue, and when the name of Charles Stanley was called, I jumped up and boldly went forward, passing him, without looking.

I was favoured by Lieutenant Wolff being engaged in shaking hands with one of the Marylanders and eating an apple with his back turned to the major when he called the name of Charles Stanley, evidently not hearing it, and which I did not permit him to call the second time. I therefore passed through unmolested. As heretofore stated, my appearance tallied pretty well with the rest of the Marylanders and Bob Brantley's appearance was in striking contrast with theirs.

After getting on the boat and mixing with the Marylanders, I was congratulated by them on my success and promised a good time when they reached home. As soon as all were aboard, the *New York* weighed anchor, when, the next morning, running down the coast on the Atlantic, we were told that we would have to remain down in the hold on the second deck until they could wash decks. They closed down the hatch and only permitted us to come on the main deck when we discovered that we were at Point Lookout, Maryland, under the guns of a thirty-two-pound battery, and the Potomac flotilla, and were then told to march out, and were led into what we called a "bull pen," where we found about ten or twelve thousand prisoners quartered in little A tents on the sand of the seashore, with nothing else to protect them from the winter's blast.

Had we suspected their motive, we could have easily overpowered the guard on the big steamer, beached and burned her and scattered out in Maryland, without taking a parole. At Point Lookout our camp was laid off in State divisions, a row of little A tents on each side of a wide street with a cook house for each division at the head of it. We were here furnished rations the same as we had at Fort Delaware, by marching in and taking our position at the long table in front of each ration. Sometimes we had a cup of what they called bean soup, but it was always my misfortune to get a cup of bean water, the cook failing to stir up the soup and thoroughly mixing the beans with the water. Besides this, we had three crackers and an inch of meat. This we had twice a day, as at. Fort Delaware, and considerable suffering on account of hunger was thereby entailed.

As stated, we were quartered in tents by State Divisions. Coming there with the Marylanders, under a Marylander's name, I started with the Maryland Division, but in connection with this, soon joined the

Texas Division, Tennessee Division and Louisiana Division and drew rations with every one of these divisions, thereby securing three extra rations which I divided among my messmates.

In order to improve my time, with nothing else to do, I decided to try to learn the French language and for this purpose, joined a Louisiana mess, the men belonging to the Seventh Louisiana, who were Creoles and spoke nothing but French in their mess. In a short time, I was enabled to understand some of their talk and they, as well as I, thought I was getting along fine, and I believe if I could have continued with them six months, I would have spoken French fluently.

While at this point General Butler was appointed Exchange Agent, this in response to the clamour of the people in the North, demanding exchange, as their people were dying in our prisons, as well as our people in theirs; but, the policy of their War Department, sanctioned by Abraham Lincoln, was not to exchange a prisoner if they could avoid it. They did not want to reinforce our army from that source when our country was about exhausted for men. To carry their point on this they cared very little for their men in our prisons and even openly claimed that it was a protection to their army to enforce non-exchange even at the sacrifice of the men in our prisons.

General Butler being placed in charge of the exchange, the Federal Government knew that they could throw the odium of refusal to exchange on the Confederate Government, because General Butler had been outlawed by our Government through President Davis' proclamation ordering him executed whenever captured, on account of his dastardly conduct while in command of New Orleans, which earned for him the name of "Beast" Butler. They well knew that his appointment as Chief Exchange Agent would forever place a barrier against exchange.

At this time General Marsden was in command at Point Lookout, and a Captain Patterson, aided by Sergeant Finnegan, in charge of the prisoners.

After the arrival of the Marylanders at Point Lookout, the Federal Government decided to relieve the crowded condition of Fort Delaware by transferring more prisoners to Point Lookout, which was done to a considerable extent.

General Butler, for political reasons, as well as to show his interest in the prisoners, made us a visit, and when his arrival was announced, proceeded in company with General Marsden and their respective staffs, to ride over to our enclosure. We were then called on by Captain

Patterson, announcing his approach, to cheer him as he came inside. As soon as the big gate was thrown open and he rode in, perhaps five thousand prisoners had collected at the gate, many of them calling out, "Boys, here is the 'Beast;'" to which he paid no attention or to the name of "Mumford," the man whom he hung in New Orleans for tearing down the United States flag placed on his house on their first occupancy of New Orleans.

When he and General Marsden attempted to enter the First Division, which was the Louisiana Division, the men called out "New Orleans." By this time such a crowd had gathered in this division that it was difficult for them to ride through, when General Butler decided not to go any further and returned to General Marsden's headquarters.

About two weeks later General Butler returned and entered the prison enclosure with General Marsden and their respective staffs; all armed with pistols, and having also an escort of about fifty cavalry. They were determined to push through the Louisiana Division, when again the insults thrown at them on his first visit were repeated. In reaching a Sibley tent, where a part of a company of the Louisiana Guard Battery were quartered, one of the young men, seeing General Butler passing in front of the tent, rushed out, took Butler's horse by the bridle and stopped him, proposed three cheers for Jeff Davis, which were given with a will by our ten thousand throats, then proposed three groans for the "Beast."

General Butler turned pale, looked at the men, seemed undecided what to do, surrounded by an angry crowd of at least ten thousand men, who although unarmed, he well knew were more than a match for him and his guards and that they would not stand any show for their lives if a single shot was fired. He decided it was best to move on and pass the incident. When nearly at the end of the division someone called "Magruder," which made him smile, as it referred to the battle of Big Bethel, which he commanded and lost to the Confederates commanded by General Magruder.

He next turned into the North Carolina Division, a brigade of conscripts, who had surrendered without firing a gun. On his entering this division the men cheered him, when he stopped and talked with them, asking how they were getting along. They told him they did not get enough to eat and were starving, and he turned to Captain Patterson and told him to add an extra cracker to the rations, which brought another cheer. He then passed through the division, being cheered frequently by these conscripts and returned to General Marsden's headquarters.

In punishment for the insults offered him in the Louisiana Division, he sent a regiment, composed of illiterate negroes from the plantations in North Carolina, to guard us. The immediate guard of the prison were on beats on a platform outside of the prison walls, which exposed their heads and shoulders to the prisoners inside of the walls. There were also guard beats at the head of every division between the tents and the cook houses. These negroes were very poorly drilled and disciplined, but fit tools in the hands of a vindictive enemy.

As the men in the prison had never seen any negro troops, they gathered along these different beats to watch their performance. They came into the prison for guard duty, carrying their knapsacks as they were afraid to leave them in their camp, fearing that some of the other troops not on duty would rob them. A guard at the head of the Texas Division, tired of carrying his knapsack, deposited it at the end of his beat; as soon as his back was turned, one of the men picked it up and ran away with it.

The negro, returning on his beat, discovered his knapsack gone and created a general laugh among the spectators by his puzzled look. Finally, he said, "Men, you better give me back my knapsack or I'll call Marse Lieutenant." The men again laughed, when finally, he called to the guard up on the fence, "Central, Oh Central! Call Marse Lieutenant and tell him one of dese here white folks stole my knapsack," when in due time the officer of the day came in on horseback, dashed up to the guard and asked what was the matter. The guard said, "Marse Lieutenant, some of these white folks stole my knapsack," which created additional laughter and merriment.

The lieutenant called on the men to return the knapsack, and said that if they didn't, he would order a search of the camp. This they could not afford to have done. In the meantime, the negro said if they would just give him back his "bacca" and guarretype, he wouldn't care anything about the balance. The men then returned the knapsack to keep the camp from being searched.

Our troubles with this negro guard commenced the first night, when they shot into the camp whenever they heard any noise. They were undoubtedly instigated by their officers and the white soldiers.

There were a number of attempts to escape, one novel plan being evolved by the Marylanders. The smallpox broke out inside of the prison, and a pesthouse was established on the main land in the piney woods, about three or four miles from the Point.

I forgot to mention Point Lookout is a peninsula, connected with the mainland by a very narrow strip, where a strong fort was located, and where these negroes were quartered. We also had an ordinary hospital inside of the enclosure, immediately in charge of Confederate surgeons, but supervised by a Federal surgeon, who would receive their report every morning on the conditions of the sick, the number of the dead, etc. A couple of Marylanders would blister their faces and hands with hot wire, giving it the appearance of smallpox; the Confederate surgeon would point out these two cases having developed smallpox during the night, when they were ordered out to the pesthouse.

They were then carried in a one-horse cart out to the pesthouse in the piney woods, where they only had one guard on duty with his beat in front of the door. The Confederate surgeon immediately in charge, at this pesthouse, would add a couple of boxes in connection with others, for the dead that had passed away during the night, and would report these two men among the other dead of the night. These boxes were then buried by Confederate convalescents, and that was the end of it. The two Marylanders, during the night, had slipped by the single guard with his beat in front of the door, then managed to cross the Potuxan River, either by swimming or floating on planks or logs, there being an only bridge which had a strong cavalry guard and could not be crossed without the countersign.

When I was made acquainted with the scheme by Judge Wilson of the Hood's Texas Brigade, who was a Mason and had a number of Masonic friends among the Marylanders, there were two men out then and after giving them a reasonable time to get away, he had made arrangements for he and I to go out next, but alas, the two men out then were captured and exposed the whole plan, which put an end to it.

Another plan of escape was attempted by others, that of wading out in the bay on dark nights, in water deep enough to barely expose their heads, but when they got opposite the fort those shrewd Yankees had cast an anchor about a quarter of a mile out, to which was attached a rope and the rope attached to a bell inside of the fort, so when the prisoner, wading along in the deep water, would strike this rope, he would ring the bell, which invariably resulted in his discovery.

Other attempts at escape by some of the Marylanders, through bribery of the guard at the gate leading out on the bay shore, invariably failed. The guards would take the bribe, then report the case when he permitted the prisoners to pass out of the gate. The escaping prisoners would then be charged on by a lot of cavalry in waiting around the corner of the fence and shot down by them.

General Butler next conceived the idea to go to Richmond with a batch of prisoners and attempt an exchange, not for the purpose of relieving the prisoners, but simply to test his own case with the Confederate Government. On his arrival at City Point, it seems some arrangement was made that enabled him to deliver these prisoners, presumably in a fair exchange for prisoners held by us. In this batch of prisoners were a number of Marylanders, who thoughtlessly published in a Richmond paper their sufferings and hardships, as well as ill treatment at the hands of the Federal authorities, and particularly denounced Captain Patterson, who had charge of the Point Lookout prison, in most bitter terms. By accident Captain Patterson got hold of a copy of a Richmond paper containing these charges and with it, went to the Maryland Division, read it to the men and told them if further exchanges were had he would see to it that the Marylanders should be the last to leave there.

After this, the Marylanders in the prison, having denounced the article as ill-advised and improper, began again to court the favour of Captain Patterson and, after several months, concluded that they had about succeeded in regaining his confidence. One morning they were notified to get ready to go to City Point for exchange. Of course, there was considerable enthusiasm among the Marylanders and I decided to go out with them, in the name of Stanley.

We were marched out and carried into another bull pen, kept there five or six hours, when we were permitted to return into our old quarters and found the Tennessee Division had been placed aboard the flag of truce boat and sailed for City Point. It is hardly necessary to say that I was the greatest disappointed man among them, because I also belonged to the Tennessee Division.

In about two weeks the Louisiana Division was called for, to which I also belonged and availed myself of the Louisianan's name, the owner of which was dead, and passed out with them.

At the mouth of the James River, we passed a fleet of gunboats and ships, and in due time arrived at City Point, where we anchored in midstream. The exchange agent, Major Mulford, immediately went ashore and telegraphed to Richmond our arrival. We were anchored here several days, expecting hourly a Confederate boat to put in its appearance with the equivalent of Federal prisoners to be returned in exchange. After several days, having been told that our boat surely would arrive the second day, and as it had not put in its appearance, we decided that there was a hitch somewhere and that we were liable to be carried back. We expected, hourly, a couple of gunboats to come in sight to escort us back to Point Lookout.

The situation, to us, began to look gloomy, and created a feeling of desperation. We were determined never to be taken back to look inside of another prison. In accordance therewith we soon made up a party of about a hundred, agreeing to overpower the guard on the boat if the Confederate boat didn't make its appearance by ten o'clock next morning.

On the cabin deck of this boat were quite a number of Confederate officers, among them General W. H. Fitts Lee, who had been wounded and captured. He was a son of General Robert E. Lee, and to him we communicated our intentions and asked their support. He replied, urging us to make no such attempt, that everything was all right and the object of our trip would be carried out without doubt. I told the men that we could not afford to accept his advice; that we had too much at stake, and I construed General Lee's position to be prompted by what he conceived his duty as a Confederate officer. I urged them, by all means, to carry out our plan.

The next day about noon I was sound asleep under the stepladder leading up to the hatch, when awakened by considerable tumult around me. I discovered about a half dozen men on the ladder, ready to make a charge on the upper deck, where the guards were located. It so happened that the man at the top of the ladder hesitated and by way of encouragement, I called to him, "Don't you stop there; put your shoulders under the hatch and throw it off." He proved to be an Irishman who said, "The divil, you say; you come up here and take my place."

There was nothing to do but climb up the ladder and take his place. I soon put my back to the hatch and sent it up, whirling on the deck, and jumped on the deck myself. The guard on duty threw his gun down on me, telling me to go back or he would kill me. I called to the men, "Come on, boys," but none would follow. I noticed General Lee in the front part of the boat, motioning to me, "Go back; go back." It is hardly necessary for me to say that I felt like a fool and went back.

There is a member of our camp here today who states that he was present, close to General Lee, and saw me; his name is J. W. Middleton.

Our boat finally made its appearance and while it moved up very slowly towards our boat for the purpose of throwing a gang plank across, for us to pass over, a party of the Louisiana Guard Battery, a company of highly educated young men from New Orleans, appeared on the upper deck with a Confederate flag belonging to the Seventh Louisiana, tacked on to a piece of scantling in the centre. General Lee and Colonel Davis of the Eighth Virginia were at one end of the line. These young men, who were splendid singers, with fine voices, struck up:

> *Farewell forever to the Star Spangled Banner,*
> *No longer shall it wave over the home of the free,*
> *Unfurled in its stead to the bold breeze of Heaven,*
> *Thirteen bright stars around the palmetto tree.*

These lines constituted the chorus of the song, which was sung with a great deal of spirit, and joined in by many of the men and officers. I forgot to mention that while the boats were coming together the Federal prisoners began to twit our boys about going back to live on corn dodgers and bacon, but when they heard this song, they were dumbfounded, ceased their guying and simply stood speechless.

On our arrival at the Rockets, a place of landing in Richmond, we were met by a great many citizens, mostly ladies in carriages, and a company of Richmond cadets, escorted us to the Capitol Square, where we were met by President and Mrs. Davis, who shook hands with every one of us. Mrs. Davis was in tears. We were then regaled by a speech from Governor Smith of Virginia, standing on the platform in front of the Capitol, when among other things he said, "They have called me from the tented field to preside over the destinies of this great commonwealth, because they say I am too old to be there; but I deny the charge and want it distinctly understood that among Yankees and women, I am only five and twenty."

Those who are acquainted with Governor Smith's history, knowing him at that time to be a man about sixty-five or seventy years old, commanding a brigade in the army when he was elected Governor, will not be surprised at his expression. Governor Smith was generally known as "Extra Billy." I will take occasion to mention that when I put my foot on Dixie soil it proved the happiest moment of my life up to that time; I felt like kissing the ground that I stood on.

President Davis, in his speech to us, told us that we were only paroled, and could not enter the service again until duly exchanged. He requested those that lived on the West of the Mississippi not to go home on a visit, pending this exchange, stating that he hoped we would soon be called on to return to our respective commands, as we were greatly needed in the army.

With me, this admonition was not needed, my only ambition was to get back to my command and again mount my horse and resume my duties. For this purpose, I sought out Senator Oldham from Texas, who went with me to the War Department and secured me a pass from the Secretary of War, to go to Greenville, East Tennessee, where I learned the Rangers were camped and in due time made my way over there and found them in a deep snow.

CHAPTER 11

The Inhumanity of the Federal Government

In reviewing my prison experience and observation, I find that I omitted to mention a case at Bowling Green, which will give the reader a fair idea of the danger of capture in territory occupied by the Federal Army and now take occasion to recall the case of John R. Lisle, a sergeant in Morgan's command, who was permitted to visit his home near Russellville, Kentucky, on a short furlough and was shot down in his own home, in the bosom of his family, by some Tory neighbours, the ball striking him on top of the head, which temporarily stunned him and while on the floor, senseless, they rushed in and secured his capture. He had on a new gray Confederate uniform and when searched, had an order from General Morgan to notify all of their men whom he met or had an opportunity to convey the instructions, to report back to their command, having overstayed their furlough.

I got acquainted with Lisle as soon as I entered the prison and found him a very bright, intelligent gentleman. He was then being tried by court martial on the charge of being a spy and convicted on this order of Morgan's, ordering men back to their command. During the trial he made a pencil memorandum of the proceedings of the court martial and finally, losing his temper one day, blessed out the court martial, telling them that he was satisfied they were after his blood and to stop their mockery of a trial, to go ahead and take his life, lead him out and shoot him. The court martial found him guilty and assessed his punishment at death by hanging.

As soon as the findings of the court martial were returned from General Burnside's headquarters, approved, he was taken down into the lower room and had irons forged on him, taken over to the court house under special guard to await the day of his execution. While at the court house his wife and oldest son, a boy about fifteen, were permitted to see him, when he smuggled the memoranda, he had made of the proceedings of the court martial to his wife, with instructions to send his boy to General Bragg's headquarters, then near Tullahoma, Tennessee, with this memoranda, satisfied that our government would demand his exchange as a prisoner of war, putting some Federal officer in confinement, as hostage. After he was taken out of the prison, we were not permitted to learn anything more about his fate.

During my imprisonment at Point Lookout, Maryland, a batch of about five hundred prisoners from Johnson's Island were received there. Hastening to the gate to watch their coming in, thinking perhaps I might see some acquaintances, I met John R. Lisle, who had just been released from a dungeon at Johnson's Island, where he had been ever since he was moved from Bowling Green in irons—confined in this dungeon and for the first time then treated as a prisoner of war.

There is hardly a doubt but designating a couple of Federal officers as hostages for his safety, had the desired effect and saved his life. I left him at Point Lookout with the balance of the prisoners, from whence he was finally sent around for exchange. I had a letter from one of our prison companions near Bowling Green, about eight years ago, saying that Lisle finally returned South and to his home in Kentucky, where he died only a few years before this letter was written.

In order to give the reader an idea of the intense hatred on the part of the Lincoln Government, it might be well here to note that in the very beginning of hostilities they adopted a policy to degrade the Southern Army in the estimation of their own people, as well as that of foreign countries. In order to carry out such policy the War Department issued an order that all executions of Confederate soldiers convicted by court martial, should be by hanging—a felon's death—which order was never modified and was carried out in its letter and spirit, never in any case permitting an exception.

In this connection I would mention a case in point, which occurred while I was a prisoner and has repeatedly been reported in the papers of the North and South. The case was a Colonel Johnston of the Confederate Army, in conjunction with a lieutenant, whose name I have forgotten, entering the Federal lines as spies. Colonel Johnston was armed with a fictitious order from Secretary of War Stanton to proceed to Murfreesboro, Franklin and Nashville, Tennessee, and inspect the Federal works at these places. They called one evening at Franklin, presented the Secretary of War's order, which seemed to be genuine, when the colonel commanding received them very courteously and rode around with them, inspecting his works.

Colonel Johnston also stated to him that he was just from General Rosencranz's headquarters, where he had inspected the works around Murfreesboro. After the inspection of the Franklin works Colonel Johnston told the colonel in command that he was compelled to go to Nashville that night and insisted on leaving at once for Nashville, although dark had set in. The colonel tried to persuade him to spend the night with him but all to no purpose. After Colonel Johnston and the lieutenant had been gone perhaps a half hour the colonel got suspicious and wired General Rosencranz for information, and General Rosencranz replied that there had been no such men there, that evidently, they were spies, to not fail to capture them and order a drumhead court martial.

The colonel then immediately ordered his horse and with a sergeant, pursued Colonel Johnston and the lieutenant, caught up with them some six or eight miles on the road to Nashville, and insisted that they must go back with him and spend the night, which they did. On their arrival at the colonel's headquarters, he immediately had them searched and found ample evidence on their persons that they were Confederate soldiers, acting as spies, notably the sword of Colonel Johnston's was inscribed "C. S. A.," and Colonel Johnston readily admitted they were spies.

During the session of the court martial Colonel Johnston made himself known to the colonel commanding, who then recognised him as a classmate at West Point. He then made an eloquent appeal to the court martial to save the life of the lieutenant, telling them that he was unaware, when they started on this expedition, of its object and finally begged them to have him shot, to permit him to die a soldier's and not a felon's death. He said to the colonel, "When you rode up, we both had our pistols out, under the capes of our overcoats and could have killed you easily, thereby saving our lives, but the thought of killing an old classmate without giving him a chance for his life overruled my better judgment and I decided that I might talk out of it, thereby sparing your life," but all to no purpose, his pleadings were ignored and he had to meet his fate by hanging.

After the defeat of the Federal Army at the first battle of Manassas, many wagonloads of handcuffs, put up in barrels, were captured, which were intended to be placed on the entire Confederate Army when captured, and marched into Washington City, wearing these bracelets.

Among Mr. Lincoln's earliest proclamations was the one declaring medicines contraband of war, thus depriving millions of sick of medicines, one of the most brutal and inhuman orders ever published by a civilized government.

Chapter 12

I Rejoin My Command

Recurring to the meeting of my comrades at Greenville, Tennessee, where I found them camped in a deep snow, when they had me relate my prison experience, etc.: They had just received orders to move to Dalton, Georgia, where I, having no horse, proceeded by rail. On my arrival at Dalton, I found the largest, best equipped army I had ever seen in the Confederacy, mostly quartered in tents. Our advance line occupied the top of a range of mountains, presenting precipitous fronts towards the enemy. This range of mountains was somewhat in the shape of a horseshoe, largely surrounding Dalton with probably a half dozen gaps, which were strongly fortified by our forces, except Snake Creek Gap on our left, nearly on a line with Resacca, a railroad station immediately in our rear on the only line entering Dalton and our only means of supplying the army and enabling retreat. I found General Joseph E. Johnston in command, with General Hardee, his second in command and General Hood, commanding a corps, immediately in front of Dalton.

Not having any horse and unable to secure one, I met a friend, Captain James Britton from Lebanon, Tennessee, who commanded Hood's escort, who told me that he had several horses in camp, doing nothing, the owners of the horses being sick and confined at the hospital; if I would come and stay with him that I could ride any of the horses. This I gratefully accepted, telling him that I would only do so with the understanding that I would be treated as a member of the company doing duty.

While on this duty, moving out with the escort one morning with General Hood and staff, to his headquarters just in the rear of Railroad Gap, I witnessed the meeting of General J. E. Johnston, W. J. Hardee, General Cheatham, General Hindman, all with their respective staffs, at General Hood's headquarters, which were under an old work-shed with a workbench under it. General Johnston and staff were the last to arrive. After dismounting and shaking hands with the different generals and members of their staffs, as also General Hood, he handed General Hood his crutches. General Hood, it will be remembered, lost his leg at Chickamauga and was ever afterwards on crutches.

Generals Johnston and Hood then moved up the road about three hundred yards out of our hearing and were soon engaged in a very animated discussion, which lasted perhaps three-quarters of an hour. When they returned Generals Johnston and Hardee mounted their horses with their respective staffs, returning to town, and gradually the rest of the officers dispersed, going to their respective stations.

CHAPTER 13

Middle Tennessee and Kentucky

On reflection, I find that I omitted about a year's service in Tennessee and Kentucky, before my capture near Bowling Green and will insert this now.

After destroying trestles and bridges between LaVergne and Nashville, under General Forrest, and capturing a railroad train at LaVergne, on which Colonel Fordyce was captured, we were ordered back across the mountain to Chattanooga, where we commenced scouting and picketing on the Tennessee River. We frequently extended our scouts almost to Guntersville, with the Federal Army massing and camping just across the river. General Mitchell commanded at Huntsville. He gave out that he was building a gunboat, with which to capture Chattanooga, and had the people of Chattanooga badly alarmed about it, but when finally, he got his gunboat ready to move up the river, a scout of about twenty Texas Rangers were sent down to meet it with shotguns, taking a position on top of a high bank, opposite the mouth of Battle Creek, which was in plain view of this high bank.

The gunboat approached and proved to be an ordinary small river boat, lined with cotton bales on the edge of the decks with the troops aboard, lying around carelessly on the side of this barricade of cotton bales, some of them playing cards. When the boat came very close to our bluff, we turned loose our shotguns on them and drove the boat into the mouth of Battle Creek, where it remained and was utilized by the Federal Army as a bridge for crossing the creek. This proved the end of General Mitchell's famous gunboat, with which he threatened to capture Chattanooga. It was driven out of commission by Terry's Rangers' shotguns and relieved the people of Chattanooga of their anxiety.

While picketing down on the river road with a companion, we stopped at a blacksmith's shop near Nicajack Cave and had our horses shod; just across the river was a camp of Federal infantry and artillery. The river at this point we judged to be about three-quarters of a mile wide, perhaps more; the railroad continued to run on the banks of the river, after passing the Narrows with the first depot out of Chattanooga, Shell Mound. After having our horses shod, we rode down to the railroad on the banks of the river, the grade of which was high enough to protect us and our horses. We discovered a soldier at the river, filling some canteens and to see him run, we fired our pistols across, which of course made him run to his camp.

Soon after, we heard the artillery bugle and immediately a gun opened on us with shell, which always struck the Nicajack Cave, some three-quarters of a mile in our rear, the country between us and Nicajack Cave being flat and open. We soon moved down to the little brick depot at Shell Mound and opened on them from there, when they perforated it with their shells; we then moved down to a box bridge across the mouth of the creek running into the river and had them make that a target. It is hardly necessary to say that we enjoyed this, somewhat, having a duel with our pistols against their piece of artillery. We were entirely protected and didn't consider that we were under any danger whatever of being hit.

While picketing on this main road, General Morgan ran down on a locomotive as far as Shell Mound, just before our escapade with this artillery and came very near having his engine struck by a shell, but he succeeded in getting back to Chattanooga with his locomotive.

We were soon ordered back to Middle Tennessee, under General Forrest, where we operated around McMinnville, Manchester and along the railroad. After an attack on the outskirts of Manchester one morning, which Colonel Forrest decided was too strong for us, we withdrew further down the railroad, where we charged a block-house, the first we ever attempted to capture and the first we had ever seen.

But, although some of our men got right up to the house, we were unable to force them to surrender, and were forced to give it up as a bad job. While engaged in this venture, a large force of infantry, cavalry and artillery had moved out on the road from McMinnville and were about to cut off our line of retreat. When we got in sight of this force, hurrying to get out of this corner, they raised a shout, which I must say made me feel very uncomfortable, knowing that they outnumbered us perhaps five to one, but we succeeded in dashing across the main road, where we wheeled and charged their advance column, bringing them to a halt, permitting others of the command to cross, that were virtually cut off, but they did capture a large fine looking negro man, who was the servant of General Forrest. His name was Napoleon, and he was devotedly attached to General Forrest.

In connection with his capture, they also captured two fine horses belonging to the general. They carried this negro to Louisville prison and did their best to persuade him to take the oath of allegiance and join them, but he steadfastly refused, as he was devotedly attached to General Forrest and was finally, through some special arrangement, exchanged and returned to the general. The last I knew of him I heard of him in Louisville prison, when he was sent around for exchange.

After operating a while longer in Middle Tennessee without any important captures, we got information that General Bragg had crossed the Tennessee River at Chattanooga and was moving across Cumberland Mountain, driving the Federal Army before him and we were instructed to harass the enemy as much as possible. In accordance therewith we would attack their infantry (moving with their artillery, ordnance and wagon trains by divisions on several of the main roads). We would dash into their rear, forcing them to stop and draw up in line of battle, when they would commence shelling us and we would move out of the range of their artillery rapidly, further up the road, striking another column perhaps in flank, leaving the first mentioned column shelling the woods for an hour or more after we had left.

In this manner we kept them harassed and impeded their rapid movements, while General Bragg, with the main army, was moving as rapidly as possible on their flank, crossing the Cumberland River higher up on his way to Glasgow, Kentucky. The Federal Army made a short stop at Nashville, collecting all their forces, and then moved from there towards Mumfordsville, Kentucky, on Green River.

While in pursuit of one of these Federal columns on top of a mountain not far from Woodbury, we struck a point on the pike where it was built across a deep ravine; the crossing protected on the side by a rail fence. Just as we entered the narrow point in this lane, General Forrest, who was riding in advance of our regiment, discovered a vidette of the enemy in the woods on the far banks of the ravine, and he immediately had some men dismounted on both flanks, to drive them in, satisfied that the enemy were going to make a stand on the other side of the ravine.

He determined to charge them, horseback, for which purpose we formed fours and prepared for the charge by tightening our saddle girths. Just as we were ready to move on them, a masked battery of four pieces opened on us and drove us back, as we stood no chance of reaching it in massed formation of fours through this narrow lane on the Pike.

The first shell cut off a leg below the knee of D. Rugeley, one of the finest looking young men we had in the company, and one of the best. He was held on his horse by his companions, on our retreat, when the enemy's cavalry charged us and, for the moment, created a little confusion. When Colonel Wharton discovered Rugeley's plight, holding the lower part of his leg by the foot and being assisted by a comrade on each side, holding him on his horse, he was completely overcome with the sight, rode up and fell over on D., with both arms around his neck, crying, when D. said to him, "Colonel Wharton, this is no place to take on in this manner. Leave me and save yourself."

This aroused Wharton and wheeling his horse, called on the Rangers to rally and drive back that cavalry and save D. Rugeley, which it is hardly necessary to say, was done in short order. This is perhaps the only instance where Colonel Wharton was seen to lose control of himself and can only be explained by the fact that D. Rugeley's father and he were most intimate friends, and on parting with Rugeley's father had been enjoined to take special care of his boy.

An instance of appreciation of our services was illustrated near Murfreesboro, Tennessee, through which place we had just passed in pursuit of a large Federal column. In passing through a lane a few miles north of town, where a number of ladies had congregated to see us pass, an old lady among them was cheering us and clapping her hands, when she was heard to remark, "Oh, daughter; just look at our soldiers, grand men as they are, all covered with dust so they can hardly be recognised; God bless them! I wish they could stay long enough so I could wash their clothes." This old lady perhaps had never seen a washtub in her life, as judging from the magnificent house which appeared through the woods, and its surroundings, she was no doubt raised in wealth and affluence. It was such expressions as this, on the part of the ladies, that made us good soldiers.

After our army reached Glasgow, the enemy had concentrated a strong force at Mumfordsville, which was strongly fortified and which they determined to hold at all hazards. Nashville was not evacuated by them, but a force of ten thousand men, strongly fortified, with Andrew Johnson, demanding of General Nelson to hold this place at all hazards, which was done. While our army was at Glasgow, which was only about twenty-five miles from Bell Station, McDonald, a member of our company, proposed to me to go by and see the Smith family, at whose house he had been sick and to which I agreed, and for this purpose called on Colonel Wharton to give us a pass, which he refused, saying that no one could be permitted to pass our lines unless they had a pass from General Bragg, countersigned by General Polk.

We told him, "Colonel Wharton, we feel in duty bound to visit these people," and gave him the reason, telling him that we would make the attempt without a pass.

He said, "Graber, if you do and you are caught, Bragg will have both of you shot."

I told him, "All right; catching before hanging."

We started out at night, telling him "If you miss us you'll know where we are." We started out the main road towards Bell Station; when about a mile we struck an Alabama picket and asked the lieutenant commanding to allow us to pass through, telling him the circumstances that prompted our determination to visit our friends.

He said, "Rangers, you know we would do anything we can for you, but our orders are very strict and we cannot disobey them."

We then moved back out of sight, struck out into the woods on their flank, passing around them and made our way to the Smith home, about four miles from Bell Station. It is hardly necessary to say the old lady and her daughters, the only ones left at home, were delighted to see us, and especially to hear from the army. They had not heard from their boys, who were in Breckenridge's Brigade, nor their father, who was with them. It will be remembered he left his home with McDonald in a wagon and carried him to Bowling Green, when he was convalescent from his spell of pneumonia. We remained at the house nearly a half day, when we heard heavy firing at Mumfordsville and immediately mounted our horses and started for there.

Arriving at Mumfordsville about night I was unable to get any information of our brigade and we decided to go into the battle with the infantry the next morning, but during the night the Federals surrendered. About daylight we mounted our horses and entered the fort through an embrasure and soon struck the hospital tents, where McDonald dismounted to try to find some liquor. While I never indulged in strong drink, it was hard to keep McDonald from it. While holding his horse, waiting for him to come back, Colonel Wharton rode in, at the head of our regiment, from the opposite side of the fort from where we had entered and on seeing me, simply said, "Hello, Graber; you beat us in," and smiled. I expect we were the first Confederates inside of the fort.

It seems that General Chalmers, the evening before, had made a determined attack on the works and was repulsed with heavy loss. The colonel commanding the fort, learning that General Bragg had arrived with the whole army, completely surrounding him during the night, decided it was better to surrender than to risk another engagement the next day, as he had only about four or five thousand men.

After leaving Mumfordsville, our cavalry under Forrest continued on the main road through Elizabethtown and on to Bardstown, Kentucky, out of which place we drove the Federal cavalry. They retreated to Louisville. We were camped at Bardstown several days, awaiting the arrival of the infantry and while there, formed the acquaintance of a number of good people, which means friends of the South. At Bardstown we found the home of Judge Newman, whose daughter, the wife of my old friend, Cannon, then lived at Courtney. Before they had removed from Hempstead, a year or more before the breaking out of hostilities, her sister, Miss Josie Newman, made a visit to Hempstead, where she formed the acquaintance of quite a number of young men that were in the army with us.

On our second day's sojourn a Mr. Tom Clay, belonging to Company K of our regiment, whose home was in Washington County, and who had been intimately acquainted with Miss Josie during her stay at Hempstead, proposed to me to call on Miss Josie, to which I agreed. Alighting in front of their house, Miss Josie happened to be standing in the door and recognising us, rushed to the gate and invited us in. Just then a little boy came along and asked me to give him a little silk Confederate flag some young ladies had presented me with the day before and I had sticking in the browband of my horse's bridle.

Fearing the little boy would take the flag while we were in the house, I suggested that I had better take this in with me. Miss Josie then said, "That flag can't come into our house." Up to this time we were unaware that they were Union people.

My friend, bowing to her, said, "We will certainly not go into a house where our flag is not welcome," and we declined to go in.

By this time her mother had come to the gate, when Miss Josie introduced us. Mrs. Newman having heard my name, through the Cannon family, quite often, she insisted on our coming in, when we told her Miss Josie's objections. She chided her for her discourtesy and told us to come in and bring the flag, when my friend said to Miss Josie, "We will compromise the matter with you and go in, if you will sing

Dixie and Bonnie Blue Flag for us," which of course she had to agree to do and, while singing these songs, I sat at the end of the piano with my little Confederate flag in my hand and when she sang the chorus, I would wave the flag.

After two days' sojourn we moved on up towards Louisville, part of our force dividing and occupying the town of Taylorsville on our right; the balance of the command camping near Mount Washington on the Bardstown Pike. Here General Forrest received an order from the War Department to personally report to Richmond and turn the command of the brigade over to Colonel Wharton. In about a week the Federal forces advanced out of Louisville. They were said to be a hundred thousand strong, while another force moved out of Cincinnati, about sixty thousand strong, with a view of cutting us off from retreat to Cumberland Gap.

CHAPTER 14

Bardstown Engagement—I "Swap" Horses with a Federal

The object of General Bragg's advance into Kentucky was to form a nucleus for Kentuckians to rally around, our War Department having been importuned by leading Kentuckians to do this, claiming they would have a hundred thousand men to join us as soon as we could reclaim their territory. On this point, however, they were mistaken, as we gathered only about six thousand recruits and they all wanted to serve in cavalry. They joined us largely about half equipped for cavalry service, many of them with citizen's saddles and shotguns or squirrel rifles and, while on the subject, I might mention here that over half of them deserted us before we passed through Cumberland Gap and soon after they found that we were unable to hold Kentucky.

General Bragg moved in there with about thirty thousand men, exclusive of General Kirby Smith's force of about twelve thousand, which moved on Cincinnati and fought the Battle of Richmond, where they completely defeated the Federal Army of about twenty-five thousand strong, capturing, killing and wounding nearly half, with the balance driven into Covington and Cincinnati.

While at Bardstown, General Bragg, finding that the real object of his campaign was a failure, decided to turn it into a raid; to collect valuable stores and move out again, through Cumberland Gap.

When Colonel Wharton took command of the brigade, succeeding General Forrest, General Wheeler with another brigade occupied the Taylorsville Pike, both brigades holding the enemy in check in their advance as best they could. Our little force at Taylorsville was drawn over to the Bardstown and Louisville Pike, where they met the balance of the brigade at Mount Washington. While at Mount Washington, drawn up in line, eating our lunch, a large force of Federal cavalry made a dash on us but were soon repulsed and driven back. In this engagement a messmate of mine, Roland Chatham, received a pistol ball right in the centre of his forehead, just over the eyes, the ball penetrating his skull and burying itself in the brain. This however, did not knock him off his horse and he remained with us until after the enemy was driven back.

Passing to the rear with his wound bleeding, he was noticed by some ladies in Mount Washington, displaying his pistol, when they were heard to remark, "Just look at that poor Texas Ranger; shot through the head and still he wants to fight." In this connection I would state that Chatham was sent to the hospital and finally to Texas, never having been completely disabled on account of this wound, and with this ball imbedded in the brain, lived to a good old age, dying only a few years ago at Bryan, Texas, where he raised a large family. Here he started and operated a cotton gin manufactory, which proved a great success and enabled him to amass a considerable fortune. During all his lifetime his wound remained open but never affected his mind. This was, perhaps, one of the most remarkable cases on record.

The Federal advance through Mount Washington and Taylorsville continued daily as soon as it was light enough to discern anything. The enemy's skirmishers would advance and, supported by their line of battle and artillery, would drive us from positions we had taken up. We would then fall back to another good position, perhaps a mile, and defend that as best we could, again to be driven from it in the same manner. I forgot to mention we had with us in this brigade, the First and Second Georgia and the Tennessee Battalion, under Colonel Baxter Smith, who is still living at Nashville, Tennessee.

When within nine miles of Bardstown, one morning (dark and drizzling rain) the enemy failed to make its appearance at daylight. Waiting until about nine o'clock, Colonel Wharton got suspicious, and sent a scout in our rear, who struck a large cavalry force of the enemy of about eight regiments, occupying the pike near the Fair Grounds. Returning, full speed, the scout reported to Colonel Wharton this condition. Immediately placing himself at the head of our regiment, drawn up immediately across the pike, Colonel Wharton sent couriers to the balance of our regiment and to a section of little brass six-pounders (originally the property of the Arkansas Military Institute) commanded by Captain Pugh of our regiment, a western Texas cowman, instructing them to come on and catch up with our regiment as fast as they could.

Wharton at the head of the regiment in column of fours, struck a lope and soon arrived in sight of this body of the enemy's cavalry. He then ordered a charge and when at a junction of a dirt road with the pike, about two companies of this cavalry formed in an orchard behind a rail picket fence, which are rails stuck in the ground, picket fashion, and fired on our flank point blank. About thirty or forty of us turned on them, halting in front of this picket fence with our bridle reigns thrown over the horns of our saddles, and with a six-shooter in each hand, began to empty saddles. This caused them to break and enter a lane in their rear, having already let down the fence to provide for such an emergency, and fled up the lane in a northerly direction from whence they had come.

Colonel Wharton with the balance of the regiment dashed into the solid body of the enemy in his front and scattered them. It soon developed that they were panic stricken and were driven over the open country, interspersed only by rail and rock fences, in detached bodies of twenty and fifty, and so on, by only a few Rangers, driving them like cattle on the prairies. Here was one of the most brilliant cavalry engagements we were ever in and resulted in our capturing a great many prisoners.

When the regiment passed through Bardstown somewhat hurriedly, passing by the Newman residence, Miss Josie Newman, who was standing at the gate, watching them go by, saw a Major Jared Gross, a former acquaintance, loping up the column. She recognised him, clapping her hands and calling out, "Goodbye, Jared; I'm glad to see you running," when the next moment she recognised a Federal, Major Watts, riding behind one of our boys, a prisoner, his face badly bruised and his clothes torn and soiled, having had his horse killed under him. This sight immediately brought her tears and she went back into the house, crying. She was a kind hearted, good young lady, full of spirit in her Union sentiment.

Now, to go back to the party of Federals in the orchard, fleeing up the lane from the direction whence they came: Captain Mark Evans, commanding one of our Western companies, and I, were the first ones to enter the lane and drive these fellows. We were followed by quite a number of others, who stopped at the fence with us when first fired into. In running up the lane we ran over a number of six-shooters and belts with sabre and six-shooters attached. The six-shooter was always a valuable capture for us, as we could readily sell it to men in the army who had money, which we were always in need of, and although we were virtually maintaining ourselves without the aid of the government, we could not afford to stop and pick up these pistols, as everything depended on crowding these Federals, who outnumbered us at least ten to one; but, as before stated, they were panic stricken, which sometimes happened to the best of troops.

After passing about a mile up this lane, I noticed a very fine pistol. I recognised it as a Tranter, an English pistol, self-cocking, of which Colonel Terry had four, and I was always anxious to secure a pair of them. My first impulse was to stop and get this pistol; then again concluded not to stop, as so much depended on our crowding them, but, after passing it perhaps thirty or forty yards, I decided I would go back and pick it up, anyway. For this purpose, I wheeled and as my horse's position was across the lane, in turning, one of our men just behind me, struck my horse's neck and broke the headstall of my bridle, dropping the bit out of the horse's mouth. He wheeled and ran after Evans and the Federals, running faster than ever I had known him to run before, and he would soon have carried me right in among them.

But when near Evans I called to him to stop my horse; at the same time one of the Federals dismounted from his horse and surrendered. He and Evans together stopped my horse, and as there was no time for swapping bridles, I slipped over on his horse, handing him my bridle rein which was still around my horse's neck with the bit attached; grabbing his pistol, I went on my Federal horse and told the Federal to wait and turn mine over to some of the boys behind.

Continuing up this lane we discovered a bunch of about twenty-five or thirty, some hundred and fifty yards to our right, in a field, headed by an officer riding a magnificent horse and in magnificent uniform. We soon arrived at a big gate on our right, just beyond where another fence connected with the lane fence, this fence running due east, and which this bunch of Federals had to cross. When we reached this gate Evans said to me, "Run through that gate and head off this bunch," which I did, I forgot to mention that this party was driven by only about a half dozen of our men.

After passing through the gate I stopped, took position almost immediately in front of them and when the officer got near the fence, I threw my pistol down on him and demanded his surrender, to which he paid no attention, but threw off the top rail, the rider of the fence, and made his horse leap the fence, passing right in front of me, running through an orchard and I have never been able to understand how he succeeded in avoiding the limbs of the trees without butting his brains out.

When the balance of his men came up and attempted to jump the fence, the first man broke it down and furnished an easier way for the balance to cross but, being headed off by me, they were forced to take right down the fence east, followed by our boys, whom I cautioned several times to hold their fire until the Federals would bunch up. To this, however, very little attention was paid and with my additional pistol, my shots held out longer than theirs.

Now, it must be understood that having to load our pistols with loose powder from the powder flask, which had a gauge attached, then ramming down the ball with a ramrod attached to the pistol, then putting a cap on the nipple, it was necessary to stop and reload, as an attempt at reloading, running, would have spilled the powder and caused confusion; hence, one after another of our boys dropped behind to reload. This found me alone, just after the Federals and I had turned the corner of a stone fence, starting due north again.

When about a hundred yards from this stone fence I fired my last shot, when one of them looked around, discovered I was by myself, called on the others to "turn on him; there is only one by himself; give him h——." I wheeled and the Yankees wheeled. When we had run back only about fifty yards, two of our men, who I think were Geo. W. Littlefield and Beardy Miller, turned the same corner of the stone fence. When this bunch of Federals saw this, they again wheeled, running north. When Littlefield and Miller came up to where I was, they said, "Come on; come on."

I said, "No, I have got to stop and load my pistol," which I proceeded to do, they continuing after this bunch of Federals. Having about three or four chambers of my pistol filled with powder and standing about fifteen yards from the fence, seven more Federals came around the same corner of the fence, running between me and the fence, after I had drawn back my horse about ten steps, giving them more room. If I had had one load in my pistol, I would have demanded their surrender, which I believe they would have done, but they never said a word to me nor I to them, and went flying after Littlefield and Beardy Miller, who were after the first bunch.

I forgot to mention that before we had reached this far, we heard heavy firing of infantry and artillery. We knew it was infantry by their first volley; then a very rapid, scattering fire, as also rapid cannonading in the direction of the Fair Grounds, which we concluded to mean that the balance of our brigade were passing down into Bardstown, around this infantry and artillery, which had been sent in support of their cavalry.

After having completed the loading of two of my pistols, I discovered a bunch of about eighty or a hundred Federals running towards me, cut off by the long fence running east. When they struck the fence, in place of crossing it, continuing in their course north, they turned right down the line of fence east, on the south side of it. By this time the firing at the Fair Grounds had become more scattered and distant, and the artillery had ceased firing, but I was afraid to venture back the way I came, by myself, therefore, decided that I would let down the fence, getting on the south side of it, follow this last bunch east, until I was about four or five miles east of Bardstown, then turn due south and strike the Springfield Pike, on which I knew our infantry were moving from Bardstown to Perryville.

I finished loading my pistols, then crossed the fence and started east in the wake of these Federals, keeping a sharp lookout ahead and, after riding about three or four miles, passing through woods-lots and fences, I emerged from the woods, up on a ridge, and discovered these fellows about a quarter of a mile below me in a field, drawn up in a line, facing in my direction. I resorted to a ruse, taking off my hat and waving it behind me, then started at them, but this would not work and immediately they started after me. I turned south and put my Federal horse to his best and soon got out of sight.

Having run in this direction some three or four miles, coming out of a woods-lot through a big gate to a large, white house I stopped and called, hoping to get some information about the best way to get to the Springfield Pike. After calling some little time, an old gentleman came out of the door, to the front porch, when I called to him that I was a Confederate soldier and wanted some information about striking the Springfield Pike, four or five miles east of Bardstown. Having heard the firing of the infantry and artillery, which no doubt greatly alarmed him, he talked so fast and rambling that I was unable to understand him, and I begged him to come to the gate, which he started to do.

When about half way, I heard the woods-lot gate creak, looked around and here were my Federals, coming single file, which of course started me again, running south into a short lane running east, and when at the mouth of this lane, only about three hundred yards long, I looked across the corner of this man's field and found about a dozen or more of these fellows bunched up at his gate, talking to the old man. I immediately turned south again, putting my horse to his very best. When about three miles from there, I struck a lane with a dirt road running towards Bardstown. I kept a sharp lookout for the Federals behind me, whom I never saw again and don't believe they followed me any further.

Looking up the lane east, I discovered five Confederate cavalrymen coming in the direction of Bardstown and when they got up to where I was waiting for them in the lane, having crossed the fence, I found that they were three Georgians and two of our own regiment. I then tried to get them to go back with me, telling them that I believed that we could pick up quite a number of prisoners, but the Georgians were unwilling; they too, had heard the firing at Bardstown and did not think it safe for us to go back in the direction of where I left these people scattered over the different fields.

I now suggested we strike south again until we reached the Springfield Pike, which we did in due time and struck Anderson's Division of Infantry, reporting to General Anderson our engagement and telling him I was satisfied we could pick up many prisoners if he would only send back with me a couple of companies of cavalry. He stated he did not have a man to spare and was unable to do so, but told me to wait there, that General Hardee would come up pretty soon and might act on my suggestion.

In about half an hour General Hardee, with his staff, came up, and I reported the engagement to him and found he had had no particulars. Being unable to tell him whether the balance of the brigade with the two little popguns had got through safely to Bardstown, made him somewhat apprehensive, but he was, nevertheless, gratified to know that the Rangers had come through all right.

General Hardee, in response to my request to send some cavalry with me to pick up these stragglers, said that he did not have a man to spare and told me we had better stay at his headquarters that night. The next morning, we would find our command at a certain point on this pike, he said. This we decided to do, being very hungry and tired. The next morning, we started for our camp and, on my arrival there, found my horse with the saddle, everything all right, but no one in the company could tell who delivered him or where he came from. Captain Evans, I suppose, being too much engaged in collecting his scattered forces, had not made any report on my exchange of horses. I never found out what became of my good Federal who held him for me and swapped with me. My comrades, who had concluded that I was perhaps killed, shot off of my horse, had given me out and, when I rode in on my Federal horse with the Federal overcoat and other equipments, you can imagine their surprise.

Miss Josie Newman, just before Major Gross passed her house, had called to some members of our company to know where I was and their answer was that I was left on the field, either dead or wounded and this caused her and her mother, with friends, to look over the field for several days, hunting me or my body, so Mrs. Cannon reported after a visit to her home, several years after the war.

Chapter 15

The Battle of Perryville

Referring back to the balance of the brigade we left formed on the pike, nine miles from town: Couriers were sent them and to our little battery, to follow us and catch up as fast as they could, which they tried to do. When near the Fair Grounds they fell into the enemy's infantry and artillery support, but successfully moved around them, losing only a few killed and wounded and taken prisoners; our loss in killed and wounded was very small.

The cause of our being cut off was through General Wheeler, who had occupied the Taylorsville Pike, moving into Bardstown the night before, sending a courier to Colonel Wharton with a dispatch ordering him to move in also. This courier was captured, which of course, proved valuable information to the enemy and on which they acted by throwing this heavy cavalry, infantry and artillery forces across our line of retreat.

This brilliant achievement of Wharton's extricating his brigade from this trap, secured his promotion to that of Brigadier-General, the same as Forrest's exploit in the capture of Murfreesboro had secured his commission as Brigadier-General.

After leaving Bardstown our army continued its movement towards Perryville, its rear covered by our cavalry, all under the command of General Joe Wheeler. We pursued the same tactics that we did between Louisville and Bardstown, taking up favourable positions only to be driven from them by the large force of the enemy, usually by their superior artillery and heavy flank movements, thereby retarding their advance and giving our infantry, artillery and wagon train ample time to keep out of their way, also enabling some part of the cavalry to collect valuable army stores, such as provisions, stock, etc.

At Perryville we were forced to call a halt and give battle, our right wing, commanded by General Polk, becoming actively engaged about two o'clock in the evening.

The battlefield selected was one of the most favourable to both armies that could have been wished for, except that the extreme left wing of the Federal Army was caught without water until they succeeded in reaching a spring. Both lines of battle were on wooded ridges, intervened by a gentle valley from one and a half to three miles wide, these ridges terminating not far from Doctor's Creek where there was considerable water, and which was commanded by our lines. At the head of the valley another wooded ridge sprang up about equidistant between the terminations of the two first mentioned ridges.

About ten o'clock we were ordered to our extreme right, commanded by General Cheatham and our line of march in the rear of the infantry line was discovered by the enemy, causing a concentration of their artillery to such an extent that we were forced to drop to the rear out of their sight. Finally, we were ordered up on this wooded ridge commencing in the centre of the valley, as a corps of observation, to watch the enemy's extreme left and frustrate any flank movements they might undertake.

I forgot to mention that the artillery on both lines opened about daylight and gradually developed on both lines to about one o'clock, the infantry of both lying down and keeping out of sight. While on the ridge as stated, acting as a corps of observation, General Wharton, with his field glass, discovered a body of Federal cavalry, loaded with canteens, at a spring at the foot of the mountain they were occupying and called to the command, "About a half dozen of you get off your horses and drive that cavalry away from the spring."

As the mountain or ridge we were on, on the side next to the enemy, was very rocky and precipitous, the necessity of dismounting was apparent. I, with five or six others, obeyed the order and we were soon down in the valley, charging this spring, when this cavalry, with their long-range Spencer rifles, took position behind a rock fence and opened on us. We had only one long range gun, in addition to six-shooters and knowing that the eyes of our own command, as well as Cheatham's Division of infantry were watching us, we never considered a halt, but charged right on to them and, with our pistols, drove them away from the spring.

We followed them around the foot of their ridge, past a house in the rear of the ridge, then down a line of fence, while they passed into the field and finally into a cedar thicket. We decided that we had better retire. We had started to do so, when one of these fellows came out of the thicket, riding a grey horse and called to us, waving his pistol. We turned loose on him with our pistols and drove him back into the thicket. We again started to retire, when he made his appearance again, pursuing the same tactics, when one of our boys, who had an Enfield rifle, the only gun in the party, crept down the outside line of the fence, unseen by them, until about even with the thicket and when the fellow made his appearance again, the third time, he fired on him, tumbling him off his horse.

This brought a shout from our party, when simultaneously with our shout, a battery opened on the extreme left of the ridge, almost right over us, but they were not shooting at us. Still, we knew unless we hurried out of there, we would be caught, and immediately proceeded to do so. When we got in sight of the ridge occupied by our cavalry, we discovered the object of their artillery fire, which was shelling a party General Wharton had sent around, leading our horses, to bring them to us. Before we got half way across we found our regiment sweeping around the foot of the mountain, across the valley, up on the enemy's ridge and as soon as they were out of sight in the dense woods on the ridge, they fell into the enemy's infantry behind a stone fence, which poured volleys into them and it is hardly necessary to say, badly scattered them, and they left a number of killed and wounded on the field.

In the meantime, General Cheatham and staff had been seen crossing the valley to the point where our regiment was engaged, followed by his strong line of infantry. General Cheatham called to our scattered forces to "take this cavalry out of here and let my people take a hand," which they did as soon as they got within range of this stone fence. This fence was defended by the enemy's infantry at close quarters with clubbed guns and bayonets, but they finally yielded and were driven, inch by inch, off the mountain to their rear.

This was the opening of the Battle of Perryville and occurred about two o'clock in the evening. Among the dead left temporarily on the field was Captain Mark Evans, shot through the centre of the head. The reader will remember that a few days before he saved my life and assisted me in swapping horses with the Federal in the Bardstown fight.

After rallying his forces General Wharton moved around in the rear of this wooded ridge and, while moving parallel with this ridge in the valley beyond, discovered an ordnance train in a lane about a quarter of a mile to our right, and prepared to charge it. Immediately a battery of four pieces opened on us on our flank, compelling us to withdraw, as we were satisfied that this battery was supported by a heavy force of infantry. Under this fire of artillery, we had a complete set of fours cut down by one cannon ball or shell that passed through the bodies of four horses, cutting off both legs of one man below the knee, but not injuring the three other men, who mounted behind other comrades and rode off the field. This set of fours was just in front of the set of which I constituted a part and, on the spur of the moment, I stopped with our wounded friend to assist him. When attempting to hand him my canteen, to give him water, my horse pulled back completely out of his reach, preventing giving him water, which I could not throw to him, as the stopper of the canteen was lost, when Jared Gross, seeing our predicament, came back to assist me.

Our command, in the meantime, had gone forward into a piece of timber, out of sight of the artillery. When Jared rode up pretty close to me, I suggested that we had better keep apart as this artillery had the range on us, and we had barely separated when they fired another shot which cut the side of the mountain and would certainly have got us both if we had failed to separate. We were compelled to leave poor Duncan on the field, where he was afterwards attended by our surgeon and taken to a house and left inside of the enemy's lines the next day. We never heard of him anymore, assuming that he died, as the shock was too great, in connection with the loss of blood, for him to survive.

Chapter 16
I Refuse to Become a Teamster

While at Corinth, immediately after the Battle of Shiloh, we were ordered to furnish two wagon drivers and called for volunteers, having two wagons to the company. There was not a man in the company that would agree to drive wagons and we were instructed to draw lots, when, with my usual luck, I drew lots to drive wagons, which was a four-mule team; and I had never done any driving before. The other party was Jared Gross, who also objected to driving mules. I told General Wharton that I didn't leave my home and everything I had to come out there and drive a mule team and that I wouldn't and couldn't do so. He said, "Now, Graber, you know you agreed to this drawing and it is not right or fair for you to refuse." I told him that I knew it was mean, but I did not expect that it would fall to my lot to drive this wagon, when he finally told me, "If you do not obey this order, I will have to have you court martialled."

I told him, "All right, Colonel Wharton, you may punish me as much as you like, but I am not going to drive that wagon."

Someone then proposed to hire a couple of men and pay them fifty dollars a month each, which was done, and Duncan, with another man from Brazoria County, whose name I have forgotten, volunteered to take the job.

After crossing the Tennessee River at Lamb's Ferry, we left our wagons and considerable private baggage with cooking utensils and tents, at Bear Creek. A few days after, the Federal cavalry crossed the river and captured the whole outfit, except the men in charge of the same. This was the last of our luxuries, tents, cooking utensils or wagons never being issued after that, except to our headquarters or the commanding general and his staff, who employed Duncan to drive the headquarters wagon.

Having been engaged in this, and fearing that the war would end and he would have to go home and report he had never been in any engagements, Duncan decided that he must go into the battle of Perryville with us, where he lost his life, as stated.

After our experience with the ordnance train and battery, our command followed in the rear of our infantry line, which slowly, but gradually, drove the enemy until dark, capturing several batteries of fine guns. By one of the batteries, we found the body of General Jackson, a Federal general from Kentucky, who, when he found his infantry had abandoned the battery, seemed determined to throw away his life and, single and alone, dashed up to one of our infantry men, cutting at him with his sword, when the man shot and killed him.

After dark we tied our horses in the edge of a woods, to a rail fence which enclosed a large cornfield, where the desperate fighting stopped.

We then went into the field and secured some corn for our horses. As the most of the corn was destroyed by the lines of battle, we had to pass over a good deal of ground to get sufficient corn for our horses. At the point where I stopped gathering, having secured as many ears of corn as I could carry in my arms, the dead lay so thick I believe I could have stepped from one to the other within a radius of ten or fifteen feet. Among them I noticed the dead body of a magnificent looking man lying on his back with his eyes open, seemingly looking at the starry firmament. Noticing that he wore an officer's suit, I turned up his collar which disclosed two stars, denoting his rank as lieutenant-colonel. I afterwards learned that he commanded a Tennessee regiment in Cheatham's Division.

During the night an armistice was had by mutual consent, for the purpose of taking care of the wounded and burying the dead. We were ordered to destroy the small arms left on the field, which were very thick, by breaking the stocks on the trees, which job we soon abandoned because many of the guns were loaded. The batteries captured by our people were exchanged for our own guns, as we only had horses to carry off the number captured, leaving our inferior guns spiked on the field.

The Battle of Perryville, for the number engaged, has always ranked as one of the most desperately fought battles of the war, equal to Shiloh, Chickamauga and others for desperate fighting, and which the respective losses of the two armies fully sustained.

The battle of Perryville proved such a blow to the Federal commander that it made him more cautious in his rapid advance. Our infantry during the night commenced their retreat with the wagon train, artillery and everything belonging to them, moving towards Harrodsburg, where we were met by General Kirby Smith and his army, coming back from Cincinnati. At this point we found a very large amount of pickled pork in barrels, that had been collected for removal with our army, but had to be abandoned and was largely destroyed by our cavalry, still covering the retreat, as heretofore.

The enemy at this point crowded us pretty close and came very near forcing a general engagement again, which no doubt would have proven disastrous to our arms, because they outnumbered us at least four to one. Our cavalry service continued to cover the retreat except with occasional branching out to different points where army supplies were stored, notably Lebanon, where I was sent with a detail of three others to a man's house by the name of Penick, who had a large plantation and owned a great many negroes. He was said to have a great deal of bacon, which we were instructed to have carried to Lebanon.

On arriving at the house, I went in and told the gentleman our business. He met us in the hall, joined by his wife and daughter and in answer to our demand that he have his negroes hitch up his wagons and load the meat, he spitefully told us that he had hid out his mules, negroes and bacon and said, "Get it, if you can." In reasoning with him, trying to persuade him that we would certainly find his hidden stuff, he became very insulting, when I finally told him he was taking advantage of us, knowing well that his grey hair and the presence of the ladies would protect him from our resenting his insults, but told him if he had any boys to bring them out and we would settle the matter with them pretty quick. He said, "I have two boys, but they are in the army and if ever they meet you, they will meet you like men."

I asked him what branch of the service they were in, when he told me they were in the cavalry. I then told him that we had a cavalry fight a couple of weeks before at Bardstown, where no doubt his boys were engaged, when on his further enquiry about the engagement, I told him how we scattered them all over the country, killing and wounding a great many. The ladies burst into tears and went back into their room, and the old man had nothing more to say about his boys.

I then again tried to persuade him to give us at least one wagonload of bacon, promising him that if he would send his team and a boy to drive it to Lebanon, he would surely have them returned, when he again refused in a spiteful, insulting manner. I told him that we had understood he had some six or eight yoke of work-oxen and in Texas we knew all about handling oxen and we would go into his pasture and drive them up and hitch them to the wagons that were at the house, but this was only a threat. We gave him up as a bad job and when we reached the pike about three miles from there, we met a citizen who told us that Wheeler's cavalry had evacuated Lebanon and burnt all the meat stored there, which we were induced to believe, and decided to ride back to the Harrodsburg Pike and get with our command, which we did.

Our army then continued to retreat, the main part of the army moving towards Crab Orchard, where we struck the Cumberland Gap road, while the army, under Kirby Smith, was struggling over Big Hill, and had still to join the main army at the junction of the roads at Pitman's. The army then moved into the mountains on the Cumberland Gap road, which, owing to the character of the country, was generally restricted to a single wagon track. This stretched out our columns of retreat for perhaps twenty miles or more and cut up the road very badly, frequently causing wagons to stall.

Two infantrymen consequently were detailed with every wagon, of which we had thirty-eight hundred, laden with provisions and valuable stores. This detail of two with each wagon was ordered to assist any wagon that was stalled by taking hold of the wheels, thereby helping the team to pull the wagon out of the rut.

A division commander was detailed every day to take charge of the wagon train and artillery and keep it moving. When a wagon stalled, the whole line of retreat, infantry, wagons and artillery behind it, would have to wait until it would move again, thereby seriously impeding our line of march and causing the cavalry in the rear desperate fighting sometimes to hold off the enemy.

It was reported of General Cheatham, when he had charge of the train, that one of his wagons was stalled, and he put spurs to his horse and rode up the line and reached the wagon. The driver was whipping his mules and the two infantrymen were standing by the roadside, resting on their guns. At the sight of this, he jumped off his horse, took hold of the spokes of the wagon wheel and tried to turn it, but all to no purpose. The two guards still stood resting on their guns. General Cheatham lost his patience and turned around and slapped one of the guards in the face. This happened to be an Irishman, who said, "Be God; if you were not Gineral Cheatham you couldn't do this."

General Cheatham pulled off his sword belt, coat and hat and threw them down by the side of the road and said, "Now, there lies General

Cheatham and here is Frank Cheatham; now light in." They say that at this invitation the Irishman lit in and got the best of the bargain, of which General Cheatham never made any complaint. The two men then took hold of the wheels in conjunction with General Cheatham, and started up the wagon, and with that the whole line of retreat.

This incident was currently reported and generally believed by all who knew General Cheatham, but I would not be willing to vouch for the same, as it is almost past belief.

After leaving Crab Orchard, General Buell dispensed with his cavalry, as they were unable to cope with ours and moved only with his infantry and artillery in advance. To enter into the details of the rest of this campaign, would require too much space and will only say that the brigade of General Wharton, which always includes the Terry Rangers, in conjunction occasionally with other cavalry, were expected to and did succeed in retarding the pursuit of the enemy, restricting his advance to from six to eight miles a day only, thereby protecting our infantry column, as well as the artillery, ordnance and thirty-eight hundred wagons loaded with valuable army stores.

On this retreat the infantry were called on only one time to fire a gun. We met the enemy in a general engagement at Mount Vernon, Barren Valley, Rocky Hill, Bushy Mound, Wild Cat, Pitman's Road, Little Rock, Castle River and many other points, inflicting on them considerable loss.

This mountain service on the part of the Rangers proved a most severe tax on their endurance, on account of being deprived of rations. At one time, for nearly two days, we depended on picking up raw corn left in the camps of artillery and wagons, where the horses and mules had been fed. A number of times, after fighting all day long, we had to go out into the hills ten or twelve miles to find forage for our horses before we could retire to get a little rest. Our camping places were frequently by the light of the enemy's fires.

To give the reader a better idea of the valuable service we rendered, I will quote an order issued by General Wheeler, read to us at Cumberland Gap, October 23, 1862.

General Order Number Three:
Soldiers of the Cavalry Corps, Army of Mississippi:
The autumn campaign in Kentucky is over, your arduous duties, as the advance and rear guard, for the present, are finished. Your gallantry in action, your cheerful endurance in suffer-

ing from hunger, fatigue and exposure, render you worthy of all commendation. For nearly two months you have scarcely been for a moment without the range of the enemy's musketry. In more than twenty pitched fights, many of which lasted throughout the day, you have successfully combated largely superior numbers of the enemy's troops of all arms. Hovering continually near the enemy, you have engaged in no less than one hundred skirmishes.

Upon the memorable field of Perryville, alone and unsupported, you engaged and held in check during the entire action, at least two infantry divisions of the opposing army. By your gallant charges on that day, you completely dispersed and routed a vastly superior force of the enemy's cavalry, driving them in confusion under their artillery and infantry supports, capturing in hand-to-hand conflicts many prisoners, forces and arms.

Your continuous contact with the enemy has taught you to repose without fear under his guns, to fighting wherever found and to quietly make your bivouac by the light of his camp fires. On this continued series of combats and brilliant charges, many great men have fallen. We mourn their loss. We commend their valour. Let us emulate their soldierly virtues.

Joseph Wheeler,
Chief of Cavalry.

CHAPTER 17

Omissions in Preceding Chapters

After leaving Cumberland Gap our army again moved into Middle Tennessee, with headquarters at Murfreesboro. Our cavalry in the advance camped near La Vergne, at Nolandsville and Triune. The enemy concentrated at Nashville, from whence they sent out foraging parties, supported by large infantry forces with which we had daily engagements, restricting their foraging within a small area of country. At Nolandsville, where General Wharton made his headquarters, we camped nearly a month, when Lieutenant Decherd was instructed to select about fifteen men and cross the Cumberland Mountain, for the purpose of buying fresh horses, which were very much needed. I was ordered to go with this party.

While camped near Winchester, Tennessee, intending to cross the mountain the next day, we heard the distant roaring of the guns of the Battle of Murfreesboro, which was not expected so soon when we left the command, and which proved a great disappointment to our party, as we felt that every man was needed for such an event. We, therefore, hastened back to the army, which we found evacuating Murfreesboro, and reported. Of the Rangers' part in that great battle I will not mention in this, as that is of record in the general reports of General Bragg and others, and will only say that they fully sustained their character as one of the leading regiments in this army, capturing prisoners, artillery, wagon trains, etc., and finally covering the retreat of the army off the field.

Our army then continued its retreat through Shelbyville to Tullahoma, our cavalry still operating on the north side of Elk River. Before crossing Elk River, a courier reached General Wheeler from General Forrest, after Wheeler had crossed the bridge, requesting him to hold the bridge until he (Forrest) could cross with his command. Promptly on receipt of this information, General Wheeler, with a portion of his command, notably the Fourth Alabama Cavalry, re-crossed the bridge to the north side, determined to hold the same until General Forrest had crossed with his command. Before Forrest reached Shelbyville, however, General Stanley, with a heavy force of cavalry, outnumbering Wheeler's little force ten to one, charged and forced them back across the river, cutting General Wheeler off from the bridge.

General Wheeler spurred his horse to the bank and over it, into the dangerous river, which had been swollen by excessive rains, making a leap of not less than twenty feet, with Stanley's cavalry shooting after him and continuously firing on him until he reached the opposite bank. This was, perhaps, the most miraculous escape he had during the war.

Before reaching Tullahoma, a Captain Gordon, who had distinguished himself near Bardstown, where he held in check a whole brigade of the enemy's infantry on the Bloomfield Road for a whole day with only twenty men, was ordered to select twenty men from the Rangers and enter Kentucky, for the purpose of gaining information of the disposition of the enemy's forces, preparatory to a general raid by our cavalry. The history of this trip, which resulted in my being wounded and captured and held a prisoner just one year, lacking a day, I have already recorded, and by an oversight, it crept into this history ahead of the proper time.

Recurring to the hard service sustained by us in the mountains between Crab Orchard and Cumberland Gap: The last night we were on picket duty our company had dwindled down to seven men and I happened to be on vidette with a messmate, John Cochran. Just at daylight, when the enemy usually made its appearance, we were relieved by two others of the command and when we reached the reserve picket, discovering a grassy spot in the middle of the road, I told Cochran I must try to steal a little nap, and laid down on this grassy spot, holding my horse by the bridle, when I was awakened, only about ten minutes after, by Cochran stooping down from his horse and jabbing me with his pistol.

The reserve picket had formed a line across the road, just a little back of where I was sleeping and were firing on the enemy's advancing skirmish line, the noise of which failed to awake me and it was only his prodding me with the end of his six-shooter that got me awake. I had just time enough to swing on to my horse and get out of there. Here Cochran's prediction, frequently made, that he would bet Graber would wake up some fine morning with a Yankee bayonet sticking in him, came very near being verified. I merely mention this to give the reader a fair idea of our complete exhaustion for the want of sleep, continuous hunger and arduous duties.

CHAPTER 18

General Johnston's Failure to Strike—Sherman

Recurring to my service in Captain Britton's company, acting as escort to General Hood at Dalton, Georgia, where I described the meeting of the several generals with General Hood at his headquarters in the rear of Railroad Gap: On our return to camp that night after supper, Captain Britton suggested he should go up to headquarters and pump Major Sellars on the meaning of the meeting that morning. He reported on his return from a visit to headquarters that General Mower, commanding Hooker's old corps, had moved down to Snake Creek Gap during the day, which was located about nineteen miles in our rear and about ten miles west of Dalton.

General Hood plead with General Johnston that morning for permission to move out of his works through Railroad and Rocky Face Gaps with his corps and defeat Sherman's Army before Mower could return to reinforce them. Captain Britton said that he would bet our army would be in full retreat that night, falling back to Resaca, which prediction was verified, as, by daylight next morning, our infantry and artillery were engaged with the enemy at Resaca, where we came very near losing a large part of our army by having their retreat cut off.

Had General Johnston yielded to General Hood's plan, there is no question but what he could have destroyed Sherman's Army; here was a golden opportunity lost by General Johnston, and was the beginning of the downfall of the Confederacy.

After about two weeks I succeeded in getting a horse with the regiment and continued with the regiment during the whole of the North Georgia campaign, the details of which I will not venture to insert, as they will be recorded fully in a history now being written by Colonel Ben P. Weems of Houston.

During the siege of Atlanta General Sherman started out two cavalry expeditions, one under a General Stoneman to move around the right wing of our army, and one under General McCook around the left wing of our army, both to unite on the Macon line of railroad, and to destroy and tear up the same, then move on to Andersonville and release our prisoners. Had these expeditions proven a success, with an army of probably twenty-five or thirty thousand released prisoners turned loose in our rear, it would have wound up the Confederacy. At Atlanta, General Hood took command of our army, not exceeding thirty-six thousand muskets and, to use his words, "This army through General Johnston's retreating from Dalton, had become an army of laborers by day and travellers by night," while the army at Dalton, including Polk's corps at Rome, numbered eighty-six thousand muskets, and was better equipped and organised than any army the West had ever had. The North Georgians and Tennesseans, largely constituting this army, with their families inside of the enemy's lines, were anxious and eager for an advance, and there is no question of doubt had General Hood been permitted to give battle at Dalton, our army would have recaptured Tennessee and Kentucky.

Referring back to the enemy's cavalry expedition out of Atlanta: General Stoneman, with a large part of his force, and a lot of convalescents in the town of Macon, Georgia, were captured near Macon by General Iverson, commanding Georgia cavalry. General Wheeler with our brigade, Ross' and Roddy's, forced McCook to a general engagement on the evening of the second day between Noonan and Philpott's Ferry, where they finally surrendered, with the exception of himself and staff, and Colonel Brownlow and some other line officers, who swam the river that night and made their escape.

General Wheeler issued an order that night for no man to cross the river after these fellows, when I, with several of our regiment, decided there must be some mistake about it and crossed the river to try to catch these fellows, specially anxious to capture Colonel Brownlow. Immediately after crossing the river, we found a quartermaster's clerk, so he represented himself to be, left wounded at a house. His wound, however, was not very serious we thought. He had on a magnificent pair of boots, which just about fitted me and I had been unable to secure boots, only wearing shoes, when I proposed to him to exchange with me, which he readily did. While he was pulling off his boots, the lady of the house came in and opened a tirade of abuse on me for taking a poor, wounded man's boots. I told her I had but just come out of a Federal prison where they treated us worse than that and I was satisfied that my shoes would prove more comfortable to this man at Andersonville, than the boots, to which our prisoner agreed.

We then continued our pursuit on the main road to Wedowee, the county seat of Randolph County, Alabama, occasionally taking a prisoner, whom we would turn over to reliable citizens, to be taken to West Point where we had a garrison. We were unable to secure many prisoners, probably not exceeding eight or ten, as those afoot would hear us coming in the road and dart into the brush, while their officers impressed every horse, they could lay their hands on and soon outdistanced us with their fresh horses.

At Wedowee we found a tan-yard, where I purchased a lot of good leather, sufficient to rig a Texas saddle. We had some men detailed to make saddles, who were experts in such work and moved down with the army as fast as it retreated. Our first shop was at Ackworth, Georgia, where they did a good deal of work, but were prevented from turning out anything extensive ever after, for the reason they were unable to get leather. I paid one hundred and twenty-five dollars for the leather I got at this tan-yard. Colonel Harrison promised me, after my return from prison, that if I would furnish the leather, he would have rigged for me one of the finest saddles that could be made, which was the inducement for me to carry this roll of leather on my horse's back.

Going back into the town from the tan-yard, we stopped at a hotel to get some dinner. This was one of the ordinary country hotels with a porch in front and large square columns under the porch. While eating dinner, I had a seat at the end of the table where I could see out on the street. The hotel was located somewhat under the hill, away from the square, when I discovered Carter Walker, one of our party, who had finished dinner, behind one of the posts with his pistol out, talking to someone on the street towards the courthouse. Having his pistol out suggested to me that there was trouble ahead, so I jumped up and told the boys to come on.

As we got out on the porch, we discovered about fifteen or twenty men on their horses near the courthouse, with one of them talking to Carter Walker, about fifty yards distant from us. As soon as we came out, he retired and when he got back with his crowd, said something to them and immediately they wheeled and left town. This proved to be a party of bushwhackers, who were not anxious for a fight with us. We now decided to return and when a few miles from town, we heard of an old gentleman, whose name I have forgotten, the only Rebel citizen in that section, whom we decided to go and see and get some information from.

After reaching his house and getting acquainted, we decided, on his urgent request, to stay with him that night, as we were very tired, as were also our horses, and we did not suppose there was any great need for our services immediately after the destruction of the enemy's cavalry. This old gentleman had had considerable trouble with his Tory neighbours, who came to his house several nights and opened fire on him, which he, his old lady and his daughter, a barefooted girl of eighteen, returned with their squirrel rifles through port holes cut in the logs of his house.

On the information of our old friend, we decided to visit the house of a Tory neighbour of his, across the mountain, who belonged to the Tory regiment in camp at Rome, which we did. Riding up to the house in blue overcoats, we called for a drink of water, when a lady invited us in, supposing that we were Federal soldiers. In our talk with them, there being two other ladies in the house, we represented that we were Federal spies on our way to Andersonville to make arrangements about the escape of our prisoners there, which created quite an interest with these women, who told us that a large number of young men of the neighbourhood belonged to the First Federal Alabama Cavalry, stationed near Rome, and quite a number of them were expected home pretty soon on a furlough.

We then arranged with them to tell their boys about our visit and tell them that we expected to return there in about ten days, as we would probably need their assistance and we wanted to confer with them. Our idea was that we would return there at that time, with our company, and capture the whole outfit.

After making complete arrangements, we started back towards Philpott's Ferry, where we again recrossed the Chattahoochie and, on our arrival at Noonan, found that Wheeler had moved over to Covington, on the Augusta road.

Riding all that day in a drizzling rain, we called at a house for the purpose of getting some feed for our horses and something to eat for ourselves. Night had already set in. We asked the gentleman if he could take care of us that night, give us a place to sleep on the floor, as we never slept in a bed, and get something to eat for our horses and ourselves. His answer was, "Certainly, gentlemen; light and come in." I told him before we got off our horses that we were about out of money and did not have enough, perhaps, to pay our fare, when he stated that if his wife had anything left from supper, we could have it and he would give us some shattered corn for our horses. We, of course, didn't feel very comfortable under such liberality, but decided to stay, nevertheless, and sleep down in his barn, some distance from the house.

While we were waiting for his wife to gather what she had left from supper, he asked us if we were that command the other day that fired on the Federals when they were tearing up the railroad near his house. I told him that we were, and he said, "They were in my pasture trying to catch my horses, when they heard the guns fire and you ought to have seen those devils run." When we went in to supper, we found a little piece of cornbread and a little butter, all they had left from supper, so the woman stated, not enough to satisfy one man's hunger. We did not sit down at the table, didn't touch anything they had to offer us, and went down to the crib to get the shattered corn for our horses, which he consented for us to take, fed our horses and laid down to rest for the balance of the night.

Next morning, we got up early and without going to the house, proceeded on the road towards Covington. Here now, was a fair illustration of the want of appreciation of a Confederate soldier, with a selfish lot of people, whom we occasionally met. Rest assured it was very discouraging to us. The idea of coming all the way from Texas to fight for and protect these people! He had told us that we saved his horses from capture by engaging the enemy near his house; you can imagine our disgust at such treatment. We now proceeded on the Covington road. When about two miles from there we came to a large, white house, a magnificent place, and rode up to the gate.

A man about twenty-five years old, well dressed, wearing a white starched shirt, the first we had seen in a long time, came out to the gate. When within twenty feet of us, espying the leather on my horse's back, tied to the rear of the saddle, he called out, "I want that leather."

I said, "If you need it any worse than I do, you are welcome to it." He said he did, he wanted to make shoes out of it. I told him that I wanted to make a saddle out if it, to ride to keep Federals off of him, when he insisted that he needed it worse. I then told him that we wanted some breakfast and some feed for our hoses."

He said, "All right, gentlemen; light and come in."

Before getting down I said, "I had better tell you that we are nearly out of money, not enough to pay for breakfast and feed, away from our command unexpectedly, but as soon as we get with them and we have an opportunity, we will send it to you."

He stated that he couldn't afford to feed us without pay, that the armies had been around him for some time and had nearly eaten him out of house and home. I told him that he needn't say anything more, that we didn't want anything he had, although our horses were hungry, as well as ourselves. As we rode off, he called after us, "I'll feed you for that leather," thus adding insult, but we decided not to notice him.

About three miles further down the road we came to another house, a somewhat humble cottage, and stopped to make some inquiry, when a lady came out to the gate and we asked how far down the road we could find a house where we could get something to eat for ourselves and feed for our horses. She asked us if we had tried at the big, white house we had passed on the road. We told her that we had and were refused because we had no money. She then insisted that we come in and partake of such as she had, telling us that she had very little left, as the commissary from Atlanta had visited her and taken all the corn she had, except five barrels, which in Georgia, means twenty-five bushels.

This, she and her two daughters had made with their own hands, her husband being in the Virginia Army. She then told us about this man at the big, white house, who had never been in the army, but had an exemption on pretence of working in a saltpetre cave and had never had any forage taken by the commissary from Atlanta, as he had protection papers, so she called them, from his general at Atlanta. I merely mention these cases to show you the condition at that time, of the State of Georgia, the worthy people submitting patriotically to all manner of abuse by some of our army officials, while some of the rich, through nefarious practices, escaped the weight of war.

Thanking this lady for her kind offer, which we could not afford to accept, we continued on this road and two miles further on struck a large cornfield with tempting roasting ears and decided to stop, build a fire, dry our clothes and roast corn for our meal, feeding our horses on the same, in moderation. We had to build our fire of rails taken off the fence and very soon were enjoying our roasting ears and the warm fire, being somewhat chilled by the rain. The proprietor of the place came up the road and, judging from his manner and looks, was pretty mad, when he said, "Gentlemen, if you had come to the house, I would have gladly given you a good meal and fed your horses, rather than to see the destruction of my rails."

I told him that we didn't believe it, that we had tried several places up on the road and were refused because we had no money and he, no doubt, noting that we were in no mood for argument, decided that he had better say no more. We then proceeded on our road to Covington. When on our arrival there we found that Wheeler, with all the cavalry having horses fit for service, had gone on a raid into Middle Tennessee, by way of Dalton, tearing up the railroad in Sherman's rear for many miles, and finally entering Middle Tennessee, returning by way of Mussels Shoals, rejoining the army below Atlanta.

After the Battle of Jonesboro, Hood started on his fatal Middle Tennessee campaign, his march to the Tennessee River being covered by our cavalry, making a feint at Rome, Georgia, to which point General Sherman had followed, confidently expecting to give Hood battle at Gadsden and never suspecting his move towards the Tennessee River. While concentrating his army at Rome, Harrison's Brigade, under Colonel Harrison, commanding our regiment, made a feint on Rome by dismounting, hiding our horses in the rear in the woods, out of sight, and advanced on the outer works of Rome, preceded by a line of skirmishers.

For this purpose, not having our battle flag with us, we used a new flag, sent us from Nashville, made by a couple of young ladies from their silk dresses, with the name of Terry's Texas Rangers worked in gold letters and some Latin words on the other side. After skirmishing with Sherman's infantry a short time, we retired down the valley, which at this point was perhaps a couple of miles wide, from the hills to the bottoms.

Falling back that night some six or eight miles, we struck a wooded ridge, running from the hills to the bottom, perhaps nearly three miles long. This ridge overlooked the country in front towards Rome, several miles. General Sherman coming out in person with a corps of his infantry, expecting to give Hood battle the next morning, discovered there was only a handful of cavalry in his front, which was Harrison's Brigade, and which he was specially anxious to capture. For this purpose, he sent a heavy cavalry force, perhaps three times our number, into our rear, flanking our position by moving through the hills on our left, then occupying nearly every road in our rear, for eight or ten miles.

During the night we received reinforcements of Pillow's Brigade, a new command, which had been in only one engagement, at La Fayette, Georgia, where they were badly handled, causing the loss of a great many killed and wounded and in consequence, they were a little demoralized. We also received a section of artillery, two pieces, under a lieutenant, whose name I do not remember.

This artillery was stationed on a hill to the left of our position, under an old gin house.

Immediately after taking position the artillery opened on the enemy, a heavy line of battle making its; appearance in the edge of the woods, about a mile distant. The Rangers were kept mounted, drawn up near this old gin house, supporting the battery, when all the rest of the two brigades had been dismounted with their horses immediately in the rear, out of sight of the enemy.

Very soon a courier from the right of our line, dashed up to Colonel Harrison and reported that the enemy were flanking us, down in the bottom, with a heavy force. Harrison abused him, told him to go back and tell his colonel if he sent him another such message, he would have him court martialled, but very soon a lieutenant dashed up from the extreme right of our line, reporting the enemy advancing in the bottom, and about to outflank us, when Colonel Harrison decided to ride down in the rear of our line and ascertain conditions for himself. Immediately the enemy raised a shout and charged. The lieutenant of the battery, concluding that his guns were in danger of being captured, limbered up and ran down to the road, where he met Colonel Harrison returning and was by him ordered to unlimber and open again on the enemy, when he succeeded in firing one shot and was sabred right over his guns by the enemy's cavalry.

In the meantime, through some misapprehension of orders, the Alabama Brigade broke for their horses, followed by the balance of our brigade, when our regiment was ordered to charge their cavalry, which we did, striking them on their flank, using our six-shooters, to which they paid no attention, simply calling out, "Clear the road for the Fourth Regulars!" This Fourth Regulars was commanded by a Captain McIntyre from Brenham, Texas, who was in the United States Army, a lieutenant, when the war broke out, having just graduated at West Point.

It is hardly necessary to say that finding the enemy's cavalry in our rear for a great many miles, resulted in a general stampede, everybody trying to make their escape out of it. In recording this engagement, I regret to have to mention the loss of our beautiful flag which, encased in a rubber cover, slipped off its staff and was found by a Major Weiler, commanding a battalion of the Seventeenth Mounted Indiana Infantry, and after many years, returned to us at Dallas, Texas, by Governor

Mount and staff, instructed to do so by a joint resolution of the Indiana Legislature, in response to a memorial, drawn up and sent by me.

In this engagement the Terry Rangers lost no prisoners, had only a few wounded and none killed, while the Alabamians' loss was quite heavy in prisoners and the balance of Harrison's Brigade had very few men taken prisoners. I made my escape by crossing the big road, being joined by about eight or ten Alabamians, one of whom was shot in the fleshy part of the thigh, which somewhat demoralised him, when he called on me, "Texas, can you take us out of here?"

I told him, "Yes, follow me; I'll take you out." I struck out straight for the river bottom, the Federal cavalry not following us, and when out of sight of the main road, in a little branch bottom, I called a halt and told the men my plan of trying to swim the river, as the road ahead of us seemed to be occupied for many miles, judging by the scattered firing a great distance ahead of us. The wounded man straightened up in the saddle and asked me if I was an officer. I told him, "No," and he said that he was a lieutenant and would take command of the squad.

I told him he could take command of his own men, but he couldn't command me, and told his men, "Now, all of you boys that want to go out with me, come on," when they all followed me, including the lieutenant.

Reaching the high ground on the other side of the branch, I discovered a house, with a lone cavalryman at the front gate, and, getting a little nearer, I recognised him as one Joe Harris, of our company, who was well acquainted in that section, having married, near Cedartown, the daughter of a Doctor Richardson, just on the other side of the river. He suggested to me that he knew of a *batteau* about seven miles this side of Rome; that we go up there, put our saddles and equipments into the boat, swim our horses across, then go to Doctor Richardson and get a good dinner; to which I, of course, readily consented. On our way to this *batteau*, following the river in the bottom, we struck hundreds of Alabamians trying to find a crossing place.

These men we took along with us and when we reached the boat, we were the first ones to cross, leaving the Alabamians there to cross as fast as they were able. Joe and I then rode to Doctor Richardson's, about ten or fifteen miles, and by three o'clock sat down to a sumptuous dinner. Here we stayed all night and the next morning recrossed the river, finally striking the main Gadsden road and finding our stampeded forces gathering at some gap, the name of which I have forgotten. Here we met General Wheeler, with the balance of his command.

We then moved down to the town of Gadsden, where we recrossed the river and spent several days resting our horses and ourselves.

General Hood, in the meantime, with his army, crossed the Tennessee River, and General Sherman returned to Atlanta, leaving Thomas' Corps to follow Hood into Middle Tennessee. Wheeler and his cavalry returned to below Atlanta, where we struck Sherman's forces moving in the direction of Macon, Georgia, by way of Augusta to Savannah. We then had daily engagements with Kilpatrick's cavalry, often driving them into their infantry. Sherman used his cavalry to forage for the army, depending altogether on the country for his commissary. To enter into detail of the many engagements had on this trip would occupy too much time and space. Our service was largely, as stated, to keep his cavalry from foraging, burning and destroying the country. In connection with this I would mention an incident at Macon:

I was at a blacksmith's shop with a comrade by the name of Freeman, who was about seven years my senior in age. While waiting to get our horses shod, we heard artillery, supported by small arms, open at our works, about a mile across the river. We immediately mounted our horses and dashed over there and just as we got in sight of the roadway through the breastworks, we witnessed a lone trooper of Kilpatrick's cavalry coming up the road through the works, having his horse shot just as he reached inside. His horse fell on his leg, from which position he was trying to extricate himself and was about to be shot by an excited militia of young and old men, who had never been under fire before, when Jim put spurs to his horse and with his pistol raised, dashed up to where this man lay under his horse, and drove off the excited militia, I, of course, following him.

He called up a lieutenant, asked his name, company and regiment; told him to take charge of that prisoner and see that he was well treated, that he would hold him personally responsible for his safety, and immediately wheeled his horse, I following him, and returned to town without giving the lieutenant a chance to ask questions. On our return I asked Jim Freeman his reasons for doing as he did, risking his own life, by being shot by the excited militia, in order to save this Federal. He answered, "He is a brother Mason." I asked him if he ever met him before. He said, "No, but I saw him give the grand hailing sign of distress, which obligates a Mason to save the life of a brother, at the risk of his own." Here was a beautiful illustration of the work of Masonry, and I told Jim Freeman the first opportunity I had of joining the Masons, if I lived through the war, I intended to be one, which resolution I carried out, joining the Masons at Rusk, Texas.

General Kilpatrick with about four thousand picked cavalry, armed with Spencer repeating rifles, which they were expert in handling, was detailed by General Sherman, after leaving Jonesboro, to forage and destroy property, under pretext of burning gin houses. They also burned a great many fine houses, the homes of rich people, on their line of march, and got their operations down to a system. He would have his engineers select a strong position along the line of march, fortify it with rails and logs and place about one thousand men in such works. His engineers then would advance some two or three miles and direct another line of fortifications in a similar manner; the balance of his command would scatter out on both flanks inside of these lines, collect provisions and forage, burn gin houses and homes, the latter of which, of course, were plundered before being consigned to the flames. In this manner he continued his operations to very near the coast.

Chapter 19

Georgia Service

At this time General Wheeler would detail a fresh brigade every morning to take the advance and move on the enemy.

When a few miles from Buck Head Creek, Harrison's Brigade was placed in advance. Striking the first line of works, we formed a line and prepared to charge, when General Felix Robertson was seen immediately to the right of our line on a magnificent horse. At the time, he was acting as chief of staff to General Wheeler, and he gave the order to forward, waving his hat and led the charge. We drove them out of their works and it became a running fight down the road with General Robertson leading, having a better horse than the balance of us. We soon struck a branch where the enemy had lined up on the other side, and they poured a galling fire into our advance.

General Robertson had his arm badly shattered by a bullet and being alone drew his horse to one side at the ford of this branch. When I saw him, he appeared deathly pale, reeling in his saddle, and a couple of the men behind me started over to assist him, but he called to them, "Never mind me, boys; crowd 'em, crowd 'em," which we did, and again started them on the run. They made another stand across Buck Head Creek near the church and set fire to the bridge, covering the fire with a piece of artillery. Wheeler then sent down a few men with long-range guns, dismounted, who soon drove the artillery away. We then repaired the bridge floor with benches out of the church and were soon across the creek, after them, with the Third Arkansas in advance.

As we were riding rapidly in pursuit, General Wheeler passing our column to reach the advance called to us, saying, "We've got them this time; Dibrell is in the rear." General Dibrell commanded Tennessee cavalry. We soon got into an old sedge field, an open country for several miles, where Kilpatrick had established a fortified camp, built a line of breastworks perhaps two miles wide, his left flank touching the road.

The Third Arkansas had formed a line of battle and was charging the breastworks perhaps two hundred yards ahead of our regiment, which emerged from the woods in columns of fours, moving rapidly to the support of the Third Arkansas. The enemy had planted four pieces of artillery in the road on our right, which poured a galling fire into the Third Arkansas, as well as our flank. The Third Arkansas finally reached the breastworks under a galling fire of four thousand Spencer rifles and drove the gunners away from their artillery, thereby silencing the same, but they were unable to cross the works and not being supported promptly, had to withdraw.

The reason of our failure to support promptly was that when we reached about half way across the open, an order came to us through Adjutant Billy Sayers for the Rangers to file to the right into the road. This divided our regiment, a part continuing ahead, the other part moving into the road and, as soon as we struck the road, a hail of grape and cannister swept it and drove us into the thick woods across the road and finally forced us to give up the attack, which was most unfortunate, as the Third Arkansas lost a good many men. Our regiment lost a few, too, and nothing was accomplished. General Dibrell was seen in our left front in the woods, unable to strike Kilpatrick in the rear on account of not being able to cross the creek. General Wheeler now brought up his entire force, making disposition of them for a final charge on Kilpatrick's flank and rear, as well as in front, and when we moved forward, we found the bird had flown; Kilpatrick had abandoned his works and fled.

We next had quite a severe engagement with the enemy's cavalry near Griswoldville, said to have been one of the most beautiful towns in Georgia, which the enemy had burned. As soon as we caught up with them, we charged and drove them into their infantry, which proved in heavy force and forced us to retire.

At Waynesboro, Georgia, we had considerable fighting in order to save Augusta, Georgia, which had one of the largest arsenals in the Confederacy and no doubt was a tempting prize for General Sherman's torch.

General Braxton Bragg happened to be in Augusta, when he conceived the idea of resorting to a ruse, which proved quite successful. He called up General Wheeler by telegraph at Waynesboro and instructed him when he was forced to give up the town, to leave the telegraph office intact, but give it the appearance of having been abandoned precipitately, then advise him promptly when the enemy entered town. Waiting a reasonable time for the enemy to take charge of the telegraph office, General Bragg called General Wheeler, when a Federal officer answered. General Bragg said:

> General Wheeler, hold Waynesboro at all hazards. Longstreet's corps is arriving. I will take the field in person tomorrow.
> Signed, Braxton Bragg.

This had the desired effect. General Sherman, satisfied he would have to give battle before Augusta was surrendered, decided he had better pass by and move on to Savannah as fast as possible. There is no question but this ruse saved Augusta, Georgia, though General Wheeler with his corps put up a strong defence, never permitting the enemy to cross Brier Creek, which was between them and Augusta.

About ten or twelve years after the war, when General Sherman was a resident of St. Louis, he gave an interview on the reason he spared Augusta, Georgia. This had been a subject of discussion by historians and especially friends of the North and was frequently attributed to General Sherman having relatives living in Augusta, Georgia. Another story was that Mrs. Lincoln, through a relative or friend, had stored in Augusta a large amount of cotton. There were various other stories, which General Sherman finally set at rest, giving his reasons for sparing the city. He claimed that one of his officers intercepted a telegram from General Bragg to General Wheeler at Waynesboro, instructing him to hold Waynesboro at all hazards, that Longstreet's corps was arriving and he would take personal command the next day.

He further stated that on account of his depleted commissary, having to depend on the country for the rations of his army, he was in no condition to give battle, satisfied that Bragg would defend Augusta to the last, therefore passed it by and hastened to the coast.

"But if the people of Augusta think that I spared their city through any love or affection for them, if the President will give me permission, I will take a hundred thousand of my bummers and go down and burn it now."

I read this interview in a St. Louis paper.

When near Savannah, Georgia, the place having been evacuated by our forces, who crossed the river at Pocatalego, Wheeler's cavalry was ordered to cross the Savannah River at a point about fifteen miles above Savannah. For this purpose, we had only one steamboat, and Harrison's Brigade was ordered to cross last, necessitating our camping in the river bottom for several days, during which time details were sent out of our brigade to collect provisions, as we were without commissary. I had charge the second day of a small detail, and after riding about twenty miles, we scattered out, each man to bring in as much as possible.

On my return to camp that evening late, without having succeeded in securing anything, only a piece of cornbread and a slice of bacon for myself, I was feeling disgusted. When about a mile from our camp, following a well-beaten path, I spied a negro man on another path crossing the one I was on and when within a few yards of me, I stopped him and asked if he couldn't tell me where there was something to eat, telling him that I had ridden all day long, trying to get something for our command and had signally failed.

The country through which we had passed for several days is the greatest sweet potato country perhaps in the South; large fields all over the country had been devoted to sweet potatoes, which had fallen a ready prey to Sherman's army and the whole country seemed to be eaten out. I told this negro, after he told me where he lived, about a half mile from there, that I was satisfied he knew where there were sweet potatoes and where there was corn for our horses. He assured me he did not and said that the Federals had taken everything that his old master had and didn't leave him a thing.

I continued to talk with him, trying to arouse his sympathy, told him of our poor fellows not having had anything to eat for several days and I had been riding all day long without securing anything, thereby working on his sympathy. Finally, he broke down and said, "Young Marster, if I were to tell you where there are sweet potatoes, old marster would kill me." I told him that his old master never would know anything about it, and he finally said he didn't think it was right, that his old master had given these Yankees everything they wanted, had plenty of potatoes left and refused to give our own folks anything at all.

"Now," he said, "if you will strike across this way," pointing in the direction of his house, entering a lane leading to the house, "about a hundred and fifty yards this side of the house, on the left across the fence, you will find some haystack poles standing, with a lot of shattered hay in the lot and if you will dig down about two feet you will strike more potatoes than you will need for several days. Up the river, in the bottom, about two miles, you will find a couple of pens of corn, enough to feed your horses for several days." He had just finished telling me, when I noticed an old man, who proved to be his master, coming our way, and as soon as the negro saw him, he said, "Fo' Gawd, marster; there he is now; he'll kill me; he'll kill me."

"No," I said "he will not; he never will know that you told me; you stand perfectly still and don't get scared." I jerked out my pistol and threw it down on him, telling him within hearing of his old master, that if he didn't tell me where there was something to eat, I would kill him, and the old man called, "Let that man alone; he don't know where there is anything to eat; there is nothing on the place, the Federals just took everything I had."

I still insisted on killing the negro if he didn't tell me where there was something to eat, and finally let him off, satisfying the old man that he hadn't told me anything.

As soon as I reached camp, I told Colonel Harrison to get out a detail of fifty men, with sacks to carry potatoes in, when he ordered Major Pearrie, our commissary, to get out the detail and follow my instructions. I told Pearrie that I was satisfied the people at the house about a half mile from there had plenty of potatoes, but did not tell him the source of my information, determined not to tell anybody. When we moved up the lane near the house. Major Pearrie halted us, went to the house to talk to the old man and negotiate for the potatoes, when the old man satisfied him there were no potatoes on the place.

In the meantime, I had no trouble in finding the lot just as the negro had described to me and when the major returned and ordered us, "About face; move back to camp; there is nothing to be had," I dismounted, crossed the fence into the lot and commenced digging with my hands and in about two feet, struck potatoes, then called to the men to come over with their sacks, which, it is hardly necessary to say, we filled up to the top. We thought we left potatoes enough to last the old man and his family for another year, and perhaps more.

We then sent up the river bottom and found the corn, on which we fed our horses. Here is another instance of the attachment of the negro to our own people, his sympathy for us controlling his actions, and I always regretted not taking this negro along with us, fearing perhaps that his old master might have suspected him of giving us information about these potatoes and corn.

After crossing the river and reaching Pocatalego, we found General Hardee and General McLaws, with the infantry out of Savannah and also artillery organisations, which were turned into infantry. General McLaws made a request on General Wheeler for a company of cavalry, preferring a company of Texas Rangers, to scout and act as escort for him, when Company B, to which I belonged, was detailed for this purpose.

One night, Captain King, inspector general on McLaws' staff, came down to our camp fire and requested me to accompany him on a ride across the swamp, to find Wheeler's cavalry, which I consented to do. We proceeded into the swamp on a corduroy road, the night being one of the darkest we had ever been out in, the only light onto the road was the sky appearing between the tall trees on both sides, which governed us in keeping about the middle of the road and kept us from riding off the logs into the deep mud and water.

After riding perhaps, a half mile, expecting every minute to be fired on by Sherman's advance pickets, our horses necessarily making a great deal of noise by stumbling over the logs, Captain King stopped and asked did I not think one of us could get through easier than both, as it would reduce the noise considerably. I told him that it certainly would. He then asked me if I would carry a written order to General Wheeler, which was for Wheeler's cavalry not to fail to cross the swamp that night in order to be on hand by daylight in the morning, when General Hardee expected an attack by the enemy's infantry. I told Captain King that I would carry the order, which he asked me to show every brigade commander that I might find, until I reached General Wheeler. Captain King then returned to General McLaws' camp, as he would be needed the next morning.

I rode through the swamp, crossed the bridge and after about a twenty-mile ride, found Wheeler's cavalry, first striking a Georgia brigade, to a colonel of which I read the order, when he immediately ordered his brigade to saddle up; the next I struck Harrison's brigade, who also followed suit; the next I struck Colonel Ashby's headquarters, commanding Tennesseans. I found him lying on a pallet in front of a fireplace, surrounded by his staff, all asleep. I showed him the order; after reading it and noticing that I was wet, having ridden in the rain part of the time, he made me step up to the fire, then after drying my clothes, take his pallet and sleep until it was time to cross the swamp, his command being very near the swamp.

He promised me that he would send the dispatch direct to General Wheeler, who was not far off and would have me awakened when the last were about to cross, thereby giving me as much sleep as possible. This kind treatment of Colonel Ashby's was much appreciated, but was not a surprise to me, having known him as one of the most gallant officers and gentlemen I ever got acquainted with.

Sometime after the war, meeting Lieutenant Fulkerson, the commander of our company, at Bryan, Texas, he told me that General McLaws told him a few days after this engagement that Graber's ride that night, finding Wheeler's cavalry, who crossed the swamp in time to cover the retreat of our infantry, no doubt saved our little army, only about seven or eight thousand strong. This army was composed of the infantry and artillery that were stationed at Savannah and Charleston and at different points along our line of retreat and was joined at Bentonville with the remnant of Hood's army, out of Tennessee, after the disastrous Hood campaign in that State.

While this humble individual service was nothing extraordinary, nothing more than performed by individual members of our company frequently, yet the result was such that I always had cause to feel proud of it. I forgot to mention that I crossed the swamp without being fired on by the enemy, as they had not reached that part of the crossing when I passed through.

The following letter from General McLaws was received by me more than thirty years after the incident just related, as the date indicates:

Savannah, Ga., April 9th, 1897.

My Dear Graber:

Your letter of the 5th reached me yesterday evening, and it gave me great pleasure to receive it, for I have very often spoken of the Texas company which formed my escort for a great deal of the time during that campaign, and always in praise of its daring spirit and its devotion to our cause. And there is no one in the company whose name I have mentioned more often than yours, for I saw more of you personally than of most of them, as you were sometimes connected with my scouting party.

When the Federal Army, which crossed at Fort Royal ferry, commenced its movement northward to meet the column under General Sherman, which came from Savannah, it was your company scouts which gave me notice of it, and I commenced following their movement along one side, which was the left bank of the Salkatchie. The night I left my headquarters was a very cold one, and the troops suffered considerably. I had an A. D. C, a relative of mine, whom I had found in Colcock's regiment of cavalry, and, not being accustomed to campaigning, he grumbled some as we rode along and my other A. D. C, Mr. Lamar, hearing him, asked what was the matter. He replied, "Lamar, if this is liberty, I would rather be a slave."

We arrived in time to successfully defeat the crossing at Braxton's Bridge, and I then rode on that night to Reeves' Bridge, some eight or ten miles above, and, finding everything in readiness, rode on to the bridge above. When I started from Braxton's Bridge, I had some seven or eight of Colcock's cavalry, who professed to know the country, and I had sent several of them to find Wheeler's cavalry, in order to get a force from him to help defend the crossing at Reeves' Bridge the next day, but I heard afterwards it was not done and in some unaccountable way my escort from Colcock's cavalry disappeared, every one of them.

Fortunately, I came across my inspecting officer, Captain King, a very energetic and fearless soldier, and I directed him to go on and bring over a division of cavalry under Wheeler, have them dismounted and placed in line close to the swamps on the right of the infantry force at Reeves' Bridge. I went on to the bridge above where General Hardee was in command, and he, seeming confident of holding his position, I started back to Reeves' Bridge alone, my escort having disappeared, as I have stated.

On my way back, I came across a camp of a single teamster with his team and wagon. I dismounted, told him who I was, and asked him to feed my horse and let me lie down by his fire and to wake me before daylight, all of which he consented to. Before daylight the next day, I was on my way and arrived at Reeves' Bridge very early and found that Wheeler had sent me a division of cavalry which was placed as I had directed.

I met Captain King, who told me of the daring ride of you and himself, and of your desperate venture to find the cavalry, and for which I was very grateful, for, had it not been for additional force thus acquired, the enemy would have crossed above me early in the day, for the Salkatchie had fallen so much that it had become fordable and the enemy were crossing not only above; but parties crossed between Reeves' and Braxton's bridges, and after crossing in sufficient numbers to warrant it they would have come down on my flank at Reeves' bridge, and I would have had to retire.

The presence of the cavalry prevented this. The cavalry late in the day, having exhausted its ammunition, I directed that they be formed mounted in the woods in the rear, and to charge any body of the enemy attempting to make a flank attack of the force at the bridge. This condition continued until sundown, when I directed the officer in command at the bridge to increase his force in the fortifications protecting the bridge and then to withdraw his artillery by hand, and as night approached the troops were withdrawn and I directed them to march directly to the rear and bivouac after going four or five miles. I then rode towards Braxton's bridge alone, my Carolina cavalry escort never returning to me.

As I rode along, I saw a mounted man sitting on his horse looking intently down the road. As I approached, he heard my coming and turning recognised me and spoke quickly, telling me that the enemy had crossed and were between us and Braxton's bridge. I told him to go ahead and act as scout and keep a good look-out. So, on we went until we saw a man on horseback. His horse was half hidden in a blacksmith's shop. He also was looking down the road intently, and, as I came up, he also said the enemy had crossed, and were occupying the road. I told him to join the other man and go ahead. We had not gone far when I heard the rapid gallop of a number of horses, and I thought to myself if the enemy have crossed cavalry I may be captured, so I withdrew a little off the road, so as to have a chance of running quickly to my infantry in the rear.

A considerable body appeared, dashing wildly on, each man having his pistol drawn, and, as they came near. I was saluted with wild hurrahs. It was the lieutenant with his Texas company, who told me that he had heard I had been captured, and he had determined to rescue me at the risk of the lives of all, and the men demanded it. Of course, I was much gratified, and, feeling myself secure, we rode on rapidly to find out what had been done at Braxton's bridge. As we went, the first of the parties who had crossed the river were visible but a short distance away, three or four hundred yards along the edge of the river swamp to which they had retired.

We halted where the Braxton bridge road joined the one I was on, and I sent in; my staff officer, Captain King, to tell the officer to march his command in my direction. After waiting a long time, word came that he had started his command on another road. He had become alarmed, because parties of the enemy had been seen by his command to cross the river above him, and he was apprehensive of being intercepted. I let him go, although his scare cost his men a good many more miles of marching. My escort, with myself in charge, rode on towards the Ediste, bringing up the rear. I would very much like to read your account of what took place when you were with Paysinger. He would come in after a scout between twelve and daylight at night, and would report to me at once, and he gave valuable information as to the movements of the enemy.

The morning after the Battle of Bentonville he came to my tent about three o'clock a. m., and told me that the enemy were moving on our left. I so reported to General Hardee, but he had been notified by General Hampton that the enemy were marching on my right, and I was sent with my command on the right. I then told General Hardee that I was apprehensive that there was a mistake, that I was so certain that our left would be attacked and not the right, I would not fortify it, but wait for the order to return to the left. We had not been on the right an hour before General Hardee came himself in great haste, calling for my command to hurry to the left, and we did get back just in time to check the enemy.

Of the things done in these days there are many that I would like very much to have related again by those who were participants, but it would hardly do to put them in print. The conduct of the enemy was, however, so exasperating that there was no treatment too harsh as a punishment for their misdeeds, and I have always regretted that there had not been more scouting parties organised to follow in the wake of Sherman's army and circulate on his flank. Your company acting as scouts, as well as escort, working in small parties, encouraging individual daring and enterprise, was equally as efficient as a much larger body moving in compact mass under one head.

I shall always remember with pleasure the duties you performed while acting as my escort and also the pleasure I had in my personal intercourse with you, as individuals. I always kept in my mind that the individual soldier was entitled to be treated with the respect due to a gentleman, if his behaviour warranted it. This in our Southern army. You will oblige me by assuring all of Company B of my high regard and respect for them individually as brave and honourable men, and collectively as an organised company, for I gave them a chance to show their characters in both ways, and was sorry to part with you all.

Very truly your obedient servant,

L. McLaws.

We served with General McLaws until after the Battle of Bentonville and to the time of surrender of Johnston's army at Jonesboro, North Carolina, never uniting with the regiment again, though occasionally meeting with them, notably at the Battle of Bentonville, where they distinguished themselves by one of the most brilliant charges ever made by cavalry. This charge was made without our company (as we were with General McLaws and the infantry) and resulted in the safety of the whole army by saving an only bridge across a deep river, the only means of retreat of the army. It seems this bridge was guarded by some of Hampton's cavalry, when General Sherman ordered Mower's corps to make a dash around our left flank and capture this bridge and destroy it.

While Mower was proceeding to do this by a rapid advance in the rear of our army, he had his pioneer corps with their spades and picks ready to entrench, and when in sight! of the bridge, he poured a volley on the South Carolina cavalry, who immediately abandoned it. General Hardee dashed up to where our regiment was formed, at the time perhaps not numbering two hundred men, and asked, "Who commands this regiment?"

A Lieutenant Matthews spoke and said he was in command of the regiment this morning. The general asked, "Lieutenant, can you hold those people in check until I can bring up the infantry and artillery?"

He answered, "General, we are the boys that can try," and called to the Rangers to "Come on."

Right here I would mention a sad incident in connection with this charge. General Hardee had an only son, a boy about eighteen years' old, who importuned him for a month or more, to allow him to join the Texas Rangers, and he had only given his consent that morning for the boy to join the regiment and he had fallen into rank with Company D. Another case: Eugene Munger, a cousin of our Dallas Mungers, who had borne a charmed life from the time he joined the Rangers after the Battle of Shiloh, and had never had a scratch, happened to be on a visit to the regiment, talking with some friends, when this charge was ordered. As they went in, passing by General

Hardee, his son saluted him.

The Rangers went into a thick woods, hardly suited for a cavalry charge, raising their accustomed yell and with their pistols, dashed into the first line of infantry, who on account of the sudden, unexpected onslaught, must have overshot them in their first volley. The Rangers were right among them, drove them into the second line, which became demoralised and fell back in confusion, the Rangers immediately withdrawing with quite a number of prisoners, bringing out their dead and wounded. Among the dead were Hardee's son and Eugene Munger. But they accomplished what was intended. General Hardee had brought up his infantry and artillery, which held the enemy in check until night, when the army crossed the bridge and was saved.

About an hour before the Rangers' desperate charge, General McLaws sent for me, when I found him immediately in the rear of his breastworks. He instructed me to take two or three men of the company and move around in the rear of Sherman's army and ascertain if Schofield's army, who had headquarters at Goldsboro, was moving to the support of Sherman, telling me that our army would fall back that night on the road to Raleigh and I would find him somewhere on that road. Taking three other members of the company, among whom was Virge Phelps, an old Mexican and Indian fighter, a man of extraordinary nerve, we proceeded across the bridge, then up Mill Creek towards Little River, where we found a division of the enemy camped about fifteen miles towards Goldsboro.

We then proceeded on towards Goldsboro and found everything quiet outside of the enemy's camps. We ran in vidette pickets on several roads leading into Goldsboro, when finally, we reached the town of Pikeville, the first station on the Goldsboro and Weldon Railroad. Here we stopped to make some inquiries, wearing our Federal overcoats and drawing up at a house for this purpose we asked for a drink of water. A very good looking, intelligent lady came out with a bucket and dipper and handed us water. On inquiry we found the enemy had never entered the town and none had been seen there.

Finally, this good lady asked us what command we belonged to. We told her that we belonged to the Fourth New York Cavalry, which claim we had made at several places where we had stopped for information. This woman kept looking at us and finally said, "Young man, you can't fool me; you are no Yankees, you are some of our own folks." I asked her why she thought so. "Well," she said, "I imagine Yankees don't talk like you do," which caused us to laugh, and as we then had decided to return and make report to General McLaws, I thought it wouldn't make any difference to tell her who we were and stated that we belonged to Wheeler's cavalry. This brought forth a tirade of abuse from this woman.

I said Wheeler's cavalry purposely to ascertain if the terrible name of Wheeler's cavalry had reached there. Wheeler's cavalry, through misrepresentations and frequently through the acts of Yankee scouting parties claiming to belong to Wheeler's cavalry, had gained a very unenviable reputation, so when we claimed to belong to Wheeler's cavalry, this woman said, "I wish I was a man; I would shoulder a gun and help put you down and only wish the Yankees would come in here right now and kill the last one of you."

I said, "Madam, you needn't wish for the Yankees, you will have them soon enough and get a taste of some of their deviltry." We then proceeded back in the direction of the Raleigh road from Bentonville.

CHAPTER 20

I Sell a Ten Dollar Gold Piece for Fifteen Hundred Dollars

I will recite an incident occurring while we were camped about six miles on a plank road from Fayetteville, North Carolina, which place was also a manufacturing point for war munitions on a small scale, also had a large cotton factory: The enemy were moving on two roads, converging into Fayetteville, one road opposed by Rhett's Brigade of South Carolinians (General Rhett having been captured a few days before). General McLaws sent for me about daylight and instructed me to take one or two members of the company and ride across the country to the road occupied by Rhett's Brigade, stating that Rhett's pickets had been run in the night before, then after watching the road for some time, if I found no enemy passing, to ride up the road until we met or heard of them.

We rode up the road to the eleventh milepost, when we discovered some women up in a field near a house, watching the road and decided to go and interrogate them on whether they had seen any enemy passing. I told Jim Freeman, one of the party, to stay in the road and carefully watch the direction from we were expecting the enemy and Joe Hungerford and I would go up and talk with these women, suggesting to Jim if the enemy came in sight and he had time to come to us, to do so, but if he had not, to fire his pistol and run in toward town or go back the way we had come and report to General McLaws and on his firing his pistol we would make our way across from where we were.

After reaching the women they told us they had been watching for an hour or more and had seen no passing, but had heard, the night before, that the enemy were advancing on that road. After getting this information they insisted on our waiting a little while, that they were cooking breakfast and wanted us to share it with them, which we decided to do, remaining on our horses. Very soon Jim Freeman came up to us and reported that he saw a Yankee vidette picket about a half a mile ahead of where he stood. We concluded, as we had time, that we would finish our breakfast and go down and run him in, which we proceeded to do.

When reaching the place in the road where Jim saw this Yankee, he could not be found. I then suggested that he was not a picket, but had strayed away from his command for some purpose and would no doubt be found at some house. We soon discovered a house a few hundred yards ahead, but a little swamp between us and the house prevented us from going directly to it and after proceeding a couple of hundred yards down the road, we found a dirt road coming into the plank road, but at the mouth of this road, owing to a turn in it, we were unable to see the house. I then suggested to the boys that they wait there and I would go up to the house and see if this Yankee was there.

After proceeding some little distance, the road turned and brought me in full view of the house, with this Yankee at the gate, his gun on his shoulder, just starting in. Having on my Yankee overcoat, I slipped my pistol out of its holster, intending to ride up and make him lay down his gun, when he discovered me and smiled, mistaking me for one of their own men. Just as I got ready to throw my pistol down on him the boys on the plank road started in a fast lope down the way we had come, which was notice to me that the enemy were on to them. I had but little time to decide. I knew if I shot this Yankee, it would attract those on the plank road and if I wheeled to run away from him, he would perhaps shoot me, but I decided to take my chance on the latter and broke for the plank road.

Just as I entered the plank road, I noticed a column of infantry within about one hundred and fifty yards. I wheeled to the right very suddenly, which threw the cape of my overcoat over my head, put spurs to my horse, made him do his best, expecting every moment to be shot off the horse, but they never fired a shot, simply calling, "Halt, halt!" The blue overcoat no doubt saved my life, as they evidently thought I was one of their own men. When the boys heard me coming, they stopped and after we got together, we struck across the country the way we had come and reported to General McLaws, which soon started our little army on a hasty march into Fayetteville, where we found Rhett's Brigade, who had moved in during the night, and had sent notice by a courier, which notice never reached General Hardee. Our army then passed through Fayetteville very rapidly, whatever stores there were in the place, of any value to our army, had been removed, and the bridge across the river was all ready to be burned in an instant.

After the army had safely passed over, as also our cavalry, I stopped at a store near the market-house to try to sell a ten dollar gold piece, belonging to one of my comrades, for Confederate money. This was perhaps the last gold piece we had in the command and the last of two hundred dollars in gold my comrade had sent to him from Texas. I found in this store a few yards of butternut jeans and forty or fifty pairs of knit socks, all the goods the fellow had and with his little safe half full of stacks of Confederate money. I asked him a hundred and fifty for one for the gold piece, when he offered me seventy-five for one and while dickering on this trade, we heard the guns fire up the street, when he counted me out fifteen hundred dollars, very quickly for my gold piece. I just had time to spring on to my horse and cross the bridge, which very soon after, was burned, with the enemy moving into Fayetteville.

The army then moved down the river to Averysboro, where they built an earth breastworks from a swamp, through which had passed a hurricane down to the Cape Fear River and in front of this, another, perhaps a half mile from the main works—a short line of works, which was occupied by Rhett's Brigade, with a battery of artillery. While our company with General McLaws and staff, were awaiting developments near where the roadway ran through the earthworks, General Hardee dashed up and called to General McLaws to send two of your Texas people down the line on our left and ascertain if the enemy are flanking in force, when I, in company with Lieutenant Bennett, dashed down the line until we struck the swamp, then turned into the swamp among fallen trees and brush until we became separated, when I was finally fired on by the enemy's skirmish line, which forced me to run back through this fallen timber.

But having a clear-footed horse, I succeeded in getting through to the end of the woods, and there started to run back, away from the fire of the infantry, when a Colonel Fizer commanding the brigade immediately behind the works, called me back and gave me a message to General Hardee, which I was forced to carry up the line, exposed to the fire of the main line of the enemy, which struck our works obliquely. I delivered my message to General Hardee just as Rhett's Brigade was moving inside of the works from their advanced position, protected by the gallant defence of a regiment of Georgians he had thrown forward outside of the main works. When the main line of the enemy poured a hot fire onto that part of the works where we were halted, we dashed into the woods somewhat out of range.

Here a ball struck Captain Lamar's fine mare on the back and she commenced laming. Lamar thought that she would fall with him and begged me to take him up behind me, which I refused to do, unless his mare actually fell. He still insisted on my taking him behind, when I proposed to swap, to which he readily assented, but the mare never gave out and I brought her into camp safely that night.

This animal, one of the finest in the army, was a present to Captain Lamar from a friend of his in Savannah and was said to have cost a thousand dollars in gold. After eating our supper that night General McLaws sent for me to come up to his camp fire, when he asked me to exchange back with Lamar, saying that Lamar prized the mare very highly, as she was a present to him. I told him most certainly I would do so, that I did not expect to keep her, but tender her back to him, which, of course, was very gratifying to all concerned.

CHAPTER 21

My Service with Captain Shannon

It was our custom, when on these scouts inside of the enemy's lines, to rest for a part of the night out of sight and hearing of the road, turning in when away from any settlement or house, so we would not be seen and spend the balance of the night in sleep in perfect safety, without having a guard. After spending that night in the woods, we returned to the road and found a large number of fresh horse tracks leading towards Little River. We construed these to mean that a Federal scout had passed during the night, which we decided to catch up with; charge their rear and stampede them. In about two or three miles from there our road rose up on a little bluff against a fence, then turned down the fence to the west into a lane, past a house.

In the corner of the field was a barn lot, with several barns, where we found about thirty or forty Federals saddling their horses. We immediately withdrew unobserved, under the bluff, to consult, and I suggested to the boys to go around this field, in the woods, strike the road below, wait in ambush until these fellows passed, then charge their rear, as intended. Virge Phelps refused to listen and insisted on charging them right there and then, which I conceived to be a very foolish thing to do, but finally had to yield. As we rose the bluff the second time, we discovered one of Shannon's men coming over the fence, out of the field, which we knew meant that Shannon was camped there with a lot of prisoners.

Captain Shannon was instructed by General Hood at Atlanta to select twenty-five or thirty men out of the regiment and operate inside of Sherman's lines all the time, getting information, and punishing marauders wherever found engaged in their nefarious business of robbing and burning homes.

Shannon's selection of the men he had with him soon won for him and his scout a reputation with our army, and especially with the enemy, second to no scout ever sent out by any army. Mosby's exploits in Virginia have been considered most wonderful achievements for any small body of men. The operations of Shannon's scouts have never been written, but where they were known, surpassed anything ever heard of.

Immediately after recognising this man, coming over from the field, we hunted up Captain Shannon and reported to him our work of the day before, when he stated he was going to send these prisoners to headquarters and suggested that I make my report to General McLaws by the lieutenant in charge and that we go back with him, as he expected to go over the same ground that we had passed over the day before. This we were very willing and anxious to do, having never been in any engagement with him.

Shannon made it a rule that wherever he struck the enemy he would charge them at once and when he found they were too strong for him he would run out and leave them, sometimes drawn up in line of battle, shelling the woods after he was gone. As soon as ready, Shannon moved out with our little party in the rear, they having better horses than ours, as they managed by some means, to keep in fresh horses all the time.

One of the first places we stopped to inquire proved to belong to a very intelligent old Rebel lady, who reported that an officer and a private and a negro soldier had just left her house, the negro driving her buggy, carrying off a lot of fine dress goods and silverware and valuables in the buggy and the others having threatened to hang her if she failed to tell where her money was, forcing her to give up about a hundred dollars in gold and several thousand dollars in Confederate bonds. She told Captain Shannon, "If you will just hurry up, you will catch up with them," which we did, in about two miles from there.

The first one of the party caught up with was the negro soldier driving the horse and buggy, when a member of the advance guard rode up by the side of him and shot him out of the buggy. It seemed as though the ball of his big pistol sent his body about five feet on the roadside, which made the scout smile, looking back at us.

At a house about a quarter of a mile ahead of us, we found two horses hitched, which turned out to belong to the lieutenant and the private, who had taken the old lady's money. Shannon called back, "Don't but two of you stop here." A couple of Shannon's men threw their bridle reins over the fence and rushed into the house, when immediately afterwards we heard pistols rattle in that house. We then continued on this road to where it enters the main county road, running parallel with the Goldsboro & Weldon Railroad. Just before reaching the main county road Captain Shannon halted us, when he went forward, looked up and down the road, came back, commanded, "Form fours and charge!"

I don't think I ever saw men going into a charge like Shannon's men, all breaking ranks, trying to get to the front, not knowing whether they were charging a small body of thirty or fifty men or a whole brigade until they got into the main county road, which disclosed about sixty or seventy mounted infantry with their guns swung on their backs, at the mouth of the lane, drinking and talking. The head of Shannon's column entered the body of the Yankees, shooting their way in among them. All offered to surrender, throwing up their hands with only one gun fired by them and that by a man about to enter a swamp below the field, firing back at us over his shoulder. These cowardly devils were not soldiers, only in name, they were a band of highwaymen and plunderers in the uniform of the United States and the most of them loaded down with plunder of every description.

We next proceeded on the main road towards Pikesville, taking a batch of prisoners along with us, guarded by only two or three of Shannon's scouts. We found these plunderers at every house on the way to Pikesville, a distance of five or six miles, and also in the town. Pikesville was a town of about fifty or seventy-five inhabitants, a blacksmith shop, store and post-office, railroad station and a few residences. On entering the town our party became very much scattered, as we found Federals in nearly every house. A party of about six or eight on horseback tried to escape, when I, with two or three of Shannon's boys, started after them, capturing the whole bunch.

Returning to town I noticed the house where we stopped the day before and had such a tirade of abuse from the woman, of which Shannon's boys with me, knew nothing. I suggested to them to let us go by that house and get a drink of water. The prisoners begged for water also. Riding up to the house, the door opened and my good lady of the day before put in her appearance, when I said to her, "Now, run and get your friends some drinking water; they are very thirsty."

"No," she said, "I wouldn't give them a drink of water to save their lives. Come in, sir, and see what they did in my house." I told her that I did not care to see it, but to run and get some water for her friends, when she again started to abuse the prisoners. I told her she must stop, that they were our prisoners and could not be abused by her.

After getting together the prisoners taken in this town and leaving about a half dozen men to guard them, somewhere near a hundred, we started out on a short scout on the road we had run over after the parties trying to make their escape. When about a mile and a half from town in a straight lane, having very high rail fences on both sides, we met about eighty or a hundred more, evidently on their way to town. The head of their column halted, viewing one of their dead bodies lying in the road, one of the men that was killed by our little party running after them, trying to make their escape.

I forgot to mention when starting out on this last scout that I told Shannon our party wanted to move in the advance guard, as we had hardly got a shot, his men always keeping ahead of us and we did not want to go back to the regiment and say we had been with Shannon's scouts unable to do any effective service. Captain Shannon replied, "All right; go ahead and report to Bill Smith," who was a first lieutenant and always commanded the advance guard.

When within about two hundred yards of this column, viewing the body, I asked Smith, as he was moving us quite rapidly, "What are you going to do; are you going to charge these fellows?"

He said, "Come on; come on."

I looked back and saw Shannon coming up in a lope with about fifteen or eighteen men, then noticed the Federal column getting restless and probably four or five of them break, when I said to Smith, "Now is our time," and we drove ahead, scattering the whole business, capturing a number of prisoners, besides a number left in the road.

We next collected all our prisoners in the town and found that perhaps not more than seventy per cent could speak the English language and we were told that these foreigners had just been imported from Europe, rushed through Castle Garden, right to the army. They were told by the recruiting agents in Europe that they would receive large bounties, good pay and good treatment and be entitled to everything they captured, which latter of course, proved the greatest inducement of all.

We camped with Shannon that night near the town, and parted with him the next morning, they moving in the direction of Goldsboro, while we started back to our army, which we never saw again until the night of the day of the surrender, which was several weeks after.

Chapter 22

We Receive Notice of Johnston's Surrender

After leaving Bentonville our army continued its retreat, the main part of the army finally moving in the direction of Greensboro, where it surrendered. Our little party continued to operate on Sherman's flank, when we heard that there was a large amount of meat collected by the Federal cavalry at a little place called Marlboro, and we decided to get a wagonload of this meat and carry it with us to our army. For this purpose, we impressed a wagon and team and loaded up with hams, which proved a great encumbrance to us and about the third day we left all with a poor widow woman, with her promise to hide out the hams in the woods and try to save them from capture.

We finally reached our regimental camp the night of the surrender of Johnston's army. Our regiment at first notice of the surrender, decided to make their way out. and not take parole, but General Wheeler came down and made them a talk, stating the terms of the surrender to be that the cavalry would be permitted to retain their horses and sidearms and go home unmolested, if they could show a parole; but if not they would be treated and shot as Guerillas. Under this condition General Wheeler advised them to surrender, which they decided to do.

After feeding my horse and eating a little supper, I tried to make up a party to make our way out without taking a parole, believing that the army would be sent to prison, and, having determined never to see the inside of another prison, I prepared to go out and succeeded in inducing about thirty of the regiment to go out with me. We rode all night, and next morning came to a place where we found Colonel Harrison on crutches, standing in the door. I dismounted and went in to tell him that the army had surrendered and when about half way to him in the yard, he motioned to me with his hand, saying, "Back to your command; back to your command."

I told him that we were on our way to Texas, the army had surrendered and the Rangers had decided to surrender with the army and take a parole, which brought tears to his eyes. He repeated, "The army has surrendered and the Rangers going to surrender with the army? You did right, sir, in coming out; the Rangers shall not surrender with the army; I am going to send them word to come out." He then bade us goodbye and we proceeded on our way.

That night we got to the town of Lexington, where we decided to stop for the night, camping at the edge of the town. I went into town to have some bread cooked for the party and it commenced to rain. Finally, I succeeded in finding a place where a lady agreed to cook the bread for us all. The gentleman insisted on my staying at his house until his wife could cook the bread, which would take her all night, and as a further inducement, said if I would stay, he would go with me the next morning and show me where about thirty barrels of Catawba wine was hid out, from which we could fill our canteens.

The next morning, going down to where I had left the boys in camp, loaded down with bread, I found they had gone and left me. They had evidently become alarmed during the night and, not knowing where I could be found, they decided I would be able to make my way out all right. I then struck out, taking as much of the bread as I could conveniently carry, but did not take time to get any of the wine. I took the main Charlotte road, when in about two or three miles, the road forked, one seemed about as much travelled as the other. About six miles from there, towards Charlotte, I came to a house where I found Major Jarmon of our regiment, badly wounded, with several of our men taking care of him.

These men told me that our party who had left me, had divided at the forks of the road, part of them taking the right hand, intending to go through Middle Tennessee and East Tennessee, the others going on to Charlotte, there to cross the river and go over into South Carolina. I then decided to go back to the forks of the road, take the right hand and try to catch up with the party going to Tennessee.

After following this road about two or three miles, I came to a branch, where I stopped to water my horse and immediately discovered about eight or ten old men and young boys riding horses, unshod, and with citizens' saddles. They had a few squirrel rifles and no other weapons, and were also watering their horses in the branch near me. They asked me what command I belonged to. I told them

I belonged to the Texas Rangers and my company was just ahead, when I asked them what command they belonged to. They said they belonged to General Lee's cavalry, which I knew was not true, but that they were bushwhackers and I decided to get away from them as soon as possible.

I started across the branch and at a little turn of the road I struck a trot, when two of them loped up behind me, separating, one on each side of me, one of them demanding to buy my saddle. I told him it was not for sale. The other wanted to buy one of my pistols. I told them they couldn't have anything I had; "I know what you are after and if you know what is good for you, you had better drop back and let me alone." They stopped and, I thought, started back to their party. I soon got to another turn of the road out of their sight, and struck a lope and ran about a mile and a half. I concluded perhaps they would come no further.

I discovered a woman ploughing in the field, at the far end of which was a log house on the edge of the woods, and just at the corner of the fence I noticed some fresh horse tracks turned off the road, which I concluded perhaps was our party who had gone to the house to get something to eat. I waited in the fence corner for the woman to return to the end of the row and asked if she had seen any men riding down the line of fence to the house, when she claimed she did not and while talking with her here this gang of bushwhackers came dashing up and surrounded me in the fence corner. I pulled out one of my pistols and told them the first man that raised a gun I'd kill "and I'll get a number of you before you get me, for I am an expert shot and never miss," when one of them said, "Come on, boys; let's leave the d—— fool."

I told them, "Yes, you'd better leave." Unfortunately for me, they turned right up the road, the way I wanted to go and when they concluded I had quit watching them, they turned into the woods, no doubt expecting me to continue on the road and they would then ambush me.

I first concluded that I must catch up with our party, as I was exceedingly anxious to go with them into Tennessee and it was not safe for me to go by myself, therefore decided I would ride along leisurely until I got up to the point where they turned out of the road, then, with my pistol raised, I would put spurs to my horse and run the gauntlet, which on further reflection, I concluded that I had better not attempt, as they would be bound to hit my horse in running by. I therefore turned back the way I had come.

When within about two or three miles of the main forks of the road, I struck a well-beaten path, running in the direction of the Charlotte road, which I decided to take and getting back into the Charlotte road, I would ride on to Charlotte. After riding in this path about a mile and a half, I came to a large log house, to reach the front gate of which I had to pass through a barn lot that had a large gate, fastened by a log chain wrapped around the bottom of the gate and the gate post. When I got down off my horse to unwind this chain, I heard someone speak and when I looked up I found an old gentleman on the other side of the lot with a shotgun levelled on me. I told him not to shoot, "I am a friend and want some directions."

He said, "Now, that animal isn't fit for you to ride and would be of no use to you, but you can't take her."

I told him, "My friend, I don't want your horse, I have as good a horse as I want. I only want some directions," and after talking with him a little, satisfied him that I was not after his horse, when he invited me in. I then told him about being on my way home to Texas and how I had been separated from the party I was going with and wanted to get to the Charlotte road the nearest way I could get there. He then begged me to spend the balance of the day and stay all night with him. After finding that he was a good Southern man, I decided to do so, satisfied I would never catch up with our party that had taken the Charlotte road and I needed rest very badly, as also my horse.

The old gentleman told me that that whole country was overrun by a band of marauders that had been pillaging and robbing their homes and they had had a meeting of the people in the neighbourhood and decided whenever a house was attacked, they would blow a horn and all rush to the place of attack, there to shoot down every man they found that had no business there. It is hardly necessary to say that he wished they would attack his house the night I was there, because I had four pistols and was regarded by him as pretty good reinforcement, but nothing of the sort happened. I spent a very restful and pleasant night, with a good supper and breakfast, and next day started out, by a near road, to strike the Charlotte pike, which I did some several miles ahead of where I left Major Jarman, the day before, badly wounded.

When I finally reached Charlotte, I stopped to make some inquiry of an infantry guard stationed at a big stable, who told me that the guards in town had orders to arrest every man from Johnston's army without a parole and advised me to pass around the main part of the town, into the road I was going on to. He furthermore told me that our whole Confederate Government was then in Charlotte; President Davis, with General Breckenridge, then Secretary of War; Judge Reagan, Postmaster General, and all the rest, and they had just heard the news of Lincoln's assassination, which seemed to have cast a gloom over the entire party.

I now proceeded on my way, around the town, back into the main road leading out to Bady's Ferry and when within four or five miles of the ferry, I met a citizen who had just crossed there and reported that Colonel Clarence Prentice, with about two hundred Kentuckians, had just crossed there and had been captured by a heavy force of Federal cavalry and by them paroled and permitted to go on his way home. Then further conferring with this citizen about where I could best cross the Catawba River, he told me of a *batteau* at a mill about twelve miles below Charlotte, when I decided to ride down there and cross in this batteau, which I did, putting my saddle and everything in the batteau, paddling across and swimming my mare, which landed me in a wheat field, in the State of South Carolina.

After getting straightened out again for the road I got directions to Anderson Courthouse, which I reached in due time and found Colonel Harrison, with a large party of Rangers, resting and having a good time. Harrison, if the reader will remember, was badly wounded and was just recovering, using crutches, when a party of Rangers came along after we had left, secured an ambulance and crossed the Catawba River with two *batteaux*, one on each side, thus bringing him out to Anderson Courthouse, which was his old home and where he had relatives.

After resting another day, we again struck out for the Mississippi River, passing through South Carolina, into Georgia, then into Alabama. Before reaching the State of Alabama, we heard that the Mississippi River was out of its banks and about thirty miles wide, which forced us to scatter out and lay up at different points, until the river ran down so that we could cross. I had promised a messmate, Joe Hungerford, whose home was at Uniontown, Alabama, that I would spend some time with him.

Riding along one day in Alabama, some miles from Marion, I was taken with a severe headache, which forced me to stop and lay up, try to get some rest and sleep. When I woke in the night I was prevailed on by an old gentleman at the house, to spend the balance of the night, which threw me considerably behind the party of men I was with.

When our party left Greenville Courthouse we decided if we struck any horses or mules, belonging to the United States Government, we would take them along with us, for the purpose of probably raising money to pay our expenses home and if we found any small parties of the enemy, we would attack them and on their surrender, would parole them, taking their arms and horses.

On riding into the town of Marion, I saw a guard in front of a livery stable, rode up to him, when he accosted me, "Hello, Texas; have you come after mules, too?"

I told him, "Yes, where are they?"

He said, "This stable is full of the finest kind of mules;" he happened to be an Arkansas man and told me that my party, who went through the day before, went out with a lot of mules, each leading two.

I told him, "All right, open the door and I will go in and get a couple."

He said, "No, you know I want you to have them, but they are in charge of Major Curry, who has a strong guard here and is waiting to turn them over to the Yankees, who are expected in here by train every minute and you had better not attempt to take any mules by yourself, as Curry, with his guards, would surely arrest you and turn you over to the Yankees."

Then I concluded best to drop the matter and proceeded to get directions, from a citizen, to Uniontown.

Stopping on the road, about five miles from Marion, to get dinner, I found at the house four Confederate soldiers—one young man on crutches, who had been wounded in the Virginia Army, the son of the owner of the place; one of the Eleventh Texas Cavalry and two Arkansas men. At the dinner table the old gentleman told me about Major Curry, a Confederate Quartermaster, who had impressed about two hundred fine mules in that section for account of the Confederate Government and had these mules in a large livery stable in Marion, protected by a guard, to turn them over to the Federals.

These mules had not been branded and the owners had plead with Major Curry to return them to them, but Curry refused, claiming it would get him into trouble with the Federals, as they would certainly get the information. The old gentleman told me that the feeling against Curry was very bitter and that he was regarded as a very mean man, persisting in his determination to turn over the mules, on account of his antipathy to his old neighbours and friendliness to the

Federals, thereby courting their favours.

Presently one of the Arkansas men proposed that we go back and take a couple of mules apiece, by force, to which we all consented. Our crippled man, not having a gun, his father told him of a rich neighbours some two miles from there who had quite a number of mules taken by Curry and was very bitter against him on that account, that he had a very fine shotgun and would no doubt loan it to him for the purpose of a raid on that stable. Stopping at this house on our way into Marion, this young crippled man secured the shotgun, when we moved on. Just before we entered town, I stopped the party and told them that I was satisfied we were very liable to have trouble with Major Curry and there was no use in starting into it without going through with it. "Now, if there is a man among you that don't want to go in, let him say so now."

They all said they were willing to go and wanted me to take command of the party. I told them, "All right, now, if you are asked any questions, who I am, tell them I am Lieutenant Jones, Company C, Eleventh Texas."

We now started in and found a big lattice door to the stable open, and as soon as we came in sight the guard rushed to the door to close it, when I dashed up with my pistol on and told him to leave that door open. I then told our crippled young man, with the shotgun, to hold that door open, to stay there and to shoot the first man that attempted to close it when the balance of our men went in to get the mules. There were two shed rooms, connected with the main room; the large room had stalls on each side. Not finding any good mules in the large room, I went to the far end and turned into one of the shed rooms, the balance of the men scattering around, hunting good mules. While engaged untying a mule in the shed room, I heard a man call to some of our men, "Who are you, and what are you doing here?"

They told him they had come after mules.

"Who commands this party?"

"Lieutenant Jones of the Eleventh Texas."

"Where is Lieutenant Jones?"

They told him I was in that shed room. In the meantime, a number of men in citizen's clothes, had entered the main room. Major Curry came around into the shed room, where I had untied a mule and asked me if I was Lieutenant Jones, in command. He said, "I am Major Curry of the Confederate States Army, in charge of these mules, with orders to turn them over to the United States Army and if you don't take your party out of here and leave these mules, I will have to arrest you and turn you over to the Federal authorities."

I told him that we would be very much disappointed if he didn't attempt our arrest, that we had come on purpose to get the mules and him, too, when he approached very near me and said in a low tone of voice, "You know this stable is full of Yankee spies now, come in advance of the army to find out what they can, and for their benefit I have to make a show of resistance."

He said, "You go ahead and take what mules you want. You Texans are entitled to them; you are a long ways from home."

We then completed our selection and led out two mules apiece, with two for our lame friend at the door, passing by a number of strangers, looking on, in the main room. Major Curry followed me outside, when I told him, "Now, if it will be of any benefit to you, Major, I am willing to give you a written statement that I appeared here with an armed force and took possession of so many mules," which he said he would appreciate very much, it might prove of benefit to him with the Yankees, and invited me up into his office with him, around on the square, where I drew up this statement and signed the name of R. F. Jones, Company C, Eleventh Texas Regiment. We then departed with our mules, back to the young lame man's home, where we separated, perhaps never to meet again.

After obtaining directions for Uniontown, on my way through Green County, Alabama, I stopped at the little town of Newbern, where I met a Doctor James Webb, who insisted on my stopping with him. He had a beautiful home; his family being away on a long visit to some other section of the State, he felt quite lonely and wanted company. I decided to accept his invitation, when he made me feel at home and my visit there for nearly two months, waiting for the Mississippi River to run down, proved very pleasant indeed, besides forming many new and pleasant acquaintances.

After spending nearly two months at this place, we had information, which we considered reliable, that the Trans-Mississippi Department had surrendered. I therefore concluded best to abandon my ride to Texas, leave my horse and arms with Doctor Webb and proceed to New Orleans, from there by steamer to Galveston. Doctor Webb succeeded in finding an only twenty-dollar gold piece, which he advanced me to pay the expense of my trip.

Armed with a parole, copied from one in the possession of an Appomattox prisoner, I proceeded to Uniontown, where I took rail for

Selma and entered the Provost Marshal's office, threw down my parole and demanded transportation to Texas, which was granted me as far as New Orleans.

Arriving at New Orleans I found that the Trans-Mississippi Department had not yet surrendered, but the agents of General Kirby Smith, who was in command of the Trans-Mississippi Department (Doctor Ashbel Smith and Mr. Ballinger of Galveston), were then negotiating with General Canby, its surrender. Here I found a large part of Hood's brigade, as also General Hood and members of his staff from Texas and General Thomas Harrison of our brigade, with some few members of the Eighth Texas, also many members of Granbury's and Rector's brigades, awaiting the close of negotiations and transportation to Texas, when finally, in about a week or ten days, the surrender of the Trans-Mississippi Department was completed and a large transport, in charge of a Federal captain, was ordered to take us to Galveston.

On arrival at the entrance of Galveston Bay we met a sloop of war going out, when our captain in charge signalled to it to return to Galveston and anchor off a certain wharf, where he expected to land our men, which he did. On arrival at this wharf, after tying up the boat, a stage was run out, when a lone gentleman standing on the wharf, claiming to be Mayor Leonard of the city, called to the Federal captain not to allow a single man to come off that boat until the trains were ready to take us into the interior. This brought forth a spirited rebuke by our Federal captain, telling him that the men were going to land and stay in the city until they could be taken out by the railroad and if they mistreated any of the men while there, he would order the gunboat to lay his town in ashes.

In explanation of the mayor's action, it seems that when the army disbanded in the interior, that a lot of bad men entered Galveston and conducted themselves badly, when the City Council met and passed an order that no more soldiers would be permitted in the city. The mayor, of course, had no idea that a large number of the men aboard were citizens of Galveston nor as to the character of the men aboard, hence his mistake.

In connection with this I recall the departure of the Bayou City Guards in 1861 for Virginia, who afterwards constituted a part of the Fifth Texas Regiment, Hood's brigade, and reflected such credit on the Confederate arms in Virginia. I happened to be present in Houston when this company, marching through the streets of Houston to the railroad depot, were escorted by a cavalry company and a large concourse of citizens—on their departure for Harrisburg, there to be mustered into the service of the Confederate States for the war.

After boarding the train a few speeches were made and a few words spoken by Captain John G. Walker, commanding the cavalry company, which I well remember, as follows:

> If you fight bravely, we will honour you; if you return safely, we will welcome you; if you die in battle I swear to Heaven we will avenge you.

Taking this in connection with our reception at Galveston, which of course, was a mistake, by accident, we can well afford to pass it.

As soon as the trains were made up for the interior, after spending a day and night in Galveston where we were treated royally by its citizens, we proceeded to our different homes and I soon landed in Hempstead among a sad, dejected and ruined people, resolved to do the best they could under the circumstances and submit gracefully to the powers that were.

It would, I consider, be entirely fitting for me to close this part of my life's history by publishing what I may call General Joseph Wheeler's farewell address to his cavalry corps (General Wheeler issued the following order to his entire command):

Headquarters Cavalry Corps,
April 28, 1865.

Gallant Comrades: You have fought your fight. Your task is done. During a four years' struggle for liberty, you have exhibited courage, fortitude and devotion. You are the victors of more than 200 sternly contested fields. You have participated in more than a thousand conflicts of arms. You are heroes! Veterans! Patriots! The bones of your comrades mark battlefields upon the soil of Kentucky, Virginia, North Carolina, South Carolina, Georgia, Alabama and Mississippi. You have done all that human exertion could accomplish.

In bidding you *adieu*, I desire to tender my thanks for your gallantry in battle, your fortitude under suffering and your devotion at all times to the holy cause you have done so much to maintain.

I desire also to express my gratitude for the kind feelings you have seen fit to extend toward myself, and to invoke upon you the blessing of our Heavenly Father, to whom we must always look in the hour of distress. Brethren in the cause of freedom, comrades in arms, I bid you farewell.

Joseph Wheeler,
Major General.

Official:
   Wm. E. Waites,
   Assistant Adjutant General.

Terry's Texas Rangers

Contents

Introduction	169
Assembly and Organisation of the Regiment	173
Woodsonville	177
Retreat	181
Shiloh	183
Forrest at Murfreesboro	187
Many Marches and Skirmishes—The Kentucky Campaign	190
Murfreesboro	195
The Donelson Trip and Retreat to Chattanooga	197
Chickamauga	200
Wheeler's Great Raid	204
East Tennessee Campaign	206
Sherman's Wagon Train and the Affairs with M'Cook and Stoneman	212
Wheeler's Second Raid into Tennessee	215
"The Rome Races"	217
The Last Campaign	220
Conclusion	224

Introduction

It is but natural that man should desire to leave some record of his achievements for the information of succeeding generations. This desire was manifested in the infancy of the race, and is shown in monuments and chiselled stone, and in writings on skins and reeds.

Here in the South, when the great war of the '60s had terminated and the various actors in the great drama had time to look about them, the desire was universal that the record made by Southern manhood should be perpetuated. The regiment of Texas cavalry known as the "Terry Rangers" shared that feeling; and when the survivors began to meet in annual reunion this desire became manifest.

Two propositions appealed to them: one for a history which should tell of their campaigns, their marches, battles, hardships, sufferings; one for a monument which should contain the name of every man who served in the regiment. For reasons which I need not discuss here the plan for the history failed. All funds raised for either purpose were combined into one and placed in control of the monument committee. The equestrian statue which now stands in the grounds of the State Capitol in Austin is the result.

The desire for a narrative still survived, however, discoverable in many personal sketches of events, some taking the form of memoirs, written by various members of the command. I have long contemplated such a work but have felt the lack of ability. It is now perhaps too late to attempt anything like a complete history of the regiment, as the necessary data can hardly be procured. Yet, when my former comrade, D. S. Combs, appealed to me to write something that would supply his children and grandchildren with some knowledge, however imperfect, of the part borne by the Rangers in the great war, I unhesitatingly promised to try it and do the best I could. I wish with all my heart I could make my story as complete as it ought to be, for I firmly believe that a well written narrative of the regiment's wonderful career would be the most entertaining book in the literature of war.

As a first step toward the accomplishment of the task I had undertaken, I wrote to Comrade Combs asking him for such data as he might have or such as his personal recollections might supply; also, as to the scope and form of the work as he wished it to appear. His answer is so kind and trusting that I here insert it and, as the lawyers say, make it a part of the record. His letter, written from his home in San Antonio, is dated January 5th:

> My Dear Lee:
> Yours of the 26th of December came duly to hand, and I should have replied sooner but I have been strictly on the go for the last ten days, and I have neglected many things that should have had attention.
> Now, Lee, I wish to state with all the sincerity of my heart, that all I want is plain statements of facts; and while I give you a brief outline of my movements, from the day I was sworn into the service of the Confederate States to the close of the war, I simply do this that you may know where D.S. Combs was, and it is a matter of indifference to me whether my name is mentioned a single time in your story of the doings of the regiment, and, more especially, of the part old Company D played in that drama.
> I was very fearful that the war would be over before I saw a live Yankee. So, Charley McGehee and I went fifty miles from home to join a company, and joined Ferrell's company between Bastrop and La Grange. According to my recollection this was in the latter part of August, '61.
> "From that day to the day I left the regiment, I was not away from Company D more than ten or twelve days, and then on account of sickness; once at Shelbyville for five or six days; at another time near Nolensville for about the same length of time.
> My initiation was at Woodsonville, and the last of the chapter was at Mossy Creek, Dandridge, and the brick house where N. J. Allen was killed and the artillery duel where Captain Littlefield was wounded. This, I think, was early in January, '64. Here I drew a furlough, and in company with Ike Jones, Bill Fisher and Jeff Burleson, I struck out for home. On my arrival at home my parents and sisters insisted that I ask for assignment

to duty on this side of the Mississippi. I had lost one brother by sickness at Searcy, Arkansas, one had been killed at the battle of Chickamauga, one badly wounded at Port Hudson, and another desperately wounded at Mansfield, Louisiana.

Accordingly, I applied to General E. Kirby Smith for such assignment, and he gave me orders to report to General Magruder at Galveston for assignment to duty in any cavalry command I might select. I chose Colonel J. S. Ford's command on the Rio Grande. I was attached to Captain Carrington's company in Major Cater's battalion, and was with that command in the last fight of the war. This was between Brownsville and the mouth of the Rio Grande, and was about two weeks after General Smith had surrendered the Trans-Mississippi department, but the word had not reached us.

I am glad to say that in this last fight of the war the Confederate arms were victorious. A few days after this we got word that the war was over. So, we folded our tents and quietly and sadly turned our faces homeward. As a company or battalion, we never surrendered. We simply laid down our arms and tried to forget the past and all its disappointments.

Now to go back and come over the story as it actually occurred, I will simply say that I was never wounded during the war, but particularly unfortunate with my mounts. I had three noble animals killed under me, two at Murfreesboro, one at College Hill, opposite Knoxville, also one wounded at Mt. Washington, near Louisville, Kentucky.

I was with you at Farmington and at Nolensville, where Ferg Kyle led his line of dismounted men, deployed as skirmishers, up against a solid line of blue, a regiment of infantry, who poured a galling fire into our ranks and caused us to reel and stagger like a drunken man.

I was with you at Woodsonville, Shiloh, Murfreesboro, Bardstown, Perryville and Chickamauga. Also, at Murfreesboro when Forrest with his little band swooped down on the two camps and took them in out of the damp.

Again, Lee, I will say that I wish you to handle the story in your own way, and I will be perfectly satisfied. What we want is the doings of the *company* and *regiment*. I care not for individual mention. If you and I are satisfied I care not whether others are or not.

I wish to emphasise this statement. I appreciate more than you know your willingness to undertake this for me, and will gladly remunerate you as far as it is in my power to do for the time you put in on the work.

Mrs. Combs and I wish to thank you and your daughter for the kind hospitality to us during the reunion, and hope you may both find it convenient to visit us in the near future. Wishing you both a pleasant and prosperous New Year, I am,

        Always yours,

                                  D. S. Combs.

If I had regretted my promise or had wavered in the slightest from my intention, this letter would have renewed in me the purpose to do my best. Yet I do not see why anyone who writes as well as Comrade Combs should desire another to write for him. I would not, with intention, do injustice to anyone; I know I cannot do justice to many deserving the highest praise; but I must say that the regiment had no better soldier than D. S. Combs.

Since this work was well under way Comrade A. B. Briscoe of Company K has kindly placed at my service a large lot of MS. of his personal memoirs. I have used this in several instances, of which due credit is given in the proper places.

Austin, May, 1911.

CHAPTER 1

Assembly and Organisation of the Regiment

When in 1861 it became evident that war between the sections was inevitable and imminent, B. F. Terry, a sugar planter of Fort Bend County, and Thomas S. Lubbock, of Houston, determined to be in the fight from the start, hurried to Virginia, at their own expense, where they participated in the first battle of Manassas, rendering distinguished services as scouts before the action and in pursuit of the routed enemy afterward. Later the War Department gave them authority to recruit a regiment of Texans for mounted service in Virginia. Returning to Texas they at once issued a call for volunteers.

The conditions were exacting. Each man must furnish his own arms and equipment—a gun of some sort, Colt's repeating pistol, a saddle, bridle and blanket. Notwithstanding these requirements, the response was so prompt that in less than thirty days the ten companies were on their way to the rendezvous at Houston. Some of the companies had the full complement of one hundred men, rank and file, and in a few more days all would have been full. Probably two or more regiments could have been raised at that time if the call had been made.

The personnel was of the very highest. Sons of leading families, many of them college graduates, professional men, merchants, stockmen, and farmers, served in the ranks as privates, all young, in their teens and early twenties. Rank was scarcely considered. The supreme desire was to get into the war in a crack cavalry regiment.

Since I write without data and from memory only, I must necessarily deal more particularly with the company of which I was a member, known as Company D in the regimental organisation. It was recruited largely from Bastrop, with contingents from Hays, Travis and

Burleson counties. This organisation, full at the beginning, always one of the largest for duty, sustained the greatest loss in killed of all the companies of the regiment. The first officers elected were:

Captain, Stephen C. Ferrell.

First Lieutenant, Charles L. Morgan.

Second Lieutenant, Jesse W. Burdett.

Second Lieutenant, William R. Doak.

The assembly for the company was to be in the town of Bastrop, and notice was given that on a certain morning the march would begin. The men from the adjoining counties reached Bastrop the night before.

It was a bright, sunny August morning. The people, *en masse*, turned out to bid us goodbye. Men, women, children, with tears in their eyes, said, "God bless you!" when they clasped our hands as we stood in line. This painful ordeal over, we mounted and rode away on what we believed was a few months' adventure.

Alleyton, sixty miles away, then the terminus of the railroad, was reached without any very exciting adventures. We sent our horses back home and took the train for Houston. The trains were then run to Harrisburg, but we were dumped off in the prairie at Pierce Junction to await a train from Columbia. The hours passed, and the night. We slept little on account of the mosquitoes, which were more numerous and voracious than any I ever met elsewhere. Next morning, as there was still no train, we walked into Houston, a distance of nine miles, pushing by hand the freight car with our saddles and baggage. Here we went into camp in an old warehouse and met some of the other companies.

From McLennan and adjoining counties Captain Thos. Harrison led a company which became Company A. Captain John A. Wharton had a full company raised chiefly in Brazoria and Matagorda Counties. It became Company B in the organisation and continued the largest in enlistment. Companies C, commanded by Mark Evans; E, by L. N. Rayburn; and I, led by J. G. Jones, were recruited in Gonzales and surrounding counties. Many of these were stockmen and expert horsemen. Company F was from Fayette and commanded by Louis M. Strobel. Company G was from Bexar and Goliad Counties. Its first captain was W. Y. Houston. Company H was from Fort Bend County chiefly, and commanded by John T. Holt. Company K, Captain John

G. Walker, was from Harris and Montgomery counties, and was full. The word "chiefly" ought to be used in telling where the companies were recruited, for all of them had men from several counties. Here, too, on the 9th of September we were "mustered in," swearing to serve "so long as this war shall last."

From Houston to Beaumont, over a newly constructed railroad, it took nearly all day to make eighty miles. From Beaumont, by steamboat, down the Neches and up the Sabine to Niblett's Bluff; thence a hundred miles on foot, through water much of the way; thence forty miles in carts. It is easy to remember this cart ride. The wheels were six or seven feet high. Motive power, oxen, two pairs to each cart. Engineers, little bow-legged Creoles, each armed with a long, sharp-pointed pole. The vehicles had no springs. As there were no seats, the six or eight passengers in each conveyance had to stand on their feet. At New Iberia, on Bayou Teche, we were transferred to boats, and went down between the beautiful banks of that stream to Brashear, now Morgan City. From there we went through an almost continuous sugar farm to New Orleans. The trip from Houston to New Orleans took over a week. It is now made in less than twelve hours, in a palace car.

In New Orleans we learned that our destination was not Virginia, but Bowling Green, Kentucky, where General A. Sidney Johnston was trying to assemble an army for the defence of that frontier. This was pleasing to us, as General Johnston was a Texan, and personally known to many of us.

The box cars in which we left New Orleans had been used for shipping cattle, and were not overly clean. Our seats were rough planks without backs. In this luxurious fashion we rode for twenty hours until we reached Nashville. There we encamped in the fair grounds. Ladies in great numbers visited us, and for their entertainment our most expert horsemen gave the first really-truly "wild-west" entertainment ever seen east of the Mississippi.

At Nashville our first death occurred, Thomas Hart, whose loss saddened us greatly. He was a promising young man, not personally well known to me.

We had expected to receive our horses here and go on horseback to Bowling Green, but one night Colonel Terry received orders to bring on his regiment "at once." At 1 o'clock in the morning we marched to the station and waited till 2 p. m. for our train. That same afternoon we reached Bowling Green. Our horses were driven through from Nashville by a detail sent back after them. We now received tents, camp utensils and wagons. Here, too, the companies were formally organised into a regiment by the election of the following field officers:

Colonel, B. F. Terry.
Lieutenant Colonel, Thomas S. Lubbock.
Major, Thomas Harrison.

The following staff officers were appointed:

Adjutant, M. H. Royston.
Quartermaster, B. H. Botts.
Commissary, Robert D. Simmons.
Chaplain, R. F. Bunting.
Surgeon, Dr. John M. Weston.
Assistant Surgeon, Dr. Robert E. Hill.
Sergeant Major, W. B. Sayers.

Terry was a native of Kentucky, about 40 years old, of great force of character, firm and self-reliant. His appearance was commanding, and in all ways, he was fitted for high rank.

Lubbock was some years older than Terry. He was a native of South Carolina. He was small of stature, pleasant and affable, and made a favourable impression on us. At that time, he was in poor health, soon had to go to Nashville for treatment, and we never saw him more.

Harrison was a native of Mississippi. He was a lawyer by profession. A small, nervous, irascible man, who proved to be a fine soldier, became a brigadier general of cavalry, and distinguished himself on many fields.

Winter was now at hand, and the climate was trying on young men raised, as we had been, in the far South. Many fell ill of measles, mumps, pneumonia, and other diseases peculiar to raw levees. Scores went to the hospital, and not a few under the sod. Still the spirits of all, from the youngest private to the resolute colonel, were of the highest, and all were anxious to meet the foe. Such as were able drilled daily, mounted guard, and performed other duties incident to camp life in time of war.

Chapter 2

Woodsonville

Terry, anxious to be doing something, was ordered to lead the regiment to the front on picket and scouting duty. On the 17th of December, Brigadier General Hindman led an expedition to Greene River. When he reached that stream, he found the north bank in possession of the enemy's outposts. He deployed some infantry skirmishers, who engaged the enemy at long range but with little effect. Called himself from the immediate front, he left Colonel Terry in charge with instructions to decoy the enemy up the hill and away from support to a point where our infantry and artillery could be used to better advantage.

The enemy allowed themselves to be decoyed, and came across in large numbers. Terry, however, was not the man to invite visitors and then leave someone else to entertain them. Sending Ferrell with about seventy-five men against their left, he led the rest against their right. We charged, yelling, each man riding as fast as his horse could go. Terry fell, dying almost instantly.

Ferrell led his force into an open field against a body of the enemy, who rallied behind a straw stack and such fences as they could find, pouring a galling fire into us. On our part it was a furious but disorderly charge of comparatively undrilled men into one of the best drilled regiments of the Federal Army. This was the Thirty-Second Indiana Infantry. The officers and men were Germans, who had probably learned their tactics in the old country. They were ignorant of the English language. They were brave fellows, and stood like veterans till shot down.

In view of the great disparity of the forces engaged and the losses sustained, this was one of the most remarkable of all the conflicts of this very remarkable war. One of the very few actions where mounted men engaged infantry on their own ground. It also shows of what stuff the Southern volunteer was made. In support of these statements, I invite attention to the official reports. The first is by Colonel Willich. Omitting some unimportant details, it is as follows:

> But now ensued the most earnest and bloody part of the struggle. With lightning speed, under infernal yelling, great numbers of Texas Rangers rushed upon our whole force. They advanced to fifteen or twenty yards of our lines, some of them even between them, and opened fire with rifles and revolvers. Our skirmishers took the thing very coolly, and permitted them to approach very close, when they opened a destructive fire on them. They were repulsed with severe loss, but only after Lieutenant Sachs, who left his covered position with one platoon, was surrounded by about fifty Rangers, several of them demanding of him three times to give up his sword, and let his men lay down their arms. He firmly refused, and defended himself till he fell, with three of his men, before the attack was repulsed.
>
> Lieutenant Colonel Von Trebra now led on another advance of the centre and left flank, when he drew down upon his forces a second attack of the Rangers in large numbers, charging into the very ranks, some dashing through to the rear, which might have proved disastrous.
>
> In the fight participated three field officers, one staff and sixteen officers of the line, twenty-three sergeants and 375 men. Our loss is one officer and ten men dead, twenty-two wounded and five missing. According to reports of our surgeons several of the wounded are beyond hope of recovery.

I have omitted from the foregoing interesting and more or less instructive details of the parts played by Lieutenant Colonel Von Trebra, Major Snachenberg, Captain Wilchbilling, Adjutant Schmidt, Lieutenant Mank and other heroes whose names are hard to spell and harder to pronounce. Valiant men all, and all doubtless recommended for promotion. As will be seen hereafter, to fight with the Rangers was to be in line of advancement in this world or the next.

I now give General Hindman's report from the Confederate side:

> The firing ceased for about half an hour, and I went in person to select a suitable place for camp, leaving Colonel Terry in command, with instructions to decoy the enemy up the hill, where I could use my infantry and artillery with effect, and be

out of the range of the enemy's batteries.

Before returning to the column the fire from the skirmishers recommenced. The enemy appeared in force on my right and centre. Colonel Terry, at the head of seventy-five Rangers, charged about 300 of the enemy, routed and drove them back, but fell mortally wounded. A body of the enemy about the same size attacked the Rangers under Captain Ferrell on the right of the turnpike, and were repulsed with heavy loss. (Attack was really made by Ferrell on the enemy, advancing under command of Von Trebra, as Colonel Willich reports.—G.)

"My loss in this affair was as follows: Killed, Colonel Terry and three men of his regiment; dangerously wounded, Lieutenant Morris and three men of the Texas Rangers; slightly wounded, Captain Walker and three men of the Texas Rangers and two men of the First Arkansas battalion.

From General Hindman's report it will be seen that the Rangers had 150 men in the fight, seventy-five with Terry, seventy-five with Ferrell; there being, in fact, two charges. Our loss was twelve altogether. Colonel Willich reported that he had, officers and men, 418 engaged. He had eleven killed, twenty-two wounded and reported five missing, a total of thirty-eight; his missing being prisoners in our hands. Thus 150 men charged 418, inflicting a loss of thirty-eight, sustaining a loss of twelve. Of this number Company D lost five: W.W. Beal and Frank Loftin killed, L. L. Giles mortally wounded, L. B. Giles and John R. Henry slightly wounded.

If a complete record could be obtained, I believe a similar disparity of losses would appear in nearly all the engagements in which we bore a part. The splendid horsemanship of our men, and their skill with firearms, made them easily superior to any foe they went against. In this fight our loss was irreparable in the death of our gallant leader. Had he lived he would, without doubt, have reached the highest rank and would have achieved a fame second to none. We had other brave leaders, but none like the matchless Terry.

In the election of officers which followed the death of Terry, Lieutenant Colonel Lubbock was advanced to the command of the regiment, and Captain John G. Walker became lieutenant colonel. Lubbock, who was at that time in bad health, died a few days later. Captain John A. Wharton was chosen to fill his place.

Wharton was a man of ability, of a distinguished family, liberally educated, a lawyer and a captivating public speaker. Enterprising and ambitious, he never forgot during a wakeful moment that the soldier who survived the war would be a voter. He distinguished himself on many fields and became, successively, brigadier general and major general.

About this time Lieutenant Morgan of Company D resigned and Fergus Kyle was elected first lieutenant. Kyle was subsequently promoted to captain, and made a very efficient officer, distinguishing himself on many fields.

The regiment now resumed its duty of guarding the front. The weather was cold, varied with rain, sleet and snow. The men suffered greatly. Some suffering, as to the weather, I escaped, having received a slight wound. I was sent to the hospital at Nashville, Tennessee, where I stayed two days, going from there to the home of a relative, where I spent nearly seven weeks. In the care of my kindred, I had all the comforts and some of the luxuries of life. I reported for duty just before the retreat from Bowling Green.

The burial squad informed me that my poor horse, who received some of the lead intended for his master, and yet had no personal interest in the row, had five bullet wounds. He fell under me near the straw stacks. I rode off the field behind John B. Rector, who halted in a shower of bullets and kindly assisted me to mount.

CHAPTER 3

Retreat

The word is not reassuring to seasoned soldiers. To new troops it is very depressing. Johnston's line was broken on the right at Fishing Creek, and was threatened on the left at Donelson. Bowling Green was, therefore, untenable, and now we must fall back behind the Cumberland.

The Rangers must cover the retreat. It was snowing the morning we left, and the enemy were throwing shells into the place. Our march to Nashville was without incident. We crossed the Cumberland in the night and camped just outside the city. We now learned that Donelson had fallen, and the retreat must be continued. We were ordered down toward Donelson to guard in that direction, and to afford succour to such as had escaped the surrender and might be making their way south.

Returning, we found the army at Murfreesboro, but it moved on by Shelbyville, Huntsville and Decatur to Corinth, Mississippi, the Rangers guarding the rear. The weather was bad and the progress slow, but the enemy did not press us. We crossed the Tennessee River on the railroad bridge, which had been floored for the purpose. When we went into camp rations of bacon and flour were issued to us. Our wagons and camp equipment being somewhere else, we were confronted with the problem of preparing this flour for the immediate consumption of the chronically hungry soldier.

If necessity is the mother of invention, hunger is a most capable handmaid of the good dame. An oilcloth is spread on the ground, and on this the flour is kneaded, but how to bake it was the question. Some rolled the dough around a stake or ramrod, which they stuck in the ground by the fire, but the stuff would slip down. Some of us tried a flat rail, and that answered very well. First heating the rail thoroughly, we stuck our biscuits on it, set them before the fire, and watched them brown, our appetites growing keener all the while. The treatment of the bacon was easy. We broiled it on a stick held before the fire or above the coals, and that is the best way it was ever cooked.

At Corinth we had a few days' rest. Absentees came in, and the morale improved.

Buell did not follow our line of march, but moved by the more direct route through Franklin, Columbus and Pulaski, intending to unite with Grant at Pittsburg Landing.

CHAPTER 4

Shiloh

Johnston planned to attack Grant before the arrival of Buell, and had brought together the largest army ever before assembled in the Confederacy. He had the force under General Hardee from Bowling Green, the remnant of Zollicoffer's army, Bragg from Pensacola with a fine corps of well drilled and well-equipped troops, and Polk from Columbus with a light force, altogether nearly 40,000 men. They were to attack an army of veterans flushed with the victory at Donelson.

Johnston ordered the army to move on the morning of April 3, but some of the troops did not get away until that afternoon. It was said that this delay was due to the inexperience of both staff and men. Johnston had intended to attack on the 5th, but the army, delayed by the bad roads, did not arrive in time. Thus, we lost twenty-four fateful hours—twenty-four hours of as precious time as was ever lost in war.

Our regiment reached the front on the 4th and was ordered to guard the left wing of the army. In detachments we guarded every road, trail and opening around the whole left front and flank, with strict orders that none of us be allowed to sleep at all. Soon after nightfall it began to rain. It poured down in torrents, and the night was pitch dark. Whether in the saddle, on post or in camp, we could hardly have slept in that downpour. It was a long, dreary night, but morning, a bright spring morning, came at last.

The regiment assembled once more, very wet and uncomfortable. Our arms, too, were wet and, fearing they would fail us in action, we implored Colonel Wharton to let us fire them off. With no thought of possible consequences, he consented. Pointing to a wooded hillside, he said:

"Go off there and shoot."

We discharged all the firearms we had. It sounded like a brisk skirmish. The colonel was immediately summoned to headquarters.

Camp rumour said that his interview with his superiors was rather stormy, that he was severely reprimanded. It is a fact that on his return he made us a speech, telling us that by yielding to our importunities he had committed a serious blunder which had subjected him to unfavourable criticism by persons in the higher military circles. He seemed to be much perturbed mentally. He asked us to wipe out the stain by our gallant behaviour in the coming engagement; asked us to ride further into the enemy's ranks than any other regiment. I think most of us audibly promised to do what he asked; and we kept the promise as far as circumstances would permit, as will be seen.

The whole army had arrived by Saturday afternoon. Early Sunday morning, April 6th, the forward movement began. The enemy were either in bed or preparing breakfast, and were taken by surprise. I know the surprise has been denied by so eminent a person as General Grant, but as he was sleeping at Savannah, nine miles away, he is hardly a competent witness. Thousands of us saw camp kettles and coffeepots on the fires, beds just as the occupants had left them, blankets spread and clothing strewn about.

It is not my purpose to describe the Battle of Shiloh. I wish merely to speak of some principal incidents. It was a continuous advance of the Confederates nearly all of the day, Sunday. The roar of big guns and the rattle of musketry was unceasing.

The Rangers were kept in column just in the rear of the left wing, and had no part in the conflict till late in the day, when our eagerness to take part in the fight was gratified by an order to clear our extreme left, and assail the enemy, who was then retiring through thick woods.

We had to cross a muddy branch. At first two abreast could get over, but it soon became so bad that only one at a time could cross, and then it was a good long jump for a horse. Not half of the regiment was over when the leading files rushed up the hill through a small open field. Turning to the right they came to a high rail fence behind which was a line of blue. From this line came a most destructive fire which emptied many saddles. John Crane of Company D was killed. Clint Terry, a new arrival, brother of our former colonel, fell mortally wounded.

We were too few to make any impression, although some of our men dismounted and began throwing down the fence. A few even crossed into the wood. The firing was so hot that we beat a hasty retreat in spite of the appeals of Colonel Wharton and other officers, who did all they could to stop our flight.

We didn't stop until we were out of range, when we re-formed at once. Thus, our second encounter with the enemy met with a repulse. I may say, however, that this charge, if it be proper to call it a charge, was not without good results to our cause. Several years since I received a letter from Colonel Chisholm, who was then on the staff of General Beauregard. He wrote that it was he who led the regiment in that advance; that the object of it was to detain the enemy until other troops could be brought up; that for this purpose the movement was measurably successful.

That afternoon we learned with sorrow of the death of General Johnston. This we then regarded as a great calamity, and time has not changed our opinion.

We were not engaged again that day. We spent the night on the battlefield, amid the dead of the enemy, subsisting ourselves and our horses from the abundant supplies on every hand. Though it rained another downpour, and though we had no shelter, we slept as only tired soldiers can.

Reinforced by Buell's 40,000, the enemy assumed the offensive next day. The Confederates only resisted, as best they could, to get off their wounded, their trains and artillery, over muddy roads. The Rangers were dismounted to aid in resisting the forward movement, losing several men. John H. Washington of Company D was shot through the hips and left on the field for dead; but under the care of Federal surgeons he recovered, and is living today.

Tuesday, the 8th, two companies of the Rangers, under Major Harrison, with part of Forrest's men, all under the command of Forrest, made a brilliant charge on a mounted force of the enemy, believed to be a large escort of a general officer, and ran them back to the main force of infantry.

The pursuit now ceased and, without further molestation, we returned to Corinth. Here we remained two or three weeks, and received some recruits, the first since leaving Texas. Company D got six, T. A. W. Hill, William and A. J. Kyle, George T. McGehee, T. M. Rector and S. M. Watkins. They were quite an addition to our force. All were fine soldiers and continued to the end. There was much sickness, caused by bad water. Everybody was anxious for more active service.

The regiment was now ordered into Tennessee. Crossing the river at Lamb's Ferry, we captured a detachment of the enemy, guarding a railroad bridge, after a hot fight, in which we lost several men. Captain Harris of Company I was killed; also, William DeWoody of Company D. There is one incident of this affair which I shall never forget. Among our prisoners was a captain of an Ohio regiment. He had six bullet wounds in his body. He sat up in the boat as we crossed the river, and walked unassisted up the hill on the other side.

CHAPTER 5

Forrest at Murfreesboro

We were now ordered to Chattanooga. Here we were placed in a brigade under the command of Colonel N. B. Forrest. At this time but little was known of this great soldier. He had not then become famous, and there were not wanting officers of high rank who predicted disaster as the result of his operations. Without the advantages of education, he possessed strong common sense, unfaltering courage, energy that never flagged, and unbounded confidence in himself. Under his leadership our metal was not to grow rusty for lack of employment.

Setting out from Chattanooga on the 8th of July, we crossed the Tennessee River and the Cumberland mountains into middle Tennessee. On the 11th we reached McMinnville and remained until the afternoon of the 12th. Here Forrest made his regimental commanders acquainted with his plans. His objective was Murfreesboro, over forty miles away, garrisoned by a force of the enemy estimated at 2,000 men, under the command of Brigadier General Crittenden.

Late in the afternoon we started for an all-night ride. At Woodbury we halted and fed our horses, resuming the march at midnight. We reached the vicinity of Murfreesboro at daylight on the 13th.

Now occurred one of those unfortunate blunders which often mar the best laid plans; probably made by Forrest himself. Colonel Wharton with the Rangers was to attack a camp of the enemy on the Liberty pike north of town. Forrest, who had been riding at the head of the column, turned aside to allow us to pass. When six companies had gone by, he fell in with his staff and escort. Thus, it happened that nearly half of the regiment followed Forrest into the town and out to the westward.

The courthouse was garrisoned by a company of the Ninth Michigan Infantry, who poured a hot fire into our ranks from the windows. Forrest and the Rangers rode on, but the sound of firing had aroused the good ladies from their beds; looking out they saw the dear defenders of their cause. Without taking time for very elaborate toilets, they rushed into the streets just as the Georgians came up. Pointing to the courthouse, they begged them to attack the hated foe. With a "Hurrah for the women!" these perfectly green troops dismounted, broke down the doors, and captured the garrison, but with severe loss.

When Forrest discovered that he had with him only a handful of Rangers, he turned back to look after the rest of his command. Captain Ferrell, now the ranking officer, led us through the suburbs of the town towards the right, or north where he thought to find the regiment. While we were passing through a field of standing corn, the artillery of the enemy opened on us at short range. The first shot struck William Skull of Company G, taking off both legs and passing through his horse, killing both instantly.

We found the main part of the regiment about half a mile east of the town, on the road by which we had come. They had made a spirited attack on the enemy, but were too weak to get any favourable results, and had retired, Wharton being wounded. As soon as the regiment was united Wharton sent the adjutant, M. H. Royston, and ten men to report to Forrest for orders. I was of this party. We found Forrest in the town. He spoke with some show of irritation:

"Tell him to bring his men up here."

During all this time he had been attacking the enemy with the forces at hand, but there was little result of a decisive nature.

Some of his chief officers had advised him to be content with what he had already accomplished and withdraw; but he was not of the withdrawing kind. Preparing for a final assault, when the Rangers came up, he delayed the attack long enough to send a demand for surrender to the camp of the Michigan regiment. This was promptly agreed to. He now sent a like demand to the Third Minnesota. Colonel Lester of that regiment asked for an hour's time and an opportunity to consult with Colonel Duffield. This officer was seriously wounded. Forrest allowed half an hour and the privilege of the interview. As Lester was going to the room of Colonel Duffield opportunity was given him to see our strength. When the half hour was up, he surrendered his entire force.

The troops surrendered consisted of fifteen companies of infantry, six of the Ninth Michigan and nine of the Third Minnesota; seven companies of cavalry, four of the Fourth Kentucky and three of the Seventh Pennsylvania; and two sections (four guns) of Hewett's battery: in all 1,765 men.

The brigade commander, General Crittenden, was found hiding in a room at a tavern.

The spoil was immense; a large number of wagons, with military stores and equipment of all sorts.

The merits of this enterprise are very great, but it must be admitted that had the enemy all been together, under a resolute commander, they could have beaten us. They had nearly 1,800 men of all arms, infantry, cavalry and artillery—a miniature army—while Forrest had a little over 1,300 men, some of them absolutely green troops.

In regard to this affair, General Buell, commanding the department, published a very caustic order, of which a short extract is here given:

> Take it in all its features, few more disgraceful examples of neglect of duty and lack of good conduct can be found in the history of wars. It fully merits the extreme penalty which the law provides for such conduct. The force was more than sufficient to repel the attack effectually.

CHAPTER 6

Many Marches and Skirmishes—The Kentucky Campaign

We rested at McMinnville three or four days, and then started a hard ride with little rest for Lebanon, a distance of fifty miles, intending to surprise and capture a force of 500 cavalry stationed there. On the morning of the 20th, we dashed into the place, but the enemy had been warned and had left in a hurry for Nashville.

We remained one day and night in this beautiful little city, recipients of the unbounded hospitality of its splendid people. They fed us on poultry, roast pig, ham, cakes and pies like "mother used to make," and filled our haversacks for the march.

From Lebanon our route was by "The Hermitage," so long the home of Andrew Jackson. Here a short halt was made, and many of the men visited the house and grounds. Mounting, we moved on to Stone River, seven miles from Nashville, where a small picket force was captured. Thence we crossed over to the Murfreesboro turnpike, only four miles from the city, and destroyed four railroad bridges, capturing the guards—in all about 120 men. We then turned off in the direction of Lebanon, and camped for the night after riding for a few miles; here we paroled our prisoners. Passing around Murfreesboro we marched to McMinnville, where we rested till the 10th of August.

We then advanced to the line of railroad, captured the pickets and burned a few bridges. The enemy had now begun to erect stockades for their guards at the bridges. There was one not yet finished, and Forrest tried to capture it but failed. Captain Houston of Company G was killed in this attack.

Moving in the direction of Altamont we camped in a cove near the mountain. The enemy advanced in force on all the roads. We had to take the dry bed of a creek which ran parallel to one of the roads on which the enemy was advancing. We travelled in this creek a mile or two, and then emerged into the open. A battery of the enemy, on the McMinnville road, not more than 600 yards away, opened fire upon us. The very best of troops, who will charge anything, are often thrown into a panic by an attack from an unexpected quarter. We broke into a run and were soon out of range, though in considerable disorder.

Marching leisurely to Sparta, we joined forces with Bragg's army, then on the move into Kentucky. Forrest was ordered to guard the left flank and harass the rear of the enemy in his retreat to Nashville. We came up to their rear guard at Woodbury, and chased them clear up to Murfreesboro, but could only run them through the place.

Bragg soon moved by Glasgow and on to Mumfordsville, getting in ahead of Buell and on his line of march. He had a strong position, but for some unaccountable reason turned off and let the Federal Army pass on to Louisville. Forrest kept on the left and in close touch with the enemy till the army turned aside, when we went on to the vicinity of Louisville. Forrest was now relieved and ordered to Tennessee, and Colonel John A. Wharton was placed in command of the brigade. We kept close up to Louisville, in observation of the enemy's movements. Had a small but spirited skirmish at Mt. Washington, as related in the introduction.

Early in October Buell began to move with some vigour. An enterprising brigade of cavalry got between us and our main army. They took position at Bardstown and thus we were "cut off." When intelligence of this move reached Wharton he called in his outposts, threw his command into column, Rangers in front, Company D leading. At a gallop we started for the seat of trouble. The enemy had chosen a strong position at the mouth of the lane in which we were traveling, and had their courage been equal to their enterprise they could have given us a warm entertainment.

When we came in sight of them our bugle sounded the charge and we went at them as fast as our horses could carry us. They broke almost at once, firing only a few shots. It was now a chase for miles. We caught over 200 of them, and strewed the woods with their dead and wounded. General George H. Thomas, of the Federal Army, says they lost about "twenty killed and wounded, and a great many missing"; these "missing" were our prisoners. Our loss was small—I cannot recall the casualties. It was one of the softest snaps in the way of a fight that we had during the war.

Some amusing incidents nearly always occur, but the laughter rarely takes place till all danger is past. After the long chase we, as well as the enemy, were very much scattered. John B. Rector seeing a lone Federal, rushed up and demanded his surrender. "Surrender yourself," replied the man, levelling his pistol. Now Rector had discharged every chamber of his pistol and promptly complied. Just then Bill Davis dashed up. He was a large, fierce looking man, on a powerful horse not less than sixteen and a half hands high. He broke out, "John, why the —— don't you disarm that —— ——Yankee?"

"I am a prisoner myself, Bill."

Quick as a flash Davis was at the fellow's side and bringing his pistol against his head broke out, "Give up them pistols, you —— —— blue-bellied —— ——."

The shooting irons were promptly handed over and the prisoner escorted to the rear.

In the language of the great American game, it was pure "bluff" all around for all the firearms were empty, but Bill Davis was always loaded to the muzzle with quick firing profanity which he could discharge in rattling volleys on the slightest provocation. I am glad to say, however, that he no longer goes loaded thus, for he has been a strict churchman for several years.

General Bragg published a general order highly laudatory of the Rangers for this affair, but I have found no record of it. It was read to the regiment and complimented us in high terms.

Bragg's army was widely dispersed, gathering supplies in that fertile section. Buell was pressing him, and to get time for concentration, and to get his train out of the way, we made a stand at Perryville, where, on the 8th of October, was fought one of the fiercest combats of the war. Fourteen thousand Confederates kept at bay for nearly two days the immense army of the enemy, but with heavy loss to both sides. Wharton's brigade held the extreme right and did a full share of the fighting. Among our killed was Major Mark Evans of the Rangers. Captain Ferrell of Company D succeeded him, and Lieutenant Kyle of Company D became captain.

I was in the Battle of Perryville, not with the regiment, but in a small detachment on the left while the Rangers were on the right. Hence, I avail myself of the description of "Perryville" given by A. B. Briscoe, who kindly placed his *Personal Memoirs* at my service.

> The enemy was on the west side of the creek and our army on the east. The valley between was open field and the tops

of the hills covered in places with timber. It was an ideal battlefield; there were no breastworks, but the hills on both sides were crowned with artillery. Polk was in command of the Confederate forces and expected the enemy to attack and waited for them until about 2 p.m. In the meantime, the artillery was making the very earth tremble with a duel of nearly 100 guns. We lay in a little valley a few hundred yards to the rear, partially sheltered from this storm of shells.

At 2 p. m. we were moved in column through the lines of infantry and the smoking batteries to the front. The open valley was before us with a deep creek spanned by a wooden bridge. Down we charged in column of fours across the bridge. After crossing, each squadron formed left front into line, which made us present five lines, one behind the other, and in this order, we charged up the hill, into the woods and among the Yankees. This whole movement was made in a sweeping gallop and as if on parade.

How different from the way we were handled at Shiloh! The Yankees were brushed back from the hill and woods and when the bugle sounded the recall and we returned, our own infantry and artillery had crossed the creek and were taking position on the hills from which we had driven the enemy. But again, we had lost our commander, the gallant Lieutenant Colonel Mark Evans, who fell mortally wounded at the head of the regiment.

I have copied this literally, but I am of the opinion that Evans was only major.

Bragg had secured the needed time. He now started for Cumberland Gap, leaving the cavalry to protect his rear and retard, as best they could, the onward march of the enemy. Colonel Joseph Wheeler was made chief of cavalry and had command of all in the rear. The country was timbered, broken, not very fertile, affording little in the way of food for man or beast. We had to form line and skirmish several times a day. The service was very trying. For more than a week there was no order to unsaddle.

At last Buell gave up the pursuit and started to Nashville. We went on through Cumberland Gap to Knoxville, where we had a snowstorm. From Knoxville, by Kingston and over the mountains, we went to Sparta, Murfreesboro and Nolensville. At Nolensville we had a position on the left of the army. Here some promotions were announced.

Colonel Wharton became a brigadier general, his commission dating from the Bardstown fight, the 4th of October. Harrison became colonel, Ferrell, lieutenant colonel, and Gustave Cook, major. Ferrell was soon compelled to resign on account of bad health. Cook then became lieutenant colonel and S. Pat Christian, major. In Company D, Dechard became first lieutenant and W. R. Black, second lieutenant.

We remained at Nolensville nearly two months, picketing and scouting. We passed our second Christmas, a serious and sober set, thinking of the homes and loved ones far away, and wondering if we should ever see them again.

Chapter 7

Murfreesboro

The enemy did not allow us much time for repining. Promptly on the 26th they moved out in force. We were sent forward to develop their strength. The regiment, under the command of Captain Kyle, was drawn up in a field and dismounted. Our leader conducted us over a high rail fence into an open wood of cedar trees. We went along listening to his encouraging words until we reached the top of a slight rise. Just over the crest was a solid line of infantry lying down. Kyle at once ordered a retreat. At least that's what he meant, though the words he actually used are not in the manual. He said:
"Get out of here, men! There's a whole brigade!"
We understood him and so did the Yankees, who sprang to their feet and delivered a volley, doing little damage. The high fence had not seemed a serious obstacle as we went in, but when I got back to it on the return, with bullets striking it like hail on a roof, it looked very formidable. I sprang up on it and just fell off on the other side. When I got up the command was moving off rapidly. I had started to the rear as soon as the others, but they outran me, and I didn't "throw" the race either. I turned to the left, down the line of fence, climbed another, and was now reasonably safe but nearly exhausted. I had still to go half a mile before I reached the command. My saddle felt mighty good and restful.

It was now plain that it was a general advance of the enemy, and Bragg prepared for the Battle of Murfreesboro, whither we now marched promptly. In the line Wharton's brigade occupied the left. When the ball opened in earnest he led this command around the right of the enemy's line, and within 600 yards of Rosecrans' headquarters attacked and captured a wagon train going to the rear. We could not hold it long; but we captured a four-gun battery and held on to that; moved down toward Nashville and ran into the train again.

In these operations Company D lost two killed, Sam Friedberger and Wayne Hamilton. Kenner Rector was wounded. John W. Hill and P. J. Watkins were made prisoners. Hill's horse was killed as we were retiring before superior numbers. He was away three or four months, and greatly missed, for he was a good one.

After a strenuous day of it, with a good many prisoners and the four guns, we returned to the army and were sent to the right, taking position on the right of Breckenridge's line. We saw that gallant officer and his splendid division move forward through an open field with the precision of parade, under a furious cannonading from the Federal batteries strongly posted in a cedar wood. The shells ploughed great gaps through their ranks. When the colours fell other hands seized them and bore them onward. When they reached the position of the enemy they wavered and began to give way, in order at first, but as they retreated under a distressing fire of artillery and musketry, they broke into a run. We stood there and could not help them, although every man of us would have gone to their aid with a whoop.

This charge deserves to rank with Malvern Hill, Franklin, and other useless sacrifices of life. Like the charge of the light brigade, "it was magnificent, but it was not war."

This was Bragg's final effort, and he withdrew from the contest. The only tactics he seems to have learned was to wait till the enemy came up to his lines and fortified himself; then attack and lose more men than the enemy, then sneak away. He had heard somewhere that "he who fights and runs away may live to fight another day."

Bragg stopped at Shelbyville. Rosecrans was content to stay at Murfreesboro, begging his government for more cavalry; nor did he feel safe in advancing till he had a large addition to his mounted force.

We took position on the left of the army, picketing and scouting the front, with occasional skirmishes and reconnoissances.

CHAPTER 8

The Donelson Trip and Retreat to Chattanooga

Just who conceived this wild-goose chase, I am not informed. For suffering, hardships, and barrenness of results, it is only exceeded by Napoleon's Russian campaign. On the 25th of January, General Wheeler, in command of the brigades of Wharton and Forrest, took up the line of march for Dover, or Fort Donelson. I do not know how to describe the weather, except in the language of the grammar on the comparison of adjectives: cold, colder, coldest. We crossed one little stream fifteen or twenty times in one day. The water froze on the legs of our horses until they were encased in ice above the knees; their tails were solid chunks of ice, while we had to walk to keep warm. Men and horses suffered intensely.

When we reached the vicinity of Dover, Forrest reported to Wheeler that he had but a scant supply of ammunition; and investigation disclosed the fact that Wharton's brigade was little better off in this regard. Forrest did not hesitate to advise withdrawal of our forces without attempt at action, but Wheeler determined to proceed.

Forrest attacked from the north and east, carried the enemy's outer works, and drove them into the redoubts, but with great loss of life. His ammunition was now exhausted, and he was compelled to fall back. Wharton attacked from the Donelson side, and captured one brass field gun, but he, too, was compelled to retire because his ammunition was running low. The Rangers had been sent out on the Fort Henry road before these operations were begun and so had no part in the assault.

Jordan, in his *Life of Forrest*, says:

The Confederate losses were heavy. Forrest had one-fourth of his force, or 200 of his officers and men killed, wounded and captured, and Wharton's casualties did not fall short of sixty killed and wounded.

Now the retreat began. All the command, except the Rangers, practically out of ammunition. The weather did not moderate. The second or third night a report reached Wheeler that a heavy column of the enemy, cavalry and infantry, under General Jeff C. Davis, had left Nashville to head him off. About midnight we were ordered to saddle up. It was so cold that if we touched a gun-barrel or bridle bit our hands stuck to the metal, and we had to put those bits into the mouths of our poor horses.

We reached Duck River about daylight, and found it bank full, the surface covered with floating ice. After some search a ford was found and we crossed to the south side. As Davis' command did not show up, we went into camp and warmed ourselves a little. After a rest of a day or two we moved leisurely back to our old position.

I do not know what could have been accomplished by this expedition beyond the capture of a small garrison. Certainly, the suffering and the losses of men and horses were very great. For a long time when the men wanted to reach the superlative of suffering, they spoke of the Donelson trip.

In April we moved over to the right and camped a few days at Sparta. The regiment captured a mail train between Murfreesboro and Nashville, getting about a dozen officers. The men rifled the mail sacks and amused themselves reading the letters of the Yankees. They obtained also a considerable amount of greenbacks; also a silver-mounted pistol, said to belong to General Rosecrans. My horse was lame and so I missed this expedition—and my share of the greenbacks.

Toward the last of June the Federal army, having received reinforcements, including heavy additions to its cavalry force, began another forward movement. The Rangers were dismounted to skirmish with the advance. During this action a heavy rainstorm came up; we thought this would suspend the affair, but when the rain ceased, we found the Yankees had advanced their lines considerably. Regarding this as a violation of the rules of the game, we mounted and rode off.

Their cavalry now showed unusual spirit and audacity, pressing us pretty close. On the 4th of July, at the site of the present University of the South, the Rangers had to charge and drive them back. The retreat was continued across the mountains and the Tennessee River to Chattanooga.

The Rangers took position at Rome, Georgia. There we had a few weeks' needed rest and recruited our jaded horses. Roasting ears were in season, fruit was beginning to ripen, and so we feasted on good things. The runabouts—"pie rooters" we called them—made the best of their opportunities. Bill Arp said they found every road in the county, and then some.

Dr. Bunting, our chaplain, started a series of meetings, and many embraced the opportunity to pledge themselves to the better life. The boys, from their scant pay, contributed money to buy a horse for General John A. Wharton. The presentation speech was made by John B. Rector, Wharton replying. Both speakers pledged the last drop of their blood, etc. Same old story, but a trifle stale by this time.

CHAPTER 9

Chickamauga

Rosecrans manoeuvred Bragg out of Chattanooga. He now seemed to have a contempt for his adversary, and divided his army into three columns in an effort to bring ours to bay. One crossed the mountains and took position at Alpine, forty miles south of the centre, evidently to gain the rear of the Confederates.

We were sent to look after this column. Lieutenant Baylor of the Rangers reported to Wharton that a heavy force of infantry was at Alpine. Wharton reported this to Bragg with a note vouching for Baylor's reliability. Bragg broke out:

"Lieutenant Baylor lies: there is no infantry south of us!"

In a day or two, however, he became convinced that the report was true, and made some feeble effort to attack them in detail. Nothing came of it except that Rosecrans, who now discovered that his enemy was not retreating so precipitately, took the alarm and began to concentrate his widely separated columns. The force at Alpine had to cross the mountains. It took them two days to get to the centre, now menaced by the Confederates. Imagine Stonewall Jackson in Bragg's place!

Of the larger events of the Battle of Chickamauga I shall treat very briefly. It has been truthfully called the soldiers' battle. Whatsoever of strategy or generalship there had been had miscarried and the two armies stood face to face for a trial of strength: a test of manhood. The numbers were about equal, not far from 70,000 on a side. The Federals had the advantage of position, which they had fortified. The Confederates had to attack. Never was fiercer attack and defence. Never was shown greater courage.

The enemy were driven from their works, but with frightful loss to the Confederates. Their killed numbered 2,389. The wounded 13,412; while the Federals' loss in killed was 1,656, wounded, 9,769. It was such dearly bought and fruitless victories as this which finally defeated the South.

The Terry Rangers were on the extreme left of the line and were ordered to drive the enemy from their front. This order was executed in handsome style. The enemy proved to be our old antagonists, the Third Ohio Cavalry. After the charge a message was brought to Lieutenant Dechard, of the Rangers, that a wounded Federal officer wished to see him. He rode to the spot and dismounted. When he saw the wounded man, he said:

"Why, it's my old friend, Major Cupp. I am sorry to see you thus."

"Lieutenant Colonel Cupp," replied the other, "but I've had my last promotion. You people have got me this time."

More than a year before, these officers, each a lieutenant in command of an escort for a flag of truce, had met. They met again, a few weeks later, under the same circumstances, but Cupp was now a captain. After the fight in Bardstown Dechard was in command of the guard for the prisoners, and recognized his former acquaintance. "Captain Cupp, I am glad to see you," said he.

"Major Cupp," corrected the prisoner, "but I cannot say that I am glad to see you under the circumstances."

As the cartel was still in force, he was soon exchanged, and as we have seen when he fell, Dechard was near. These facts were related to me by Dechard himself, and he was known to be perfectly reliable. These incidents confirm the old adage, "Truth is stranger than fiction."

The dying officer desired Dechard to take his watch and other belongings and send them to his relatives in Ohio, which was done a few days later by flag of truce.

Wheeler and Forrest followed the discomfited Federals up to Chattanooga. Here it was remembered that two detachments under Lieutenants Friend and Batchelor had been left on picket in gaps of the mountain away to the left of the battlefield, and I was ordered to go to them at once and direct them to join the command, which would be found on the Athens road.

There was about an hour of daylight, and I hoped to pass the ground of the terrible struggle before night, knowing that there was nothing for me or my horse until I did so. In this I was disappointed. Darkness came on shortly after I reached the scene of that awful carnage. Many of the Federal dead and wounded still lay where they had fallen. The air was freighted with a horrible odour, the battlefield's commentary on war. The wounded hearing my horse's footfalls, began calling me to give some assistance. Dismounting I picked my way to the first one. He desired to be turned over. Another wanted his canteen. The poor fellow had struggled while there was strength, and now unable to move further, was out of reach of his canteen. These were relieved and others not specially remembered here. It seemed that hundreds were calling. I was ever a coward in the presence of suffering, besides duty required that I should proceed on my journey. So, I asked:

"Are you aware that your own surgeons with their details and ambulances are here uncontrolled on the field?"

"Oh, yes," was the answer, "they come around every day and leave us water, a little food and medicine, but it is awful to lie here this way."

I mounted and rode off, feeling sad at the fate of these men dying unattended hundreds of miles from home and loved ones, but I steeled my heart by the thought that if they had stayed at home with their loved ones they would not be thus dying.

I was now lost. It was dark and my horse could not follow any road, for roads were everywhere. Artillery wheels make many roads on a battlefield. After a while I saw a light and went to it. It was the camp fire of the details for the care of the wounded. These men sat around. The ambulances and mules were near. There was a little house, too. On the porch I saw some officers in uniform. Surgeons they were. I inquired for some resident. A slender girl came to the door and in reply to my request directed me to Lee and Gordon's mill.

The moon was now rising. I was on that part of the field from which the dead and wounded had been removed, but there was wreck and ruin everywhere. Maimed and groaning horses, and no one to waste a load of ammunition to end their suffering; broken gun carriages, the debris of a battlefield.

I crossed and watered my horse in the stream at the mill. As I rode up the hill, I met two of my own company, who had been at the wagon camp cooking for the company. When they learned how far it was to the command and the horrors of the battlefield, they readily agreed to camp, for it was now late. So, I had supper, for my comrades had sacks of bread and bacon, but my poor horse had nothing. We lay down and slept under the shining moon, although but a few miles away hundreds of human beings lay dying.

On the morrow I proceeded on my journey. When I reached the first detachment under Lieutenant Friend and delivered my message, he kindly sent one of his men on to tell Batchelor: gave me some forage for my horse, and all gathered around anxious for news of the battle. Here they had been in sound of the mighty struggle, the boom of the great guns, even the rattle of small arms, while their comrades were in dire peril, but denied the privilege of sharing in their danger or triumph. They had heard that the enemy had been driven from the field, but had heard nothing from their own command. They were hungry for news from the Rangers. What part they took, and who were killed or wounded? For they knew if the Rangers had been engaged somebody was hurt.

These occurrences took place nearly forty-eight years ago, and yet their memory is clear in my mind, and when I think of my lonely ride in Chickamauga's gloomy woods, of the dead and dying, the wreck and ruin of that awful night, I am convinced that there is no more expressive definition of war than General Sherman has given.

When Batchelor's squad came up, we started to overtake the command, joining it on the following day, as well as I remember. It was then well on its way to the Federal rear in middle Tennessee.

CHAPTER 10

Wheeler's Great Raid

Our march was up the Holston River to find an unguarded ford, but the pickets were everywhere. We halted in a field at night, and Company D, armed with picks and spades, was directed to go to the river bank and there make a way for the artillery. A guide from the vicinity showed us a way across, by a ford unknown to the Yankees. We captured a few pickets.

Wheeler now divided his forces, himself leading a column into Sequatchie valley, where he captured and burned 2,000 wagons. He then overtook the remainder of the command as we descended the mountains. Our route was by McMinnville and Murfreesboro, and the way was sufficiently familiar to us, since we had travelled it so often under Forrest the year before.

When we reached the vicinity of Murfreesboro, Captain Kyle with his squadron, consisting of Companies D and F, was ordered to ride around the place, reach the railroad leading to Nashville, and try to capture a train. We came to the railroad a little before daylight, but there were no trains running; the enemy had learned that the "rebels" were in the country. Captain Kyle heard of a lot of wagons down toward Nashville and decided to take them in. This he did without resistance. The teams had been engaged in hauling wood to the garrison at Nashville, and the wagons were drawn by oxen, the only instance of this kind that we saw during the war. The oxen being fat, and also too slow of foot to go with us in any other form, were converted into beef.

We crossed over to Shelbyville pike, the scene of some of our operations in the spring. Learning that a small force of cavalry held Shelbyville, General Wharton ordered the Rangers to attempt their capture. We saddled up early, and rode briskly, reaching there about daylight, but the enemy had left. There were several stores in this place, established by some enterprising Yankees, and stocked with clothing and dry goods. Rather than have their doors broken down, the owners opened them. Winter was coming on, we were a long way from home and nearly naked, and here was our chance for winter supplies. Some of the boys got a black "Prince Albert" coat. This was presented to the chaplain, who wore it a long time.

The line of march led by Farmington. Here the enemy had taken a strong position in a cedar thicket. Over the ground were scattered large boulders. The enemy, armed with Spencer rifles, were lying behind these stones. The Rangers were ordered to charge this position. We got up pretty close; in fact, into the edge of the thicket; but they poured such a destructive fire into us that it did not take us long to discover that we had more than we could handle. We took some prisoners. We also got some of these rifles, the first of the kind I had ever seen; they would shoot seven times without reloading. The casualties are not remembered, except that Major Christian and Lieutenant Blackburn were wounded. Love, of Company C, was killed.

That night at headquarters they were discussing the incidents of the day. Wharton said the Rangers had done all that any soldiers could do; that it was impossible for mounted troops to drive brave men, armed as were the enemy, from such a position. General Wheeler said they had done all that he expected; had held the enemy engaged while our artillery and wagons ran by through a field, thus saving the command from a bad situation. Then Colonel Harrison spoke:

"It was no fight at all! I'm ashamed of them! If they cannot do better than that I'll disown them!"

A staff officer put in:

"I always thought that regiment somewhat overrated anyhow."

This aroused "old Tom," who got up, shook his finger in the fellow's face and broke out furiously:

"Who the —— are you? There is not a man in that regiment who cannot kick you all over this yard, sir!"

As he strode off to his horse, he was heard to say:

"By —— I'll curse them all I want to; but I'll be —— if anybody else shall do it in my presence!"

Moving on to the Tennessee River, we crossed that stream at one of the fords along the Mussel Shoals. From there, in a more leisurely manner, we went back to the army, still besieging the Federals at Chattanooga.

CHAPTER 11

East Tennessee Campaign

Bragg felt so sure that Rosecrans would be starved into surrender that he dispatched Longstreet to Knoxville to take in the garrison stationed there. Our division, commanded by General Martin, was sent along with him. Longstreet laid siege to the place. We were transferred from one side of the river to the other, fording the freezing water at night. We had a little skirmish on College Hill; details not remembered, except that Lieutenant Black was wounded.

It was reported that the "loyal" people up the river were in the habit of loading small boats with provisions, setting them adrift to float down the river for the use of the garrison in Knoxville, the boats being caught by a boom across the stream. Someone conceived the brilliant idea that if trees were cut down and rolled into the river above, they would float down and break the boom.

Our regiment, placed temporarily under the command of somebody's staff officer anxious to distinguish himself, was detailed for this service. A worse selection could hardly have been made for the performance of such work. Probably not one man in twenty was possessed with any skill with the axe. Young men raised on the prairies, professional men, boys from the stores, sons of planters, who had slaves to do their chopping, composed this force of axmen.

Night, a very dark night at that, was the time selected for the exploit. A light drizzle was falling. Imagine anybody trying to cut down trees under such circumstances! The staff colonel in command stopped at a house where there was a blazing fire, dismounted, and took a comfortable seat. The regiment went up on the hillside and hacked away for hours. I believe some trees were actually felled, chopped into convenient lengths, and rolled into the stream and appeared to sink in the water. All suffered from the cold. It was such foolish services as this that tended to demoralise the Confederate soldier and sap a man's courage and patriotism as nothing else will. There is something inspiring in a charge, albeit there is danger, too, with comrades falling all around; but spirited troops would choose a charge every time rather than such imbecile business as that midnight tree-cutting exploit.

When the Confederate Army was driven from Missionary Ridge, Longstreet was compelled to raise the siege of Knoxville. He retired to the eastward, taking position on the East Tennessee and Virginia railroad, near Morristown, if I remember correctly, the cavalry guarding his front.

The cold was intense. The people, in sympathy with the enemy, furnished them with excellent guides to any exposed position of ours. Hence, we had to be exceedingly vigilant. Imagine going on picket at 2 a. m. with temperature at zero or below; but the army must sleep, and the cavalry must guard the outposts. We had also numerous skirmishes, but I cannot remember the details of them.

A letter written by me to my parents dated January 4, 1864, enumerates six fights during November and December in which the regiment lost twenty-seven killed and wounded; one on the road to Cumberland Gap. This was early in November. We chased some cavalry several miles, taking a dozen or more prisoners and wounding a few without a single casualty on our side, unless someone's ears were frost bitten, for it was a very cold morning and a biting wind raged.

We had three or four skirmishes near Mossy creek. In one of these, on December 26, 1863, Captain G. W. Littlefield was badly wounded by a large fragment of a shell which lacerated his left hip for a space five or six inches by twelve or thirteen. It looked like a mortal hurt. A strong constitution pulled him through, yet he was compelled to retire from the service, and even now (1911) suffers from the wound.

On the 29th of December we were ordered to drive a force of the enemy who were dismounted and lying behind a large brick residence and the outbuildings. We had to break down the garden fence, which we did by forcing our horses against it. We drove them all right, took a few prisoners, but sustained serious losses ourselves. In Company D, N. J. Allen was killed outright. Richard Berger was shot through the face, losing the sight of one eye, and William Nicholson had a slight scalp wound.

There was another on the 24th, near the same place, and one near Dandridge, but I am unable to recall the incidents, although the letter referred to says that I participated in all of them. In all we sustained serious loss, and so far as I can see without any appreciable effect on the campaign; but as Forrest said, "War means fight, and fight means kill." Besides our blood was up and life held cheaply.

One little engagement, all one-sided, and as far as we were concerned, was more amusing than serious. Our brigade under Colonel Harrison, and an Alabama brigade commanded by General John T. Morgan, so long a Senator from Alabama after the war, were out on separate roads which, however, came together some distance in the rear of our position. The Alabama brigade, attacked by the enemy, gave way. We were called back, and when we reached the junction of the roads the enemy was passing in hot pursuit. In columns of fours, we took them in flank, killed a few, took several prisoners and scattered the remainder, for they were so completely surprised that they made no resistance. They were Brownlow's brigade of East Tennessee Cavalry and rather shabby soldiers. We had no casualties.

The service was very arduous; besides the picketing alluded to above, foraging became very laborious. The country along the streams is quite fertile and produced abundantly of food for man and beast, but cavalry troops consume rapidly, and the valleys were soon exhausted. So we had to go away out into the mountains for supplies. Often wagons could not go the roads and we had to bring supplies on our horses over mountain trails for ten or fifteen miles. These expeditions were not without danger, for these rude mountaineers were good shots, and lying in the woods, did not see their bread and meat taken with kind feelings. They sometimes fired on these foraging parties, but at long range from mountain crag or other secure position, and I believe injured no one.

As I am not relating these things in chronological order, this will be a good place to set down the facts concerning the night alarm on the banks of Pigeon River. We were in camp for several days on the banks of this stream which, though small to be called a river, was yet rather deep at that place; though it could be forded, as will be seen.

Across from our encampment, some two or three hundred yards from the banks, was a stately mansion, the home of a wealthy and refined family. I think the people's name was Smith, but I am not sure. The name will do anyhow. The head of the family, a general or colonel, was away from home, with the army no doubt. The family at the house consisted of the mother and three or four daughters, all charming ladies. They had secured a house guard to protect them from insult. Joe Rogers, being a little indisposed, was duly installed as guard. This meant good times for Joe; a bed to sleep in, three meals a day with plate, knife and fork, a stable for his black horse Nig, of which, by the way, he was very fond.

It was not long before the society men of the regiment acquired the habit of slipping out after evening roll call to enjoy a game of cards at General Smith's. One night several of them, a lieutenant, a clerk of the quartermaster's department, and one or two others, crossed the river in a small skiff and were soon pleasantly engaged in the fascinating game of euchre with the young ladies. Suddenly there was a cry of "Halt! Halt!" and pistol shots rang out on the night air. Out went the lights, and the visitors rushed for doors and windows, knocking over chairs, tables, and even the young women. They rushed to the river, plunged in and across, and made for their companies.

The first alarm was plainly heard in the camp. Sharp orders to "saddle up" were given and repeated from company to company, and the brigade was soon in line. Colonel Harrison sent Tom Gill and a small party to ascertain the cause of the row. Tom passed General Smith's, where all was dark, and went on to the picket stand. Pickets reported all quiet; no enemy had passed their post. Tom returned to the house, where he met Joe Rogers. It appeared that Joe had not run with the others at the first alarm. He had gone out the back way to look after Nig and his equipment. While getting these he heard voices, accompanied with laughter, and the voices seemed somewhat familiar. Peeping around the house he soon ascertained that the alarm had been caused by three or four Rangers. He reported the cause of the disturbance to Gill and his scouting party, and Gill reported it to Colonel Harrison.

"The old man" was furious at first, for a false alarm in war is a serious matter and a grave offense. However, after some reflection, he concluded to drop the matter, as he thought the incident would have a wholesome effect on the guilty parties. The men did not so easily let it drop. Frequently at night for some months afterwards someone would call out:

"Who waded Pigeon?"

From some other part of the camp the answer would come:

"Murray! Brownson!"

The story got into the comic papers and caused some amusement and some mortification to the victims of the joke. John Haynie, one of the best soldiers in the regiment, was the leader of the alarmist jokers. If I ever learned the names of the others, I have forgotten them.

We had now been in the service for considerably over two years, and there had been no general system of furloughs. Our regiment might have fifteen if they would re-enlist, but as we had already enlisted for the war, we could hardly perform this condition. However, it was demanded that we make declaration of our intention to continue in the service. Some of us considered this a reflection on our honour, and decided to do without the coveted furloughs.

Then some of the boys got together, made a speech or two, passed a preamble and resolutions, declaring we would never—no never—quit as long as an armed foe trod our sacred soil. This was considered satisfactory at headquarters, and the furloughs were ordered. Lots were drawn for the three assigned to Company D. These fell to D. S. Combs, I. V. Jones and J. F. McGuire, who left at once to visit their homes.

At that time the enemy was at the mouth of the Rio Grande. They evidently intended to invade the country far enough to break up a most profitable trade between the States west of the Mississippi and the outside world by way of Mexico. This traffic was carried on by means of wagons, hundreds of which went in a constant stream to the Rio Grande, loaded with cotton, and brought back supplies of all kinds. The people feared the enemy would penetrate the interior, as the State had been stripped of its defenders.

Every persuasion was used to prevail on these men to remain on this side, and they finally agreed to stay. The lieutenant general commanding the department readily agreed to the arrangement, and thus Company D lost three good soldiers. We could not blame them, for, given the opportunity, every one of us perhaps would have done the same thing.

It was during this winter that one of the saddest events of all our career happened; the hanging of E. S. Dodd by the enemy. He was a member of Company D. He was of a good family and well educated. For many years he kept a diary, setting down at night the happenings of the day. He was taken prisoner with this diary in his pocket. On that evidence alone he was condemned and executed as a spy.

Spring was now approaching. Those masters of the art of war—Grant and Sherman—were preparing to strike the final blows at the tottering Confederacy. Longstreet went to Virginia. Our cavalry went to Georgia to our old commander, General Joseph Wheeler. Our way was up the French Broad River, through western North Carolina and South Carolina, marching leisurely where there were abundant supplies. We reached Georgia as Sherman was preparing to move. On the 9th day of May, just north of Dalton, we were ordered to charge a force of the enemy, which proved to be our old acquaintance, La Grange's brigade of Indiana cavalry. We went at them in our usual style, at top speed, every fellow yelling as loud as he could. They broke and retreated precipitately.

We took more than sixty prisoners, including the brigade commander, Colonel La Grange. His horse was wounded and fell, pinning his rider to the earth just at a large farm gate. John Haynie, quick as a flash, was at his side, securing the prisoner, evidently an officer. Addressing his captor, the prisoner said:

"You have a prize indeed. I am Colonel La Grange. I did not know that you boys had got down here from East Tennessee. I knew you as soon as I saw you coming."

With the help of some of the prisoners he was released from his fallen horse, mounted on another, and escorted by his captor to Colonel Harrison. This incident came under my own observation. For the interview which followed his presentation to Harrison I am indebted to that officer himself, who related it to me several years after the war. La Grange said:

"I was in command of the brigade, and was anxious for the commission of brigadier general. Had some influential friends who were helping me. My division commander told me to go out, run in the rebel pickets, skirmish a little and send in a report, which he would forward with strong recommendations for my promotion. I came out, ran into the Texas Rangers, and am a prisoner."

"Only the fortune of war, my young friend," said Harrison. "Only the fortune of war."

Our loss was quite heavy. Among the killed were Charles T. Pelham of Company D, an educated young man, of good family and fine promise, a civil engineer by profession; D. F. Lily, a young lawyer, who fell almost in sight of his mother's home, and W. H. Bigelow, a native of Canada; both of these last were of Company G, and both educated gentlemen.

CHAPTER 12

Sherman's Wagon Train and the Affairs with M'Cook and Stoneman

The enemy, over one hundred thousand strong, under one of the ablest commanders in the Federal Army, advanced on all the roads, overlapping the Confederates, who took position after position, to be turned by the superior numbers of their adversaries.

At Resaca there was quite a spirited engagement with a part of the advance. At Cassville we took position and offered battle, but retired before the flanking movement of the enemy. Near this place Wheeler turned their left and captured a train of wagons within a few miles of Sherman's army. The Rangers were not in this capture, but when the enemy sent a force of cavalry to retake his train, we met it in the most unique engagement of the war. Sherman's great army with its hundreds of cannon, thousands of wagons and other vehicles had passed along, pulverizing the roads and fields into fine dust, which covered everything, in many places several inches deep. A single horseman riding along raised a cloud, a company or regiment, such a dense fog as to obscure everything.

We were in line on one side of a slight rise in the land. The cavalry of the enemy above mentioned were approaching on the other side of the hill. We were ordered forward, and at the top of this hill we met each other, enveloped in clouds of dust. We raised the usual yell, although in doing so we took in large quantities of Georgia real estate. We emptied our pistols into the dust, and the enemy broke. We did not pursue them very far; for we knew we were near their main army, and feared we might run into a brigade or two of infantry, as we could not see anything twenty feet away. Previous encounters had given us a contempt for their cavalry and we did not hesitate to charge a whole brigade if need be; but we had a wholesome respect for large bodies of infantry. We took a few prisoners, but did not know, owing to the dust, what other casualties were inflicted on them. We had seven wounded, including George Burke of Company D, who was shot in the shoulder.

Wheeler was determined to save his train, so he tried to march all night, but a violent electrical storm came up, rain fell in torrents, and our progress was very slow, for the drivers of the teams could not see the road, except by the glare of the lightning. After this had gone on for several hours, making scarcely so many miles, the command camped in column—I believe without orders.

Wheeler dearly loved their wagon trains. I believe it is safe to say that from the first to the last he captured as many wagons as he commanded men. Thousands were burned, but other thousands were secured for the use of our army. The Northern contractors probably enjoyed this as much as Wheeler; no doubt they would have been glad to replace all the wagons, for a reasonable consideration.

The retreat of the army continued to the very gates of Atlanta. Here the Rangers made another charge, in which Jesse Billingsly of Company D was killed.

During the last week of July, the enemy undertook to play our game, and simultaneously made two raids on our communications. One column under General McCook, with 3,500 cavalry, turned our left. They crossed the Chattahoochie near Campbelltown, passed through Fayetteville, where they burned between fifty and one hundred wagons, and struck the Macon railroad near Jonesboro, twenty or twenty-five miles below Atlanta. As soon as intelligence of this movement reached Wheeler he started for the raiders.

We rode all night, coming up with them about daylight. They made very feeble resistance and we ran over them. It was now a chase of twenty miles to the Chattahoochie again. As this stream was not fordable, they made a stand to gain time for crossing the river, which they were attempting by means of boats. Our column was strung out for several miles, Harrison's brigade in front. We were dismounted and pushed into the thick woods.

It was afternoon of the first day of August, and about as hot as such days ever get. The enemy made some resistance, but we drove them steadily some four or five hundred yards, when we heard firing in our rear where we had left our horses. So, we had to face about and fight our way back. We got mixed up with Ross' brigade, which had been dismounted as soon as it came up. After some three hours of this work, the enemy surrendered; that is, all who had not crossed the river.

Wheeler reported 950 prisoners, 1,200 horses and two pieces of artillery as the fruits of this engagement. There were many of their killed and wounded lying in the bushes. I have no information as to the number. Our regiment lost two killed and ten wounded, including one from Company D. This was V. Catron, who was shot in the leg.

The other column of the enemy, led by General Stoneman, turned our right flank and struck our communications lower down, near Macon. His force was reported to be 3,000. General Iverson of the Confederate cavalry attacked them and took 600 prisoners, including Stoneman himself, with two pieces of artillery. The remainder of their force in small detachments made their way back as best they could. Iverson did not have force enough to pursue them.

General Shoupe of General Hood's staff recorded in his diary, that the "First of August deserved to be marked with a white stone." These operations cost the enemy nearly half of the two raiding parties, and fully justified General Hood in saying that our cavalry were equal to twice their number of the enemy.

Chapter 13

Wheeler's Second Raid into Tennessee

Wheeler was now ordered to operate on the long line of the enemy's communications. Finding the posts and bridges south of Chattanooga too strongly fortified to offer any promise of successful attack, Wheeler determined to go over into middle Tennessee again. He went up along the Holston above Knoxville, and then had to cross under a severe fire of the enemy's pickets. For this undertaking there was a call for volunteers. It looked as if the whole of the Rangers were volunteering, and Wheeler had to stop them.

The fording was deep, but the enemy were easily driven from their position. A small force, not of the Rangers, was sent down toward Knoxville. They met the enemy and were roughly handled; about half of them were taken prisoners, and the exultant enemy came on at a furious rate. Our regiment was formed in an open field. Colonel Harrison took position in front. We went forward in a walk at first, and then in a trot. The men were impatient. Officers kept saying:

"Steady, men! Keep back there!"

Then we heard the popping of pistols, and all eyes were turned on Harrison. The routed Confederates came into view. Next the enemy in close pursuit. The men could now hardly be restrained. Finally, Harrison shouted:

"Well, go then! —— you, go!"

The tap of the drum on the race track never sent jockeys and racers to the front more impetuously than the Rangers went at the sound of these words. The enemy's force was small, and they faced about at once. Their horses were nearly exhausted, and we soon overtook them, capturing nearly the whole party, which did not exceed two companies.

Our march was now across the Cumberland mountains, by McMinnville, the familiar route we had travelled two years before under

Forrest, and one year before under Wheeler. Just before reaching Murfreesboro, we turned to the left and began to destroy the railroad leading to Chattanooga, over which Sherman's supplies had to be carried. We piled fence rails on the track and set them on fire. The heat caused the rails to expand and bend into all shapes, rendering them useless until straightened out; of course, the ties were burned also. In this way we destroyed some fifty miles of the road; but the enemy had unlimited resources, and kept trains loaded with railroad material at Nashville and Louisville; these were rushed to the scene of our operations. With large forces working day and night they soon got the tracks in order.

We now moved forward to the Mussel Shoals, where we were to cross the Tennessee River. In a little skirmish on the north side W. H. Caldwell of Company D was wounded in the hip. He was disabled for the remainder of the war by this hurt; never entirely recovered, in fact, walking with a limp for the rest of his life.

After crossing the river, the men of the Third Arkansas, who had shown courage and devotion on many fields, became greatly demoralized. Finding themselves nearer home than they had been for years, many of them deserted. One morning it was reported that twelve of these men had gone. A detail of twenty Rangers under Lieutenant Joiner, the whole under Captain Bass of the Third Arkansas, was sent after the deserters. I was one of this detail. Riding forty or fifty miles a day, we overtook four of them about twenty miles from the great Mississippi and made them prisoners.

On the return my horse was badly injured by falling through a broken plank in an old bridge, and I was left afoot. Joiner gave me orders to remain until my horse recovered, or until I could procure another, and then join some other command until I could get company over Sand Mountain, as that region was infested with bushwhackers and murderers. It was some weeks before I could get a mount, for horses were very scarce, but this is not a narrative of my operations.

CHAPTER 14

"The Rome Races"

I am indebted to Comrade A. B. Briscoe for a description of this incident.

General Harrison, our old colonel, was in command of the forces composed of ours and Ashby's brigade of mounted infantry and a battery of four guns. For some reason, but contrary to all former usages, our regiment was dismounted and placed near the battery, and Ashby's infantry kept mounted to protect the flanks and led horses. The fight had barely commenced when it was realised from the immense bodies of infantry in our front that it was a bad one. The battery was ordered to the rear, but just as they were limbered the Yankee cavalry poured in on our flanks and completely enveloped us.

I did not give an order to run nor did I hear an order of any kind, but I soon found myself dodging through and among the Yankee cavalry, who were shouting to us to surrender. We reached our horses, which were not over 150 yards in the rear, mounted, and after a very hasty formation charged out through the enemy, and although we made repeated rallies, they ran us back about five miles. Why the Yankees did not capture more of our men is a mystery, as outside of the battery we lost very few prisoners. To give an appropriate name to this battle we called it "Rome Races," for such it was.

In this race the colours furled around the staff and in the oilcloth were lost—not captured—as the subjoined letter shows:

Dallas, Texas, May 18, 1898.
Terry's Texas Rangers Association, Austin, Texas.
Gentlemen: I have been in Texas since 1890, and have frequent-

ly endeavoured to find some members of Terry's Texas Rangers, and finally, by accident, met with your comrade, H. W. Graber, and reported to him the finding of your flag the day after our engagement with your forces near Rome, Georgia. It happened in this way: I was directed by the general commanding to take two companies and move through the woods on the right of our line to a certain point where a country road intersected the main river road then occupied by our brigade. Just before coming into the main road I picked up a package or roll of something, threw it over my saddle, and on my return to the main command examined the same and found it to be the Terry's Rangers' flag in its case. It seemed to have slipped off the staff and been lost in that way.

At the suggestion of your comrade—Graber—I have made a request on the authorities of the State of Indiana, who have had charge of it ever since, soon after its capture, and herewith enclose you a letter from Chas. E. Wilson, military secretary at Indianapolis, which seems to indicate there is no authority with the executive department of the State to return the flag, as it is in absolute control of the State Legislature, which is a matter of exceeding regret to me, as I should like to have returned the flag to you in time for your next reunion at Austin. I am furthermore able to assure you that this flag was never displayed in the streets of Nashville, as has been reported, but remained in possession of our regiment until soon after it was found. We returned direct to Louisville, from which point it was sent by express direct to the State of Indiana.

In view of the existing unsettled condition of the country, I would suggest we let the matter rest until our country is again pacified and returned to its normal condition, when I will take pleasure in making a further effort to return this flag, which was not captured, but found, and I consider, therefore, property should be returned to its owner.

With kind regards and best wishes, hoping to have the pleasure of a personal meeting with your association, I am, with great respect,

    Yours very truly,

        J. J. Wiler,
    Maj. Com. 17th Indiana Volunteer Infantry.

This flag was returned to the survivors at Dallas in October, 1898. Its loss was very mortifying to the Rangers, as it had been presented shortly before by the ladies of middle Tennessee.

In justice to the knightly "Count" Jones, I must say that no one could have taken the colours from him without taking his life.

In this action fell Wm. Nicholson of Company D and Lieutenant Batchelor of Company C, and perhaps others, but I have no record of them.

CHAPTER 15

The Last Campaign

Wheeler's cavalry was now almost the only obstacle to Sherman's great march to the sea. They harassed his columns front, flanks and rear, picking up many prisoners; but three or four thousand cavalry could make little resistance to the onward sweep of 60,000 veterans under one of the greatest captains of modern times. Conflicts were of almost daily occurrence. The Rangers were engaged at Buckhead Church and Waynesboro, Georgia. Again, at Aiken, South Carolina. At Averysboro and Fayetteville, North Carolina, where, after a night's march, they surprised Kilpatrick's cavalry camp, but failed to bag that redoubtable leader.

In all of these conflicts the losses were heavy. Old Company D lost in killed, John Gage, P. R. Kennedy, Dave Nunn, Sam Screws and Jim Wynne. Their list of wounded, too, was large. P. R. Kyle and Geo. T. McGehee, good ones both, were badly hurt at Aiken; McArthur, Brannum and P. J. Watkins also. The other companies sustained heavy losses. Lieutenant Heiskell of Company K was killed. I wish I could name them all.

In all of these actions, the remnant of nearly 1,200 enlistments charged with that dauntless courage which had characterized them at Woodsonville, at Bardstown, at Dalton and many other brilliant fields of arms. Their old colonel, now a brigadier general, Thomas Harrison; their colonel, the knightly Cook, and the staid and ever reliable Major Jarmon, were all stretched on beds, racked with the pains of severe wounds. The command now devolved on Captain Matthews, who but a little over a year before had been elected lieutenant, promoted to the rank of captain by the bullets of the enemy which brought down his superiors, was now, at Bentonville, to lead the old regiment in the last charge, which will always rank as one of the most brilliant feats of arms in the history of wars. As I was not present, I will let Lieutenant

Briscoe tell of it, for he tells it well.

The Last Charge.

We did but little fighting the first day, as the enemy changed positions very rapidly. But the second we were engaged in some severe skirmishes all the forenoon, in one of which Major Jarmon, our only remaining field officer, was severely wounded, when we were withdrawn a few hundred yards to rest and give place for the infantry.

We had been in this position resting and eating our rations probably over an hour, when we heard the boom of artillery directly in our rear. Every man pricked up his ears, for we knew that it meant something serious. Captain Doc Matthews of Company K (my company) was in command of the regiment, which numbered about 100 men. We were standing talking of the probable cause of the artillery fire in our rear when General Wheeler galloped up and asked for the commander of the Rangers. He seemed a little excited. His order was, 'Captain, mount your men, go as fast as you can and charge whatever you find at the bridge.' These were almost his exact words.

In less time than it takes to tell it, we were mounted and racing to the rear. Within about half a mile of the bridge we passed a small brigade of infantry 'double quicking' in the same direction. We saluted each other with a cheer as we passed, for all felt that it was a critical time in the battle. As we came upon some rising ground, we had a good view of the enemy across an open field about 500 yards distant. Here we halted an instant to close up the column, and for Captain Matthews to salute General Hardee and staff, who wished to know what troops we were. Captain Matthews told him and of our orders from General Wheeler. He took a look across the field at the dense blue line and said, 'Then execute your orders.' It looked like the old regiment was this time surely going to its grave. Everything was so plain and clear you could see the men handling their guns and hear their shouts of command. Without a moment's hesitation Captain Matthews gave the order, 'Charge right in front,' and with that wonderful rebel yell we charged across the 500 yards of open field upon and among the mass of Yankees. We rode them down and emptied our pistols at close range. When the force of the charge was expended, we fell back with about 200 prisoners.

Like our other brilliant charges, it was the very audacity that brought success.

In this charge fell, mortally wounded, Wm. J. Hardee, Jr., son of Lieutenant General Hardee. Nearly a year before he, with several other boys, had run away from school to join the Rangers, but on account of their extreme youth Colonel Harrison sent them back to school. The boy would not remain in school, so General Hardee kept him with him for several months, but he fretted to join the Rangers. Finally, the father consented. The boy was enlisted in Company D and fell in this, his first action.

I reached the command shortly before the surrender. The regiment in numbers was little more than a good company. Battle and disease had claimed and received their toll; but this little remnant seemed as full of courage and spirit as when first they left their State.

The dream was over. General Lee, "yielding to overwhelming numbers and resources," had laid down his arms. General Johnston, again in command of the Army of Tennessee, agreed with Sherman to disband his army. Sadly, the Rangers dispersed, taking the roads to their distant homes.

General Wheeler issued the following order, which for intense feeling and felicity of expression is a gem:

Headquarters Cavalry Corps,
April 28, 1865.

Gallant Comrades:

You have fought your fight. Your task is done. During a four years' struggle for liberty, you have exhibited courage, fortitude and devotion. You are the victors of more than 200 sternly contested fields. You have participated in more than a thousand conflicts of arms. You are heroes! Veterans! Patriots! The bones of your comrades mark battlefields upon the soil of Kentucky, Virginia, North Carolina, South Carolina, Georgia, Alabama and Mississippi. You have done all that human exertion could accomplish.

In bidding you *adieu*, I desire to tender my thanks for your gallantry in battle, your fortitude under suffering and your devotion at all times to the holy cause you have done so much to maintain. I desire also to express my gratitude for the kind feelings you have seen fit to extend toward myself, and to invoke upon you the blessing of our Heavenly Father, to whom we must always look in the hour of distress. Brethren, in the cause of freedom, comrades in arms, I bid you farewell.

              Joseph Wheeler,
              Major General.

Official:
  Wm. E. Waites,
  Assistant Adjutant General.

CHAPTER 16

Conclusion

I am well aware of the imperfections of this work. I can only say that I have tried to tell an unvarnished tale, to do no one injustice, nothing extenuate nor set down aught in malice. Beyond a few old letters which have escaped the ravages of mice, and such official reports as I could find, I have been compelled to rely on memory—frail and unreliable at best, more so after the lapse of half a century. I beg to remind those who may find fault that it is much easier to find fault than to do good work. No two persons see events exactly alike. This is illustrated in our courts every day.

From the standpoint of the martinet our organisation could hardly be called a regiment. A distinguished lieutenant general is reported as saying that it was not a regiment at all but "a d—d armed mob." If there was ever any serious attempt to discipline it the effort was soon abandoned. Volunteers we began, volunteers we remained to the end. If any wished to evade duty, they found a way, and the punishment for evasion was light. To our credit it may be said that few ever avoided a fight. There were few real cowards among us, and they were simply objects of pity. If a man did not wish to go into a fight, he held his horse until it was over.

One reason of our almost uniform success was the superiority of our arms. It will be remembered that at the beginning the possession of a good pistol was a requisite for enlistment. If a man died or was killed his comrades kept his pistol. When a prisoner of the enemy's cavalry was taken this part of his outfit was added to the general stock, so that after a few months most, if not all, had two weapons of this kind, and some even tried to carry three or four. No other regiment of the army was so supplied.

Again, it was a noteworthy fact that the men were all good horsemen, accustomed to the use and management of horses from childhood. When three or four hundred of such men, charging as fast as their horses would go, yelling like Comanches, each delivering twelve shots with great rapidity and reasonable accuracy, burst into the ranks of an enemy, the enemy generally gave way. It did not take us long to find this out; also, the enemy were not slow to "catch on."

If it be said that other commands lost more men in battle, the explanation is simple and easy. The purpose of fighting is to destroy the enemy in battle; all drill, organisation and hard marches are to this end—to kill and wound as many of the enemy as possible. If this is granted, the Rangers invite comparison with the best in any army. It is safe to claim that the regiment killed, wounded and captured a number of the enemy at least several times our highest enlistment of nearly 1,200. If it be said that my claim for superiority is biased by prejudice in favour of my own regiment, I will give estimates of others.

In a letter to me acknowledging an invitation to one of our reunions, General Wheeler said:

> They were unceasingly vigilant, matchlessly brave and daring.

General Thomas Jordan, an educated soldier, a writer of ability, chief of staff to General Beauregard, was selected by Forrest and his principal officers to write a history of the campaigns of that great soldier. In a note in his book, General Jordan says:

> This regiment was raised and commanded by the lamented Colonel Terry, whose brief military career, beginning as a volunteer scout at the first Manassas, was full of distinction. He was killed at Woodsonville, Kentucky. The privates included a large number of the wealthiest and best educated young men of Texas, who, with many others specially trained in the business of stock raising on the vast prairies of that State, had acquired a marvellous skill in horsemanship. The career of this regiment has been one of the most brilliant in the annals of war.

Dr. John A. Weyeth, who also wrote a life of Forrest, says:

> No braver men ever lived than the Texas Rangers.

General Hood (*Advance and Retreat*) writes of the cavalry:

> I had, moreover, become convinced that our cavalry were able to successfully compete with double their numbers. The Confederacy possessed, in my opinion, no body of cavalry superior to that which I found guarding the flanks of the Army of Ten-

nessee when I assumed its direction.

I now quote Federal authority. Writing of the comparative merits of the soldiers of the two armies, in a paper on the Kentucky campaign, General Buell, while denying the superiority of the Southern soldiers over the Northern, admits it was true of the cavalry. He says:

> Another sectional distinction produced a more marked effect in the beginning of the war. The habits of the Southern people facilitated the formation of cavalry corps which were comparatively efficient even without instruction; and accordingly, we see Stuart, John Morgan and Forrest riding with impunity around the union armies, destroying or harassing their communications. Late in the war that agency was reversed. The South was exhausted of horses, while the Northern cavalry increased in numbers and efficiency, and acquired the audacity which had characterized the Southern.

Read that again. It comes very near saying that the South was overcome because the supply of horses failed. The writer is an educated soldier and student of war.

L'Envoi.

My task is done. My story is told. I have derived pleasure as well as pain and grief from the recital; pleasure in going back over the dreary waste of years to the morning of life, and dwelling in memory amid the scenes of my early manhood; pain that I cannot do justice to all who, at the call of country, periled their young lives for home and the right; grief for the heroic dead, who sleep in unmarked graves wherever duty lead to danger and death. Their matchless courage and devotion earned undying fame.

Their praise is hymned by loftier harps than mine;
Yet, one I would select from that proud throng:

Because he was my bedfellow, and I loved him as a brother; faithful in the discharge of every duty, clean, brave, and true—William Nicholson.

Reminiscences of the Terry Rangers
By J. K. P. Blackburn

When the Civil War commenced, I was in school in Lavaca County, Texas, both as teacher and pupil, where I had been most of the time for four and a half years before. I was born in Tennessee in 1837 and in the fall of 1856, when I was about 19 years of age, my father emigrated to Texas with his family of wife and eight children. I taught a little primary school in Payette County first for three months. Then I sold a horse my father gave me, got my money for teaching school, put these two funds together, and went to Alma Institute in Lavaca County for two years. I taught one year in Gonzales County, and after thus adding to my bank account, returned to my *alma mater* as pupil and assistant teacher and was there until hostilities commenced between the North and the South.

My first experience in anything that looked like warfare was had in a trip to San Antonio to help capture the Federal forces and war equipage at that place. The United States had been accustomed for years to make San Antonio an army post with a good force and plenty of army supplies under able commanders so as to be available to protect the western border from invasion. Soon after the State of Texas passed the ordinance of secession, Ben McCulloch, a frontiersman and Indian fighter, called upon the people living in the western and southern counties of Texas to meet him at the earliest possible moment at a rendezvous near San Antonio with any firearms to be had.

Without delay nearly all the men able to bear arms and to do military duty, started with a rush, riding continuously without rest or sleep until we reached the place of gathering, which if my memory serves me, was on Sea Willow Creek a few miles from the city to the north. We who were from Lavaca County reached the place late in the night, probably two or three o'clock a.m. McCulloch had already sent men to surround the Alamo, then used as a fort and an arsenal for army and military supplies.

The movement was made with much caution and secrecy. Men with rifles in hands were placed on top of the surrounding buildings so as to command the place the artillery men must occupy when they would attempt to fire the cannon. The headquarters of General Twiggs, one mile out in the country, were picketed by a file of armed men so as to prevent communication with his forces in town. When daylight came a flag of truce was sent in to the commander at the fort, a demand for surrender made, his attention called to men on the housetops and the forces now coming in to surround the fort and his army; and without firing a gun he surrendered everything he commanded. (February 16. 1861.)

In the meantime, General Twiggs ordered his carriage and started for camp without seemingly knowing what had happened while he slept. Two of our men met him as he started out, presented their shot guns and told him he was their prisoner of war and so they marched him into the Grand *Plaza* where McCulloch and his men to the number of several hundred had assembled.

I happened to be standing within a few steps of McCulloch when General Twiggs was brought in and I heard their conversation. After salutations General Twiggs said, "Ben McCulloch, you have treated me most shamefully, ruining my reputation as a military, man and I am now too old to re-establish it."

McCulloch answers, "I am serving my State, the State of Texas, Sir."

General Twiggs replied, that if an old woman with a broomstick in hand had come to him and having authority from the State of Texas demanded his surrender he would have yielded without a word of protest. "But you, Sir, without papers, without any notice have assembled a mob and forced me to terms."

So ends this episode. General Twiggs in his humiliation wept like a child and he had my sympathy and the sympathy I think of all who witnessed this meeting. The soldiers and arms and munitions of war captured—I cannot now recall numbers or amounts.

★★★★★★★★★★

In the whole department of Texas 2445 officers and men were surrendered by Twiggs. See report of Colonel C. A. Waite, U. S. Army, to Lorenzo Thomas, February 26, 1861, *Official Records of the Union and Confederate Armies*, Series I, Vol. I.

The value of the grounds, buildings and stores of all kinds surrendered in San Antonio was estimated at $781,808.39; at the other posts in Texas, $700,000. See report of the Texas Commissioners, Devine, Luckett, and Maverick, *Official Records*, Series I, Vol. LIII.—C. W. R.

★★★★★★★★★★

I returned to school, but school work seemed tame and common place and overshadowed by the tragic events on every side. War was declared by Lincoln on the seceded States, calling for troops from the other Southern States to help put down the rebellion. The Confederate Government had been formed at Montgomery, Alabama. A blaze of enthusiasm and resentment sweeping over the southland prompted patriots on every hand to get ready to defend their homes and firesides against the ravages and destruction of an insolent foe who was then moving to invade the South. The seceded States established drill and instruction camps in different parts of their borders, training men on every hand for effectual fighting.

The camps were provided with competent drill masters, mobilisation went on day after day through the spring and the early summer and on through the year, and regiments were formed and sent forward towards the seat of war until thousands upon thousands were mustered into service from every section that year, the year of 1861. I spent several weeks at Camp Clark on the San Marcos River, drilling and learning military tactics at that camp of instruction. All conversation on every side pertained to war and incidents and hopes and fears connected therewith. The question of, "Are you going to the war?" was rarely asked, but "Where will you go?"

I had a room-mate the last session in school named Foley, large hearted, intellectual and a poet, a Baptist preacher of ability, and a native of New York City. He and I discussed the question often and while we both preferred cavalry service, being good horsemen, he preferred to go west and northwest with the first regiment formed, I to go towards the east in order to be upon the main fields of battle even if I had to go with the infantry. We separated. He enlisted in Colonel Ford's Second Texas Cavalry and went to meet the enemy that was threatening Texas from the northwest. The next news I had from that Command, Foley had been killed in a charge on a battery at Valverda or Glorietta, New Mexico, (I have forgotten which)—killed by the last shot fired from that battery before its capture. Thus, passed from earth one of the noblest spirits I ever knew.

I considered a proposition from Captain Fly who was raising a company in our neighbourhood for the 2nd Texas Infantry and at one time told him I thought I might join his company when they got ready to start, but told him of my preference for the cavalry.

Weeks passed. At last, the opportunity came. A regiment of cavalry was to be raised in western and southern Texas for service in Virginia. Two Texans of wealth and leisure, B. F. Terry, a sugar planter, and Thos. S. Lubbock, a lawyer, who were traveling in the East—whether for business, pleasure, or curiosity, I know not—happened at or purposely were at the battle of first Manassas in Virginia, and rendered all the aid they could to the Southern cause. Terry acted as volunteer aid to the commanding general, and Lubbock also exposed his life in bearing messages during the contest.

About the middle of August commissions came to Terry and Lubbock from the war department at Richmond, Virginia, authorising them to raise a regiment on certain conditions, *viz.*: each man to furnish his own arms (double-barrelled shotgun and two six shooters), his bridle, blanket, saddle, spurs, lariat, etc., the government to mount the men on good horses. The men should always select their own officers from colonel down to fourth corporal and serve in the Virginia Army as an independent command.

This was the opportunity that many had wished for and in less than twenty days this call was answered by 1,170 men assembling at Houston to be enrolled in the regiment, afterwards called Terry's Texas Rangers. Colonel Terry immediately after securing the commission selected ten men in different sections and counties of the southern and western part of the State and asked them to raise a company of about a hundred men and bring them to Houston for enrolment in the army as soon as practical.

The company which I joined was made up from Fayette, Lavaca and Colorado Counties, the majority being from Fayette. L. M. Strobel, having the authority, enrolled the names and set a day for meeting at Lagrange in Fayette County for organising the company by electing officers from captain to corporal. At the called meeting Strobel was elected captain, W. R. Jarman first lieutenant, Phocian and William Tate (brothers) were elected second and third lieutenants, C. D. Barnett orderly sergeant, and J. T. J. Culpepper second sergeant. I cannot recall with any certainty the names of the other non-commissioned officers at this date.

Our next meeting was called for Houston, Texas, where we were to be sworn in as soldiers of the Confederate States. Early in September the city of Houston was filled with volunteers anxious to enlist in the Terry Rangers. One thousand men were expected to constitute the regiment, but more and more were enlisted until the number reached 1,170, an average of 117 to each company, and others, I don't recall how many, were denied the privilege of enlistment.

A Lieutenant Sparks, who had belonged to the United States Army if I mistake not, came authorised to administer the oath of allegiance to the Confederate States and enrol us as her soldiers. A little incident happened at the time which showed the feelings and determination of the men. They were lined up on three sides of a hollow square (as I now remember). The enrolling officer in the centre asked this question, "Do you men wish to be sworn into service for twelve months or for three years or for during the war?" With a unanimity never surpassed, a shout unheard of before, that whole body of men shouted, "For the war," "For the war!" not one expecting or caring to return until the war was over, long or short, and the invaders had been driven from our borders.

And now the regiment is ready for service, as fine a body as ever mustered for warfare. The majority of them were college boys, and cowboys, professional men, men with finished education, men just out of college, others still under-graduates, men raised in the saddles, as it were, experts with lariat and with six shooters, and not a few from the farm, from the counting houses and from shops. Just why the regiment did not elect field officers and become a fully organised body of soldiers at Houston I never knew.

In the absence of this organisation, the companies not being numbered or lettered, each company was called by its captain's name. Ours was Captain Strobel's company, and was sent forward as the vanguard of the regiment toward the seat of war by Colonel Terry who assumed command although he refused to be called Colonel until he should be elected to the position by his men. The election took place in Kentucky in December following.

The company was put in box freight cars and started eastward over what was afterwards to be called the Sunset Route, which at that time ran east from Eagle Lake, Colorado County, Texas, through the city of Houston, to New Iberia, Louisiana.

★★★★★★★★★★

Mr. Blackburn's memory is slightly at fault here. The railroads ran from Alleyton on the Colorado, a few miles northwest of Eagle Lake, to Harrisburg, and from Houston to Beaumont, though the track of this latter road was laid to Orange. See *Atlas of Official Records,* Plate CLVII; also A. M. Gentry to Secretary of War, Richmond, May 1,

1861, *Official Records*, Series IV, Vol. I, p. 1,109.—C. W. R.

****

Our baggage and guns were put in the cars with us, each man retaining and wearing his pistols as regularly as his clothes. At New Iberia was a gap where the road had not been built reaching to Brashear City, Louisiana, about 100 miles. Over this gap we were supposed to walk and most of the company without a murmur commenced this march.

****

This gap in the railroad ran from Orange through New Iberia to Brashear City. L. B. Giles, *Terry's Texas Rangers*, says: "From Houston to Beaumont, over a newly constructed railroad, it took nearly all day to make eighty miles. From Beumont, by steamboat down the Neches and up the Sabine to Niblett's Bluff; thence a hundred miles on foot, through water much of the way; thence forty miles in carts. . . . At New Iberia, on Bayou Teche, we were transferred to boats, and went down between the beautiful banks of that stream to Brashear, now Morgan City."—C. W. R.

****

The captain had hired wagons to transport the baggage and guns. A few men found horses they could hire for the trip and so we started with eight or ten men riding horseback and the balance on foot. The country was level, for the most part, the road was good, but innumerable lagoons or sloughs lay across this roadway from six inches to two feet deep and there was no way to cross them except to wade them. With this kind of experience, a half day found most of the men with blistered sore feet, and the further we went the more aggravated was their condition. So, the captain, who was mounted, decided by the middle of the afternoon he would mount his men by impressing horses for the balance of the journey.

That section was full of horses running in great herds on its prairies, so he and his mounted men found a herd of more than 100 head of all ages, sorts, and sizes, and penned them on or near the road while his baggage wagons were halted at little streams nearby. When the footmen reached the place, they were told to look up their baggage, take their lariats, go to the pen and mount themselves, and the evening might be spent in breaking their horses and getting ready for the march next day.

The ages of the horses were from three to eight years, many of them had never been haltered before, some few were broken and gentle, and some of the older ones had been handled some but spoiled in attempting to break them and turned out on the range to go free. Of this last class I got one, an eight year old, Claybank gelding; but whatever their condition or habits, they were all well broken by dark that night. Next morning one of my messmates, Patton by name, a school and classmate for several years, found his horse was loose and gone and could not be found anywhere near. The company was preparing to move. I went to the captain, explained the situation and asked permission to return to that pen and get another horse for Patton. He consented.

Another one of my mess-mates told me he had been lucky enough to get a horse fairly well broken and gentle and that he would exchange with me until I went on that errand and returned. The company moved off and Patton was left at camp alone to await my coming with his horse. I rode back about six hundred yards to the pen where we had corralled the horses that evening. It was empty and I inquired at the house nearby of ladies—no men being at home—for the horses. They told me they had been turned out into a very large grass pasture nearby lying out south of the house.

I went into that pasture and rode south from the residence; but concerning what happened for the balance of that day I am indebted to those good ladies for the information, for my mind suddenly became blank as to that matter and never since that time to this good day have I been able to recall anything that happened after I started out south from the house that day. About sunset I revived enough to realise that someone was sitting by me, pouring cold water on my head and I asked in surprise, "What do you mean by this treatment?" and "Where am I?"

Patton answered, "You have been dead all day and I am trying this treatment to revive you." He then told me he had waited for me at the camp until he became uneasy at my failure to return and came up to this house hunting for me and found me there in an unconscious condition. Then the kind hearted ladies told me that I had early in the morning gone out into their pasture and had driven up a bunch of horses near the house, made a dash at them and had lassoed one of them and being unable to manage the animal I was riding, the lassoed animal made a quick circuit around me, jerked me off on the ground upon my head and that they had gone out there, dragged me to the house in an unconscious condition.

They further stated the two horses thus lashed together by the lariat around the horn of my saddle on one and around the neck of the other ran off at a furious pace to overtake those gone on before, ran one on each side of the same tree, bringing on a collision resulting in the death of the one and the fatal wounding of the other. The ladies had also brought my saddle, blanket and lariat to the house.

Now night had come on. Our company was a day's journey ahead of us and we two soldiers were left to shift for our transportation the best we could. We consulted about what was best to be done. Patton had learned the family possessed two carriage horses in their barn and we paid the ladies $5.00 for their use to ride until we should overtake our company, pledging our honour as soon as we reached the camp to return them by their driver who was to accompany us. We saddled up and started at once, riding all night before we overtook the company.

We sent back the horses with many thanks and journeyed from there to Brashear City, Patton and I in baggage wagons. At Brashear City we were all put on railroad trains again and soon after reached New Orleans, where we were quartered in a cotton compress building. Next day, aboard the cars on the Mississippi Central road we resumed our journey, without any incident of note until we reached Grand Junction, Tennessee, where we received a telegram from Colonel Terry ordering us to remain there awaiting further orders from him.

About two days later another message came announcing the fact that General Albert Sidney Johnston had interceded with the Secretary of War for our service—I mean the services of this Terry Ranger Regiment—and that we should take up our journey for Nashville, Tennessee, where General Johnston had arranged for our horses and munitions of war. This change of destination brought deep disappointment and displeasure to everyone, as their hearts had been set on going to Virginia.

General A. S. Johnston was a West Pointer, had served in the U. S. Army both in the Mexican War and later on western frontier. He had a home and farm in Texas, and had resigned his position in the army when Texas seceded from the Union and accepted service in the Confederate Army, and was at that time commanding the nucleus of what was afterwards the army of Tennessee, at Bowling Green, Kentucky. To Nashville we journeyed, and when we reached the city, encamped on the old fair grounds in West Nashville. Other companies of the regiment soon followed us and in a short time the whole regiment was encamped at Nashville.

The news of our coming and stories of the marvellous acts of horsemanship of the cowboys had preceded us; and we proved to be a great attraction for the people of Nashville and surrounding country—so much so that crowds gathered in the mornings and greater crowds in the evenings every day while we were getting in our horses in that city. Every wild, unbroken, vicious horse in that section was brought in to be ridden. When one came in there was generally a rush made by the soldiers to get first chance at him. When he had been bridled and saddled one would mount him, pull off the bridle, turn him loose, put spurs to him, and bid him do his worst. Before he was half through with the performance another soldier would spring upon him as a hind-rider and after a time, depending upon the strength of the animal, he would come to a stand-still, completely exhausted and his riders were ready for the next act.

One attraction for the spectators was the ease with which the horsemen could ride in full gallop or fast run and pick up from the ground anything they wished to. To start this performance, it would be announced from the stand or some prominent place that a number of silver dollars would be strewn along on the race track for anyone that would run at full speed and pick them up. This proposition would create much rivalry and interest among those who had gotten their mounts and a half dozen, sometimes more, would enter the contest, for by this time many had exhausted their pocket change.

The money was placed by the spectators along the track at intervals of twenty paces or more apart in full view of the horsemen, and at a signal all started and generally every dollar was picked up the first dash made. Well, the spectators seemed to tire of the dollar proposition in a few days and reduced the offer to half dollars which was as readily accepted and gathered as the dollars. Later on, another reduction to 25c was made and still later the ladies would bring in many bouquets to be given away in the same manner, but the rivalry and interest among the performers never ceased and thus was an entertainment given from day to day that brought many thousands of spectators during the regiment's sojourn at the Fairgrounds.

During the month of November, I think, there broke out in camp a great epidemic of measles of a very violent form, which was no respecter of persons seemingly, for most of the members had it, some in milder form than others, but it seemed to touch everyone. To show how general it was in its attacks I quote from Henry Middlebrooks of our company. He said his mother had told him he had measles when a babe and he had measles when he was fifteen years old and he had them now so badly as to be rendered unfit for duty and was discharged from the service. Captain Strobel's company was first to lose a man from this epidemic, M. G. Harborough being the victim.

The hospitals at Nashville and many private houses were filled with the sick and dying. I was sent to one of the hospitals where for weeks I was kept alive by the best of nursing and attention of the good ladies of Nashville who, in regular reliefs, nursed the sick night and day. God bless the good ladies of Nashville. They will always have a warm place in my heart, for my own mother could not have nursed me more carefully and constantly. The epidemic continued its fight upon the regiment until the middle of December, maybe a little longer.

About that time, I reported to the regiment for duty at a little village about fifteen miles north of Bowling Green, Kentucky, Oakland by name, where I joined about 150 men able for duty. Over 1000 men had been eliminated by measles; many of them died and others were discharged on account of disability and others still to return later on as they recovered. I can't recall numbers now, but I might safely say as many or perhaps more in our regiment died of this epidemic than were killed in battle in the four years the war continued.

An incident connected with the removal of the regiment from Nashville to Kentucky I feel should be mentioned at this time. Colonel Terry as a precaution against possible trouble had arranged for guards to be placed around the camp every night to prevent the men from going up town. The men, undisciplined as they were, looked upon this as an unnecessary restriction upon their general liberty, and so some of the most determined ones would manage to get out and go up every night and sometimes they would get unruly or noisy from drink and fall into the hands of the police and be locked up; but generally, they were released after short detention and a promise of good behaviour in the future.

In this way there was some bad blood between the "cops" and the Texans, which soon brought on a crisis and bloodshed and death to some of the police force. One night three or four soldiers slipped by the guards, went up town, imbibed too freely of booze, went to the theatre and took their seats in the gallery. Captain John Smith's expected execution and Pocahontas' rescue as related in early history of the Colonies was the drama staged for the night.

When that part of the play was reached where Captain John Smith, condemned to die by his Indian captors, was bound hand and foot and his head placed upon a rock, the executioner drew back his bludgeon to strike the fatal blow, Pocahontas thrust her own body between

Smith's head and the descending bludgeon, one of the boozy soldiers in the gallery whipped out a six-shooter and fired upon the supposed executioner with the remark that "his mother had taught him to always protect a lady when in danger."

This shot missed its mark, but created consternation and stopped the play. The police rushed in to arrest the offender, the other soldiers helped him to resist arrest, and shooting began, resulting in the death of two policemen and the wounding of another one and the freedom of the soldiers to return unmolested to camp. This tragedy was reported to the Governor of Tennessee and immediately telegraphed by the governor to General Johnston, who ordered Colonel Terry to come immediately on the first train to Bowling Green and report to him. By daylight next morning the regiment was in the train on their way to their destination, nearer to the scenes that should soon be enacted between contending lines of battle. The baggage and the horses collected for the use of the regiment up to this time were sent on through the country by a detail of men with an officer in charge.

When Colonel Terry reported to General Johnston's headquarters, at Bowling Green, he was ordered to assemble his regiment at Oakland, fifteen miles north of Bowling Green. About the first business attended to in the new quarters was to hold an election for regimental officers and to cast lots for assignment of companies to their places in the regiment. This resulted in the election of B. F. Terry for Colonel, Thos. S. Lubbock for Lieutenant-Colonel, and Thos. Harrison for Major. Martin Royston was selected as Adjutant and W. B. Sayers as Sergeant Major.

Captain Strobel's company, to which I belonged, drew the letter F for its number of place in the regiment. The other companies drew other letters of the alphabet, from A to K inclusive, except J, and thereafter the companies were called and known by letters instead of by captains' names. The organisation now being complete, a roster was made out and sent to the Secretary of War at Richmond, Virginia, and an application made for numbering the regiment, and for commissions for all commissioned officers of the same. The number assigned us was 8th Texas Cavalry, when we would have been 2nd Texas Cavalry but for the two or three months' interval between our enrolment and our final organisation. The first duty assigned us was to patrol and picket all that section from Bowling Green north as far up as Woodsonville on Green River, Kentucky.

The winter came on with much snow and hard freezing weather.

The men were coming in slowly from their sick beds. Those already in camps had to do double duty, owing to their small numbers and the great amount of the work to be done. It was not uncommon for men to be compelled to stand picket in the snow several inches deep for four hours at a time and then be relieved for two hours and be put in again for four hours. This duty was very trying on the constitutions of those just recovering from an attack of measles. This unusual experience brought bronchial troubles or affections upon me, and although it did not send me to the hospital again, yet I have never up to this day gotten entirely rid of it.

On the 17th day of December, the regiment made a reconnaissance up near Woodsonville, Kentucky. The turnpike ran parallel with the railroad for some distance before we reached the village. Colonel Terry sent two companies up the railroad and the balance of the regiment kept the pike. On near approach to the village on Green River, the two companies came suddenly upon about an equal number of the enemy who were concealed behind some haystacks and a fence near the railroad, who saluted the Texans with a volley of musketry which told heavily upon them, but the Texans charged them on horseback and drove them back toward the village.

In the meantime, the balance of the regiment had come up on a rise or deviation in the pike in view of the conflict, several hundred yards from us to our right. We were halted there for a little while and sitting on our horses in column of twos when suddenly without the least suspicion of what was about to happen, a heavy volley of musketry was turned upon us from a black jack thicket on the hillside east of us and very close to us. Colonel Terry immediately ordered a charge, emphasising the order with an oath not easily forgotten, so we made a rush for those bushes concealing a considerable force with bayonets fixed ready to receive us.

With our shotguns loaded with buckshot we killed, wounded, and scattered that command in short order. Our casualties were comparatively few in numbers, but fearful in results, as we lost our Colonel, shot through the jaw, the bullet ranging up through the brain. He and his horse and three of the enemy fell in a heap. He had shot two and a ranger near him, I think, shot the third one.

This was the 32nd Indiana Regiment of Infantry we fought, commanded by Colonel Willich so we were informed by the prisoners we captured. This was our first battle and the first engagement of the Army of Tennessee. We had ridden into an ambuscade and if the enemy had lowered their fire sufficiently in that first volley, there is no good reason why we would not all have been killed or wounded. One lesson we learned from that experience that served us well in future operations. That was to have flankers out on each side of a moving column as well as a vanguard whenever we might suspect an enemy, so as to avoid ambuscades.

In the engagement at Woodsonville Captain Walker of Company K was wounded by a bayonet passing through his lower arm and slightly wounding him in the chest. What the losses were on each side, I cannot now recall. (Colonel Willich reported the loss of 11 officers and men killed, 22 wounded, 5 missing; Brigadier General Hindman, commanding the Confederates, reported 4 killed and 10 wounded. See *Official Records,* Series I, Vol. VII, .pp. 16-20— C. W. R)

When Colonel Terry was killed, Lieutenant Colonel Lubbock was dangerously sick and died in a short time afterwards, so under our "bill of rights" as we believed, we held another election for Colonel and Lieutenant Colonel and to fill some vacancies in line officers where they had resigned and gone home. At this election we chose Captain Wharton of Company B for Colonel, Captain Walker of Company K for Lieutenant Colonel and in Company F, B. E. Joiner Third Lieutenant instead of Wm. Tate, resigned. We continued our scouting, picketing, and patrolling in that section of Kentucky through that severe winter 1861 until February, 1862. In the meantime, we received boxes of heavy clothing from our home folks in Texas which was badly needed and duly appreciated, for ours was threadbare and too light for the cold weather.

Sometime in January, I think, Confederate General Zolicoffer was killed at Fishing Creek and his army defeated, and in February, Fort Donelson on Cumberland River, after two days fighting surrendered to General Grant. These heavy losses caused General Johnston to give up Kentucky and move into Tennessee and select later the Memphis and Charleston railroad as a base of operations.

When the army reached Nashville, our regiment was sent down the river to, or near to, Fort Donelson to gather up some teams and army supplies that had been rushed out there before the surrender of the fort, while the main body of the Confederates assembled at Murfreesboro, where we rejoined them after bringing those things we had been sent for. After a few days General Johnston moved his infantry and artillery southward to reach his new selected base at Corinth, Mississippi, leaving the cavalry at Murfreesboro to watch the enemies' movements and to impede as much as we might their progress south if an attempt was made to follow in pursuit.

In a few days only our regiment and a few squads of other cavalry were to be seen about the city. Among the odds and ends of cavalry men was Captain John H. Morgan, afterwards General Morgan, with a few recruits trying to raise a cavalry command for the Confederate service, and at the same time paying most assiduous attentions to Miss Ready, daughter of Colonel Ready of Murfreesboro.

One night Captain Morgan asked Colonel Wharton for a detail of two men to go with him next day on a raid within the enemy's lines up toward Nashville, telling Colonel Wharton he already had seven men armed and well mounted, and he wished him to furnish him two more good men well mounted with blue overcoats, shot-guns and pistols, which would make ten by counting himself. Colonel Wharton sent the order to Company F to make the detail wanted. Jake Flewellen and I were ordered to report to Captain Morgan next morning at sun-up, mounted and ready for the trip.

Sunrise came; Captain Morgan and nine private soldiers moved out on the Nashville pike, mounted and equipped for the trip according to instructions, except I had on a black overcoat. I had no blue one and didn't want one and never did wear one. Morgan assigned me to the rear, thinking and judging correctly too that the squad would be judged by those in front and not by one man in the rear. The enemy had moved their army out on Murfreesboro pike, ten or fifteen miles, and gone into winter quarters, and were making preparations for a movement south when spring should come. We kept the turnpike road for several miles and as we approached the neighbourhood of their encampments we turned to the right and moved through fields and woodland, sometimes, in full view of their encampments and I thought uncomfortably near them.

But the blue coats of the squad kept down any suspicion as to our identity and we kept our course until we were something like five miles from the city when we approached the pike again, where a thicket of undergrowth was near to the pike. We stood parallel to the highway in a line of battle for a short time, when a wagon train from Nashville loaded with provisions and supplies for the army drove up, guarded by a troop of cavalry, about sixteen, I think. Armed with sabres, with guns and pistols pointed at them and a fence between us, they surrendered readily and the guard and teams and drivers all fell into our hands without firing a gun.

As soon as the wagons could be fired and the teams and guards could be collected for the march, Captain Morgan ordered me and three or four others, including my fellow soldier Flewellen to take charge of them and get out of the enemy's lines as quickly as possible and not to halt for anything until we crossed Stone River, near Murfreesboro, where we should encamp and wait his return.

Our trip being without incident we reached our camping place about sundown. On the eastern bank of the stream was a large commodious dwelling with a small family in it and servants in the kitchen or cabins and plenty of provender in the barn. We put our prisoners in one of the large rooms and a guard over them and a vidette on or near the river bank; had the servants to feed all the horses at the barn and by alternating in guard and picket duty passed a quiet night.

Next morning before sunrise the vidette reported ten or twelve men advancing towards us from the other side of the river. We supposed them to be Yankees, as the enemy was generally termed by us, but as they drew nearer there were no guns in sight and we decided with much relief that it was Captain Morgan and his men with ten prisoners of war they had captured and kept in the woods all night awaiting daylight so they could see their way to travel better.

Captain Morgan, when he reached us related the events of the previous day after we had left him. He said they captured about sixty prisoners and had ordered four men to take them and follow us to Stone River and camp as he had ordered us, and that the enemy's cavalry which had gotten wind of his presence in their lines were looking for him, coming upon this second lot of prisoners, recaptured them and slew three of his men after they had surrendered, one of them making his escape.

He further told us that he and his companion had visited a picket post and he, pretending to be officer of the day whose duty required him to look after the guards and pickets of the army, had called to the commander of the post to come out of a house in which he was quartered and as he approached him Morgan placed a pistol to his breast and told him he was his prisoner and for him to make no sign or outcry to his fellows in the house on penalty of death, but to call them out by name, one by one, until all were captured without realising what had happened.

Then his companion was sent out to the picket post a short distance away and brought in the two videttes who were on vidette post, and being late in the evening, the enemy scouting on all sides looking for them, they hid themselves, sat up all night guarding their prisoners and very early in the morning had travelled on until they reached us and now without further delay everything was made ready for the further march into Murfreesboro, that about one mile distant.

We marched up the street in front of Colonel Ready's house, lined up prisoners, horses and spoils and guards across the street while Captain Morgan went in the house and invited his sweetheart and the balance of the family at home to come out on the veranda and see the fruit of his exploit. Flewellen and I were then relieved with thanks and we returned to our company, leaving the prisoners and spoils in the hands of Morgan and his three men he still had with him. Next day one of Morgan's men hunted me up and told me Captain Morgan wanted to see me at his office, so I went with him to the office.

The captain greeted me most cordially and said he wanted to thank me over again for the valuable service I had rendered during the scout the day or two before. I told him I did the best I could with the matter I had in hand and did not deserve any special thanks more than others with me. But he seemed to look at the matter differently and said he wished to give me something to be kept as a souvenir of that hazardous venture. He then told me to select a sabre, the best of the captured lot he had and take it with me as a keepsake of the occasion. I did so and took the newest and brightest in the lot and went back to my company with it, and while we served in the same army, I don't think now I ever saw him again.

Morgan was captain then, but soon his efficiency as a cavalry officer and raider was conceded on all sides and his promotion was rapid. He made many raids into the enemy's lines, even going one time into Ohio. Men flocked to his standard from Tennessee, Kentucky, Missouri, and other sections. He became Brigadier and later Major-General, I think. He married Miss Ready; was finally killed in Greenville, East Tennessee, in one of his raids in that section.

While I prized my sabre as a souvenir, I soon found it was an inconvenience to carry with my other equipments. I had a double-barrelled shotgun, two six shooters, my blanket, oil cloth, clothing, haversack, etc., to carry and I could at once see that while it might prove a nice keepsake, I had no other use for it. Later on, I had a chance to leave it with a relative in middle Tennessee to be kept for me until the war was over or until I should call for it, and in this way, it passed the war period; after the close of hostilities, I went to see my kinsman (who had died in the meantime) and recovered my sabre from his family who had taken good care of it. It now, (1919), hangs in the hall of my daughter's home in Grand Rapids, Michigan, 563 Union Ave., S. E. It is her keepsake now, to be disposed of by her as she may desire.

Sometime in March, 1862, we, the cavalry forces at Murfreesboro, broke camp and started to follow the army of Tennessee to Corinth, Mississippi, where it was being prepared to act on the defensive against the oncoming armies of General Grant and General Buell. Grant's army was at Pittsburg Landing and encamped out some distance from the landing on the Tennessee River in the direction of Corinth, near Shiloh church, while General Buell was moving his army from Nashville to the same point by forced marches to unite with Grant in his attack on General Johnston, now at Corinth, about fifteen miles south of Pittsburg Landing. Johnston's army consisted of about 40,000 or 45,000 men—my recollection Grant's nearly the same—and Buell's probably 50,000.

Johnston decided to attack Grant's army before Buell could reach him and taking one at a time, defeat them both, and I have no doubt his plan would have succeeded had General Johnston lived a few days more. After hastily collecting his forces, he moved out of Corinth, on the evening of the fifth of April and next morning before light attacked the enemy in the encampments. (Johnston's army left Corinth on the morning of April 3 and arrived in the vicinity of Shiloh late in the afternoon of the 5th.—C. W. R.) The attack was unexpected and furious from the beginning. The enemy was driven slowly back towards the river all day long, making a most stubborn resistance, but gradually they gave up their encampments and artillery and equipments until four o'clock that afternoon when the Confederates were unwisely halted by an order from General Beauregard who succeeded to chief command after General Johnston's fatal wound about three o'clock that afternoon. This closed the first day's engagement with the whole battlefield, including many arms, wagons, sutlers stores, etc., etc., in the hands of the Confederates.

We slept on the battleground that night as best we could with torrents of rain pouring down on us all night and with the gunboats on the river firing over us all night to disturb our slumbers. Many of the boys visited the sutlers stores that night and helped themselves to the edibles and as much clothing as they could use or carry off. Next morning early the Federals having been reinforced by Buell's army, made an attack on us by moving forward against our left, with what was said to be eleven lines of battle, and beat our left wing back some distance and then a movement along all of our front beat back all of our line slowly but surely all day long until night closed the fight with Federals in charge of all their encampments given up the previous day.

Thus ended two days of the most terrible fighting I ever witnessed before or since. Never did I at any other time hear minie balls seem to fill the air so completely as on this second day's fight. But the battle was not ended yet, for on the third day, the eighth of April, in the evening was an engagement between the Confederate cavalry and Federal infantry that ought always to be mentioned as the last act of this tragic event where losses on both sides amounted to more than 20,000 men. (The losses as officially reported were: Confederates, 20,699; Unionists, 13,047.— C. W. R.)

I will now recur to the regiment and company to which I belonged, in order to record their part in this bloody contest and to give some of the incidents of more or less interest that occurred at that time. (Colonel Wharton's report of the battle is to be found in *Official Records,* Series I, Vol, X, Part I, p. 626.—C. W. R.) When the battle commenced on the 6th of April our bugler sounded the assembly which brought us quickly into line. The several companies were numbered to ascertain our effective force at the beginning. Company F numbered 65 men in line, including non-commissioned officers, a captain and second lieutenant. This lieutenant had been elected by the company principally because he had slain two different men in personal combat, and was therefore regarded as a hero of heroes.

While the company was being numbered, the musketry one-half mile away was heavy and almost continuous and this officer riding up and down in front of the company remarked time and time again, "Ah, boys, that is music to my ears," making us believe he would perform many deeds of valour when he reached the firing line. At last, an order came for us to march to the front and when near there we were ordered to form columns of fours, move to rear of the enemy and make an attack from that quarter; but failing to get far enough back to take them in the rear we marched the head of the column right into the flank of the enemy's line, who, concealed from our view, were lying down behind some timber recently felled by a storm.

Being at right angles with our line of march, they could concentrate the fire of their whole line to enfilade our column from end to end; and as the head of the column neared them, they rose suddenly, poured a volley into us which reached every company in the line of march, killing and wounding men and horses clear back to the rear of column. Of course, nothing could be done but fall back and reform for further action in a different move; but I must stop to tell you about this officer to whose ears the battle at a distance was so musical. Though not touched by bullets he became suddenly sick at the sight of bloodshed and had to be sent to the rear to avoid a nervous collapse. It was his first and his last experience in battle for he resigned and returned to Texas and we never saw him again. This lesson is that "the true test of valour comes, not in use of words, but only in action in the crucible of battle."

The regiment was dismounted and made an attack on the enemy on the left flank of our army and then moved to the rear of our army for a support to other troops in firing line, and so fighting and manoeuvring was kept up until four o'clock in the afternoon when all the reserves were ordered to the firing line for a final rush to be made as we all thought to drive the panic-stricken army of General Grant into Tennessee River. We formed the line, and awaited the order to move forward.

In the meantime, the enemy immediately on our front left their line in some haste and disappeared from view over the crest of the hill near the river. While we waited with much impatience for orders to move there came an order from General Beauregard telling that the battle was ended for the day and we had captured General Prentiss with four thousand of his men and a great victory was ours. When the order was read instead of creating enthusiasm amongst the men it created indignation and disgust because it was apparent to all in the firing line that the hard-earned victory that had cost so much blood and so many lives was to be thrown away for the want of one more charge which as we thought then and think now would have resulted in a complete overthrow or capture of General Grant's army and the downfall of General Grant himself as a military leader.

But why was the Southern Army halted at this critical period? General Beauregard's excuse was it was late in the day, the men were tired and needed rest; but the truth as I saw it is the sun was still between three and four hours high and the men were anxious for this last charge to the river, which was not more than one-half mile away, I think. The men talked among themselves of the importance of the movement and their willingness to make it at the time and after events prove but too well the men were right and the commander wrong in issuing the order to halt.

I want to make a little digression from the main story to pay my respects to some erroneous history in regard to this crisis in that battle. Nelson's *Encyclopaedia* and the *History of the Mississippi Valley* by Prof. Johnson, Ph. D. and LL. D. of the Agricultural College of Minnesota, I think, both agree substantially in the statement that a hastily constructed battery on the hill near the river and the firing of the gunboats from the river stopped the Confederate's advance. (Possibly Mr. Blackburn has in mind Rossiter Johnson's *History of the War of Secession*, on his *Fight for the Republic*, in each of which a statement of the kind alluded to is made. The name he gives is evidently incorrect.—C. W. R.)

While I am still upon the earth I want to testify as eye-witness at close range, that the aforesaid battery and the gunboat's shelling had no more to do with stopping the forward movement that day than the flowing of the ocean tides or the changes of the moon had to do with it, for nearly an hour had passed since we halted before the battery was placed and before the gunboats fired the first shot and the men had scattered from their commands looking for something to eat. So, I enter my protest here and now against the careless and unauthorised way these two authors record history.

But to return to my story. There was a man, Charles Howard by name, strong physically and mentally, brave as Julius Caesar and well educated, but with the way and manners of a frontiersman, with many peculiarities. He had belonged to Company P but got a transfer to Company C for some reason I don't recall. He had gotten a nice laundered white shirt from the sutler's store the night of the 6th of April. Next morning, the 7th, as the regiment was formed to move, someone reproved Howard for tucking his shirt back at the neck, exposing his breast which was one of his habits, telling him it was a shame to treat a nice shirt in that way. His reply was, "If I get shot in the breast today, I don't want the bullet to injure my biled shirt."

Pretty soon we were ordered to move out towards the enemy and ascertain their position, their probable number, etc., and report back to the commanding general. Our movement, which was only intended for a reconnaissance, drew the fire of the enemy's pickets, for advance in their forward movement had already begun, and one ball struck Howard in the breast a little below the collar bone, going through him and lodging in the muscles or shoulder blade in the back part of his shoulder, not touching his laundered shirt.

A little later while we stood in column still headed towards the enemy Howard came riding along the column singing "Blue-eyed Mary," a favourite song of his. As he neared me, I said, "Which way,

Charles, with your 'Blue-eyed Mary' this morning?"

He replied, "To Texas, don't you see my furlough?" pointing to the wound in his breast. He rode horseback to Corinth that day, about fifteen miles, applied for and obtained a furlough soon after, went to Texas and about five months later reported back to his company for duty again, sound as a dollar.

Our next move was to the rear a short distance to dismount and join in with a Louisiana brigade of infantry to make a charge on the enemy. Our movement was down a gentle slope to the bottom of a hill. The enemy came down the slope on the other side towards us. The whole face of the earth at that place and time appeared to be blue and their many lines of battle firing over each other's head made a storm of lead that no single line of battle could resist and so after a short time the line was so weakened by losses as to compel the retirement of the remainder. But I want to relate an incident of the battle that impressed me as being out of the ordinary.

John P. Humphries, a member of Company F, a brave good soldier carried the largest shotgun I ever saw and always loaded it with about 20 buckshot to each barrel. He had a most peculiar laugh, unlike any laugh I ever heard. As we made that charge that morning there was a small oak tree near the bottom of the hill where the line made a stand. It was right in my front so I got behind the tree thinking it might save my hide somewhat. I had scarcely reached it before Humphries came up behind me. He saw the tree was too small for two to stand behind in safety, so he moved a few steps to the left and got behind another tree about the same size.

A little while after I heard Humphries laugh and looked towards him to see what had happened. A minie ball had pierced his hat close to his scalp and knocked it from his head. He grabbed it up, pulled it down hard on his head with both hands and laughed his peculiar laugh again. It occurred to me, and I mentally said, "If you can laugh at that, you will laugh at death when he comes." This repulse was the first experienced in the Battle of Shiloh. After this the battle raged pretty well all day over lines resisting with great stubbornness; but by night the enemy occupied their foremost encampments, and our army retreated that night carrying all the army supplies with them as far as was possible to do.

Next day, April 8th, the cavalry were employed in patrolling the space now behind the army and as rear guard we protected as best we could the retreat of our army to Corinth from any possible attack that might be made by the enemy's cavalry or any other arm of service that might pursue it. About four o'clock in the afternoon the enemy's infantry in force kept moving up towards us until we realised, we would have to check them by some means to keep them from overtaking the rear of our army.

A short distance ahead of us Major Harrison, now commanding the regiment, sent me to General Breckenridge's headquarters who was commanding the rear of the retreating army to tell him of the near approach of a large body of the enemy and to ask him for aid or orders. General Breckenridge's reply was, "Give Major Harrison my compliments and tell him to hold the enemy back awhile for I can't move from here yet." I rode back, delivered the message, and found the enemy had approached to within 250 or 300 yards of our position; had formed two lines of battle and had thrown out skirmishers who were making it lively for our boys who were then standing in line on horseback.

At this juncture Colonel Forrest came up to us with about an equal number of horsemen to our own, placed them on the right of our line, and being senior officer took charge of the whole line, about two hundred or more in all. He immediately decided to charge so Major Harrison rode up in front of our line, telling us to prepare for the charge, and added, "Boys, go in twenty steps of the Yankees before you turn your shotguns loose on them."

Forrest ordered forward. Without waiting to be formal in the matter, the Texans went like a cyclone, not waiting for Forrest to give his other orders to trot, gallop, charge, as he had drilled his men. By the time the Yankee skirmishers could run to their places in ranks and both lines got their bayonets ready to lift us fellows off our horses, we were halted in twenty steps of their two lines of savage bayonets, their front line kneeling with butts of guns on the ground, the bayonets standing out at right angle or straighter and the rear lines with their bayonets extended between the heads of the men of the first line.

In a twinkling of an eye almost, both barrels of every shotgun in our line loaded with fifteen to twenty buckshot in each barrel was turned into that blue line and lo! what destruction and confusion followed. It reminded me then of a large covey of quail bunched on the ground, shot into with a load of bird shot: their squirming and fluttering around on the ground would fairly represent that scene in that blue line of soldiers on that occasion. Every man nearly who was not hurt or killed broke to the rear, most of them leaving their guns where the line went down, and made a fine record in getting back to their reserve force several hundred yards in their rear.

After the shotguns were fired, the guns were slung on the horns of our saddles and with our six shooters in hand we pursued those fleeing, either capturing or killing until they reached their reserved force. Just before they reached this force, we quietly withdrew; every man seemed to act upon his own judgment for I heard no orders. But we were all generals and colonels enough to know that when the fleeing enemy should uncover us so their line could fire on us, we would have been swept from the face of the earth.

Some observations might be appropriately made at this time concerning the engagement. (The official report by Major Harrison is in *Official Records*, Series I, Vol. X, Part I, p. 923.) It was the last fight of the Battle of Shiloh. The enemy turned back from there and we had that section to ourselves. Forrest and his command never fired a gun in that battle for the reason that his military manoeuvres as then practiced did not allow his men to get there until the fight was over. Notwithstanding this fact a Memphis paper a day or two afterwards gave out the statement that Colonel Forrest with a few Texans on April the 8th had charged the enemy in force and completely vanquished them.

After Forrest gave the order to forward, we never saw him any more until we were brigaded over at Chattanooga and put under him for service. We were told that when we made that cyclone movement towards the enemy Colonel Forrest turned to his men to urge them forward faster and was struck in the back by one of the enemy's bullets fired at us as we went at them, and had to be taken off the field. (For a somewhat different version, see Wyeth, J. A., *Life of N. B. Forrest* or Jordan, Thos., *Campaigns of Forrest and Forrest's Cavalry*.—C. W. R.)

I have been asked by some persons inexperienced as to warfare why the Yankees did not shoot us all off our horses when halted so close in their front. Of course, they had no loads in guns to shoot us with and we knew it for as we approached them both lines of battle had fired at us and they had had no time to reload.

There was only one Texan wounded in that fight, Lieutenant Story of Company C, and there is a good reason for that; for the enemy fired when we were crossing a low place in the ground about fifteen yards away and most of their balls went over our heads. One of them struck and mortally wounded Lieutenant Story and one ball took a fur cap off my head leaving, as my comrades afterwards told me, a small powder marked line across my left temple. One or two more incidents of this battle and I will pass on.

In our pursuit of the flying enemy, as I rushed by a stump of a tree, ten feet high and two feet in diameter, looking at a Yankee running in my front a little distance I became suddenly aware of a bayonet near my body in the hands of a red faced Dutchman, and I could not tell whether he made a thrust at me and missed me or whether he intended to use it on me if I bothered him. I turned upon him, fully intending to kill him, but when I levelled my pistol at him, he dropped his bayonetted gun upon the ground and with the greatest terror depicted in his face, said, "I surrender."

In an instant I forgave him and let him live. I think surrender was the only English word he could speak, neither could he understand a word I said. I said, "Take that gun up and break it against the stump" and when I found he didn't know what to do and stood trembling I pointed to the gun and made signs to take hold of it and motions to strike. I got him to understand me, he broke the breech off and I motioned him to our rear and he went off at a lively gait.

I had a messmate by the name of Ed Kaylor, a good soldier, never showing any fear about him. In this battle he came upon a captain who had vainly tried to rally his men as they ran to the rear. When he found he could not get them to stop and help him he concluded he would sell out as best he could so he fired on Kaylor as he rode towards him. They exchanged three shots each; Kaylor slowly advancing upon him. When Kaylor closed in upon him he threw up his hands and offered to surrender, but Kaylor, in language not suitable for parlour topics of conversation said, "Oh H—ll you are too late" and fired another shot, killing him instantly.

An eye-witness to this pistol duel said Kaylor had a broad smile on his face during this gun play. When I heard of the incident, I said to Kaylor, "Ed, what did you see in that game that caused you to smile so sweetly at that Yankee?" He said he was not conscious of having smiled, but he surely did enjoy that scrap immensely. Poor Kaylor afterwards was killed in East Tennessee while serving under Longstreet, during the siege of Knoxville, as related by a Texan companion with him at the time, as follows: Kaylor and a companion having lost their horses (in battle or otherwise) were ordered to mount themselves again by taking horses wherever they could find them back in the mountains, for the most part of that section was disloyal to the Confederacy anyway.

As they searched the mountain section for horses, they heard that there was to be a dance given to the Yankee officers near where was one of their encampments, so they concluded to attend that dance, and mount themselves while the Yankees danced. But after reaching the place they concluded to go in the house, get the riders and take them and their horses both back with them, so they entered the room during the dancing with pistols in hands and demanded surrender of all the men who were in the room, all armed with pistols belted around them.

For a time, all seemed to go as they wished until someone cried out, "There are only two of these rebels." Then ensued a scuffle for their pistols already in Kaylor's hands and Kaylor began to shoot and several fell from his unerring aim, until someone regained his pistol, shot him and he fell dead among several he had already slain. His companion escaped and lived to tell of his taking off as here related.

But to return to the main story, the Battle of Shiloh was finished. The losses were enormous as already related. Of the sixty-five men and two officers that answered roll call on the morning of the 6th of April of Company F, only fourteen men and the captain answered roll call on the morning of the 8th of April and I was acting orderly sergeant. Now this should not be construed to mean that the other fifty men had been killed or wounded, but it does mean that those not killed or wounded were absent from roll call, most of them off on some kind of duty, such as picketing, scouting, helping the retreating army in whatever way duty assigned them.

The Confederate Army collected at Corinth, and the Federal Army at Pittsburg Landing, each army where it had encamped before the battle, and each one to plan its future operations was left unmolested for a time. Our regiment was ordered back to Tennessee going through lower middle Tennessee on to Chattanooga. We camped one or two nights at Rienzi, Mississippi, on our way. Awaiting final instructions as to our future movements, news came to us that General Price had reached Corinth with his army of Missourians and Texans.

As I had a brother with this command in Whitfield's Legion of Texans, I decided to make him a visit before we left Mississippi. It was about twenty miles I think back to Corinth, so getting some papers fixed up by my comrades as a pass to keep me from being arrested as a deserter, I went back to Corinth as my command went eastward on their journey towards Tennessee. My papers were not genuine.

I found my brother sick from exposure during the winter campaign under Price in Missouri. I stayed with him all night and next morning moved out early to overtake my command which was by this time twenty miles and two days journey ahead of me. I rode all day and a part of the night to overtake them. They had captured a small scouting party of Yankees the night or day before I reached them.

Next morning a detail was called for from Company F to take the prisoners, back to Corinth, and I was called on to be one of the guards; so back to Corinth I journeyed again, and after delivering the prisoners to General Beauregard's headquarters the following night, and resting a few hours, set out to overtake the command which was moving eastward. After about two days more I was again with the command. But now my faithful steed which I had ridden constantly since the middle of December the year before gave out entirely, worn out by constant usage and had to be left on the wayside, and I had to join the wagon train and to be snubbed as a "wagon dog" by my comrades, a common appellation given to everyone who went with the wagons, regardless of the conditions making it necessary for him to be there.

The command went through middle Tennessee and had a fight or heavy skirmish with the Yankees at Sulphur Trestle in Giles County. I do not recall any results of that fight as reported to us except Captain Harris of Company I lost his life there. Arriving at Chattanooga a brigade was organised by putting Forrest's regiment, our regiment, and two Georgia regiments, three and four, I think, together, and Colonel Forrest took charge of it for service in middle Tennessee and wherever we might be needed.

At that time elections were held in different companies to select commissioned officers where there were vacancies caused by resignations or otherwise. Company F elected two lieutenants, 1st and 2nd, J. K. P. Blackburn 1st, and A. J. Murray 2nd. While we were entitled to commissions issued by the Secretary of War, we never applied for them and never received them. In fact, I don't remember of ever having seen a commission from the government for any officer in the command. The men of the different companies knew whom they had selected and, whether they held commissions or whether they wore insignia of office or not, they always felt that they must obey the men they had elected over them. Hardly a star or bar was to be seen in the command, except in dress parade when the colonel might show his rank on a dress coat that he kept for the purpose.

Our next encounter with the enemy was in Warren County, Tennessee, near Morrison's depot where the enemy had constructed a stockade and left about three companies of infantry to protect a railroad bridge across the river from destruction by the Confederates. The stockade was built of logs twelve or fifteen inches in diameter and twelve feet long, set on end in trenches two feet deep, close touching each other with portholes cut between the logs about as high as a man's head, to shoot through.

These logs were thoroughly tamped in place and a small door left in one side for passing in and out with a screen of like make just on the inside so one going in would pass in the door and turn to left or right to get inside of the stockade. I have been thus particular in describing this fort or stockade so the reader may more easily understand why we were so easily and completely defeated by this small contingent of defenders when we attacked that fort.

When within one-quarter or one-half mile of the place Colonel Forrest formed the brigade into single line, ordered us to dismount and then rode in front of each regiment giving instructions about the charge he intended to make. When in front of our regiment he said, "I don't want but one-half of this command for this engagement"—that his scouts reported that only three or four companies were up there and that they had their dinner already cooked, and he wanted us to kill them and then eat their dinner.

Company F had thirty men in line, so the first fifteen were ordered to step two paces to the front, and the captain told me to take charge of them, so we manoeuvred for some time to get a suitable place to charge from, but could not get nearer than two hundred or two hundred and fifty yards without being exposed to full view of the enemy from the start to the finish, so we were ordered to charge at least two hundred yards through an open field upon that fort. Of course, the enemy were inside and had nothing to do but shoot us down from the start.

After approaching near enough for some of our men to make telling shots at those portholes we were driven back in much disorder to the timber, back of the field from whence we started. Our loss was estimated at 180 killed and wounded. Company F's loss was one killed and five wounded. The enemy's loss was 20 killed whom we shot in the head through those portholes. James Petty of my company was killed within ten feet of the door of that stockade. These details of the enemy's dead and the place where Petty fell we have learned from our surgeon who was left to care for the wounded at that place.

Our next move was to capture about 2,000 soldiers commanded by General Crittenden at Murfreesboro, Tennessee. We started from the neighbourhood of McMinnville, Tennessee, one evening in the summer—I don't remember the date (July 12, 1862. The fight was on Sunday, July 13.—C. W. R.)—rode until about eight o'clock, stopped, watered and fed our horses, mounted again and rode until nearly daylight to reach our destination.

Before we reached the town, we captured the videttes on the pike upon which we were moving; also captured General Crittenden in his bed at his headquarters, a nice dwelling in the town, and learned from the citizens that the enemy had an encampment of eight hundred or one thousand infantry soldiers in the suburbs of the town, about the same number and artillery out on Stone River a mile away, and a strong guard over about 150 political or citizen prisoners at the court house.

Colonel Forrest divided his command into three divisions, sending one to attack the court house, one to attack the enemy on Stone River, each division led by a few rangers, and the balance of the rangers to attack the encampment in the edge of Tennessee. The first two bodies mentioned did little except to draw the fire of the enemy and to warn them to be ready for us in later attacks. The rangers went into the encampment with a yell and attacked the enemy as they came out of the tents in their night clothes and after a lively skirmish in which many of them fell, our Colonel Wharton was wounded and ordered the regiment to withdraw.

Afterwards Colonel Forrest collected all of our regiment behind a block of buildings near the encampment, sent in a flag of truce demanding unconditional surrender of the encampment within thirty minutes and added, "If you refuse, I will charge you with the Texas Rangers under the black flag."

After a little delay they agreed to surrender and immediately Colonel Forrest sent flags of truce to other places where the troops were with .the same demand and same threat and added, "I have your general and all the balance of his command as prisoners in my hands." In a little while the whole of General Crittenden's army were our prisoners with all their artillery, wagons, teams and army and soldiers' supplies and about 2,000 soldiers. Forrest had played a bold game of bluff and it had succeeded where we could scarcely hope to conquer by force of arms; for our number was about half, and half of that number were fresh troops who had never been under fire of battle before.

An incident occurred as we made the charge along the streets in the twilight of that morning which was both inspiring and impressive.

The ladies in their night robes came out on the pavement and cheered with their shouts and their "God bless you," even when the enemy's bullets were flying about them.

All army stores and artillery, small arms and ammunition were put under guard to take them back to McMinnville, about forty or fifty miles (I cannot remember exactly). The troops were collected and a guard of two companies and a commissioned officer were called for to take charge of them and march them back to McMinnville. Companies F and D of our regiment were detailed for this purpose and I was ordered to take charge of them and see to it that they were delivered to the place of rendezvous.

I formed a column of prisoners, eight abreast and closed them up so as to allow only walking room between them, and put some guards in front on horseback, some in the rear, and the balance on each side; thus, enclosing prisoners in hollow square and gave command to move forward. I gave instructions to the guards so the prisoners could hear, "If any man makes a break from that column, shoot him down without halting him." This was near sundown and we moved without difficulty but slowly on account of the long distance the prisoners had to walk; rushing them would have resulted in breaking them down.

My guards had had no sleep now for about forty hours nor rest either, so I soon found they were asleep on their horses, and fearing the enemy might discover it and make their escape I had to use heroic methods to meet the emergency. So, I rode around that moving column all night punching or pinching the guards to keep them awake. They would generally respond by "All right" or some sign as I waked them, but as soon as I passed, they would fall asleep again so my march around that column continued on and on.

Just before daylight, I received order from Colonel Forrest to park my charge in a grass lot, put out videttes and let them rest an hour or so. So, I readily obeyed instructions. By the time that I had placed the guards, the prisoners had all fallen on the ground and were asleep. My guards also fell asleep and I after strenuous efforts to keep up and look after the business in my hands, fell asleep also, my horse remaining by me. When daylight came, I was the first to stir. I awaked the guards and then the prisoners, adopted the same formation I had before. We were soon on the march again with still about fifteen miles to travel.

We reached Forrest's headquarters about nine o'clock, turned over the prisoners to him, and asked him for the camp of the regiment. I dismissed the guard, went to camp, and found our captain and a few men with him. I dismounted, leaving my horse with the saddle and personal baggage on him for someone else to look after and fell down on the bare ground and slept until after sundown that evening without having had water or anything to eat for about twenty-four hours. The last I had was from the sutler's store the evening before. When I got up, I found my horse dead only a few steps from where I left him. He had died from exhaustion. The two days and two nights constant going on the light feed he got were too much for him and he perished in the service of his country, so to speak.

I can think of nothing of much interest occurring to any portion of our regiment until General Bragg with the Army of Tennessee made a raid into Kentucky in September, 1862, I think. The cavalry of course was to be the vanguard on this trip in order to clear up the way, and keep the commanding general posted as to what was before him on his line of march.

Our first engagement was with McCook's corps near the Kentucky-Tennessee line when our regiment was ordered to feel of the enemy in that section to ascertain its strength and size of force. This resulted in several casualties to our men and in finding it was McCook's corps marching north to be ready for General Bragg when he should get there. S. G. Clark of our company was one of the killed here. I kept a diary of the trip through Kentucky on this raid and while I lost it soon after the raid was over, I remember some of the entries made.

One was that from the day we entered Kentucky until the day we passed out of the state, thirty-eight days, our regiment in part or as a whole had been under the fire of the enemy's guns forty-two times, including Perryville Battle as one of the times. Fighting and skirmishing occurred every day and some days more than once. (The report of Gen. Jos. Wheeler of the cavalry operations in Kentucky is found in *Official Records*, Series I, Vol. XVI, part 1, pp. 893-900. Wharton's report is not found.—C. W. R.) Except at Perryville our losses were generally light, but coming so frequently they amounted to many in the aggregate.

Before I leave Perryville in my narrative, I shall relate incidents on that field not to be easily forgotten. My bedfellow during the trip was D. A. McGenagil. At Perryville, a piece of shell bursting in our line of battle struck him in the side, breaking two of his ribs. He was sent off to the hospital for repairs so I was without a bedfellow that night, and as the nights were frosty, I looked out for some other person to get the benefit of his blanket for a covering while mine should be spread on the ground for the pallet. We only had one blanket each, hence the necessity of having a partner.

The battle had continued to rage until eight o'clock at night or thereabouts, the Confederates driving back their antagonists steadily until the firing ceased. Our regiment was required to go on picket along the space where the last fighting was done. It was in a cornfield near a little branch. The Federals had withdrawn but a short distance without noise, and without fires had retired after putting out their pickets on the side next to us. We were instructed to go to the place to be picketed with great caution and keep silent. We found the place we stopped on and had to stay that night on ground covered with flint rocks from the size of a man's fist to the size of his head and many dead of both armies lying around.

The wounded had been removed, or most of them. I looked around or searched around among my company; we only had a poor star light, as it was mostly cloudy. I found Sam Woodward of my company with a good blanket and no bedfellow for the night, and we soon arranged to bunk together. I said, "Sam, you look for a place as smooth as you can find, as clear of the flint rock as possible, and let me know and we will fix for bed."

In fifteen or twenty minutes he came to me and said, "I have found a fairly good place, but there are two dead men on it."

I said, "They are as dead as they will ever be, are they not?"

He said; "Yes," and I said, "Then we will remove them a little space and occupy their place."

He said, "All right," and we went to the spot selected and turned one man over one way and the other the other way (they were lying parallel with each other), made our bed between them and slept sweetly until daylight next morning; and behold one of the dead was a Confederate and other one a Federal soldier. Both had fallen on the same spot and died near each other.

Some of our boys, nearly barefooted, were searching around among the dead for footwear, all in the darkness. They had to judge of what they were getting by the way it felt. Mullins of Company D found a good pair of boots on Wheeler, I think, another ranger who was asleep among the dead. He immediately decided the boots would suit, grabbed one of them, and jerked it off Wheeler's foot. This aroused Wheeler to consciousness and he called out, "What in the h—ll are you doing there?"

"Nothing, d—n you, I thought you were dead and I needed those boots."

John P. Humphries, of whom I have spoken before, needed footwear and went out after daylight to see what were the chances. He found a Yankee, dead, sitting against a tree, with a good pair of shoes. John got down on his knees to take off the fellow's shoes and, just as he got one unlaced and ready to pull off, took another glance at the Yankee's face and the Yankee winked at him. He left the shoes on his dead man and came to camp and told it, and laughing that peculiar laugh, said he didn't want any shoes anyway.

Next morning our army moved to Harrodsburg, Kentucky, and the other army stayed near where they had camped before, not seeming to want to follow us, except at a considerable distance from us.

One other incident of the Perryville Battle I will mention. There were two young men, about eighteen and twenty years old, brothers, named George and Simeon Bruce who came to Texas to live, from Vermont, about eight months before the commencement of hostilities. They had no relatives or interests in Texas, but when the war came up, they volunteered in our regiment, saying the South was right in its contentions, and they freely offered their lives in its defence. At Perryville Simeon Bruce was shot through the calf of his leg with a grapeshot and George was left with him to care for him. They communicated with homefolks in Vermont and told of their whereabouts and conditions.

An answer soon came back with money for every need and urging their return home. They were informed, also, that one of their brothers was a colonel in the Federal army and another one a surgeon in the same army. The family where they were staying also urged them to go home when they learned the facts concerning them. The boys didn't entirely consent to return, but said they would give it favourable consideration, not fully committing themselves to any certain course, but rather left the impression when Sim recovered, they might go home.

Sim after a long time got so he could ride horseback without much discomfort and then the boys bought horses with the money sent them and hastened South to their command and remained with it, making splendid soldiers until the war ended and returned to Texas and are there or in Oklahoma yet, or were when I last heard from them. When they returned to us, I said, "I love my country and have offered my life in her defence, but I believe you Bruce boys are truer patriots than I am." As to the losses in this battle, I cannot recall. It was quite sanguinary and losses were heavy on both sides.

After the Battle of Perryville, the Confederate Army moved towards Cumberland Gap in eastern Kentucky. The Federal Army followed at a safe distance; our cavalry was rearguard to the Confederates. Skirmishes light and heavy with the enemy's advancing column was our daily pastime, sometimes twice or three times a day. Rations became scarcer day by day as we traversed the poor mountainous regions of eastern Kentucky. The people in there were generally poor with small patches in cultivation and few live stock, and all they had to live on had been consumed by the infantry which preceded us; so, it must be clear to the reader that the cavalry suffered for want of food supplies.

They were kept too busy to make excursions off the line of march to get food so they fasted and fought for days without anything worth mentioning. I saw men trimming beef bones left by the infantry, where they had killed the beeves and issued the meat to the men, thus getting a little of the stringy leaders off of them. Then they would break them and get the marrow inside. I saw a number of men, of whom I was one, pick out the scattered grains of corn tramped in the ground by some infantry officer's horse where he had been fed a day or two ahead of us, and eat them with a relish, thus proving the adage that hunger is a good appetizer.

One day we were fighting a large force of the enemy's infantry and our colonel thinking we would not be able to check them sent to our infantry for help. A brigade of our men came back to our assistance, and General B. F. Cheatham came with them, but they reached us after we had driven the enemy back and didn't need their help. General Cheatham had eight or ten ears of corn tied on his saddle behind him to feed his horse. A hungry Texan spied him and said, "Old man (addressing Cheatham), I will give you a dollar apiece for those ears of corn."

The general with a haughty, dignified look said, "Do you know whom you are talking to?"

The soldier said "No, and I don't care a damn, but I will do what I said I would about that corn."

The general smiled, untied his corn, and threw it to the hungry men who scuffled over it as very hungry hogs would have done.

In a few more days we passed out of Kentucky through Cumberland Gap, moved on to Knoxville, Tennessee, and camped a few days to rest. The first night we were at Knoxville it snowed all night and next morning the ground and the army was covered with a three inch snow. We had no tents or covering of any kind, but our sleep was sound and restful. The leaves were still green on the trees and the contrast in colours between the leaves and the snow was quite impressive, and very unusual. This was in October, 1862, if my memory serves me correctly.

From Knoxville the army moved to middle Tennessee. Our regiment was camped at Nolensville, about fifteen or twenty miles south of Nashville. Our duty was to watch the movements of the Yankee Army now assembling at Nashville and to keep our general posted about them. We remained at this point until Christmas Day. Some of the boys were preparing to have an eggnog for Christmas when suddenly our pickets were driven in and reported a large force of infantry and artillery moving upon us. The regiment was mounted at once to meet this advance. As soon as we come in full view of the enemy they opened fire with artillery, four guns throwing what seemed to be about six-pound shells. I was in command of Company F that day, the captain being on the sick list but still in camp.

As we moved in columns of twos in front of the enemy their shells got our range pretty quickly. One shell burst in rear of my company doing slight damage, another one entered the body of a horse near my horse's head, bursting inside the horse and knocked my horse to his knees and covering him and me with blood and flesh from the other horse. Strange to say the trooper riding this torn up horse escaped without the slightest injury. His name was Glasscow of Company C; he was riding in the rear of his company in front of me. A few steps further another shell passed between my horse's head and the rear of another horse ridden by Lieutenant Black, cutting down a cedar tree as large as a man's leg, just on the left of us.

We moved further to the left out of range of this artillery, dismounted, formed a line and moved out towards, or to the left of this battery somewhat; but before we made the attack a flanking command was discovered moving to our rear on the right and we returned to our horses and rode over to the right of the first alignment to meet this flank movement and while engaging these with a furious fire another force equally strong was approaching from the front and we had to retire for a new alignment.

Colonel Harrison, passing by me as we had begun to retire before the enemy, said, "Form your company on this rise and hold the position while I form the regiment behind you in supporting distance." I called on my men to fall into line, but they had turned towards the rear and the heavy firing of the enemy from two points made it almost impossible for men or horses to get their consent to face the other way and stand still; so, I urged and I ordered with all the vehemence I possessed, sometimes getting as many as two or three to face about and make a temporary halt and then move on.

Finally, Gabe Beaumont of Company A, who had fallen behind his company in the different movements, seeing my trouble said to me "Lieutenant, I will stand; form your company on me." He took his stand, I rushed my men in line with him, and having got my men in line was riding up and down the line encouraging all I could to stay there. The enemy's bullets were flying uncomfortably thick. I heard a ball strike when near Beaumont and saw his gun fall, but he stood perfectly still until I approached him.

I asked Gabe, "Are you badly hurt?"

He said, "I think I am."

I said, "I will excuse you now. You can retire and my men will stay here without you." So, I sent him off with a man to help him if he needed help. This ball shivered his left arm just below the shoulder joint and had to be taken off at the shoulder to save his life. He was shot out of service, but he demonstrated to his comrades in arms what true bravery could accomplish. I met this brave hero many years after in Coleman, Texas. He had studied medicine after the war and made a success in that profession. A while after Beaumont was sent to the rear, the colonel sent me word to withdraw my company and fall back to my position. This ended the fighting for the day, and that night, after viewing the enemy's encampments with Company F, trying as best I could to make an estimate of their numbers and reporting the same to the colonel, we rested.

The regiment moved to Murfreesboro where two armies were rapidly gathering for one of the great battles of the Civil War. Just whether we moved that night, or fell back gradually as the enemy advanced to Murfreesboro I cannot now recall, but on the first day of January, 1863, brigade skirmish line was formed from our brigade and I was ordered to take charge of this line. The men were placed in line ten feet apart on foot in one side of an old field grown up in long weeds about as high as a man's head. The enemy were in the other side of the same field. Our skirmishers were armed with rifles or muskets for the occasion.

I was told to keep the men to their places so there would be no weak spot and no bunching of our men on the line, to keep them firing continually, etc., etc. As I rode along that long line of men—I was the only man on horseback in that line—I saw that Bill Simpson of Company F was about two feet, or three feet at the most, from a high poplar stump in line with the men, so I said, "Bill, take the stump. There it is but a little ways from your place and it may save your life or your limbs."

He looked up at me and said, "I thank you, I am doing very well here," and refused to use it. These two lines of skirmishers were in what was afterward known as the left flank of our army during the battle and as far as I am able to tell now this was the beginning of that great battle.

We were relieved after a while by some infantry and we remounted our horses to meet some Yankee cavalry that came in on our left. We charged them, drove them, and scattered them. As we returned from pursuing them my horse slipped and fell, throwing me on the horn of my saddle and producing a case of nearly strangulated hernia from a slight rupture I had had before. This fall laid me up for several days and took me off the battlefield until the battle ended and longer. Whatever else I relate of this battle or as to what happened in or to the regiment must be from hearsay and not from personal observation. The regiment was engaged all the time, sometimes in the flank, sometimes in the rear of the enemy; sometimes fighting infantry, sometimes cavalry; capturing many of the enemy and destroying much of his supplies.

One or two incidents I wish to relate happened during that conflict. A Yankee general fell into the hands of the Rangers. They asked him his name and rank.

He said, "General Willich."

"The same who commanded the 32nd Indiana Infantry as Colonel?" he was asked.

"Yes, the same, and who are you," demanded the general.

"Terry Texas Rangers" was the reply.

"*Mein Gott*," said General Willich, "I had rather be a private in that regiment than to be a Brigadier General in the Federal Army."

Willich had met the boys at Woodsonville, Ky., as Colonel of the 32nd Indiana regiment and had met them at Murfreesboro as Brigadier General and had lost out both times and was qualified to judge of their military prowess. General Willich was Dutch or German, with a foreign accent.

Colonel Harrison by this time had so long escaped personal injury from shot and shell, his men dubbed him "Old Iron Sides," because as they said he was sheathed with iron and no bullet could penetrate his body. On the second day of this battle, Billy Savers, his adjutant, sat on his horse beside him under a heavy fire. Colonel Harrison leaned over to Sayers and whispered, "I am wounded, but don't say anything about it on account of the men."

Billy wanted him off the field, but he refused to go. It proved to be a flesh wound in the hip, not very serious, and he stayed with and commanded the regiment throughout the battle. On another occasion the colonel, while standing in front of his line ready to make or receive a charge as it might happen, was looking through his field glass at a body of cavalry some distance off.

Suddenly he exclaimed, "Now boys, we will have some fun. There is a regiment out there preparing to charge us, armed with sabres. Let them come up nearly close enough to strike and then feed them on buckshot."

So, they came up with great noise and pretence, hoping to demoralise and scatter their opponents and then have a race in which they could use their sabres effectively. But as the Texans stood their ground the Yankees ran up to within a few steps and halted suddenly, giving our boys the chance they were wishing for. One volley from the shotguns into their ranks scattered these sabre men into useless fragments of a force. Many of them surrendered and our boys quizzed them with merciless questions. "Why did you stop?" "Are your sabres long ranged weapons?" "How far can you kill a man with those things?" After a conflict lasting two days with varying success and defeat for both armies, the Southern Army withdrew to the south, leaving the other army with fresh reinforcements encamped not far from the last lines of battle the evening before.

The weather had turned fearfully cold and the earth would freeze very hard at night. About the first night after we left Murfreesboro Jim Stevenson, coming off of duty late, came to the log heap fire of my mess, and asked permission to sleep near our fire. Jim was a shiftless boy whose dress was weather worn and untidy, his body generally dirty and infected with what the boys called "graybacks." So, no one would sleep with him and he didn't expect any one to divide bedding with him. We granted his request and he made his pallet down a little space from the rest of us and went to sleep.

Next morning, he slept on after daylight. I went to see how he was faring and to awake him if still living. I caught his top blanket at his head and raised it up and as it was set and frozen it stood up on the other end like a dried raw hide would do with like handling. I said, "Get up my boy, don't try to sleep all day. How did you sleep?"

He replied, "Bully," that he had two blankets last night. He had an old thread bare blanket under him and a heavy army blanket he had captured from the enemy during the battle just fought. He had slept all night without moving, as evidenced by an unfrozen streak, just the shape of his body on that blanket where he had lain on his side; the rest of that blanket being frozen stiff as a board. Jim could suffer hardships without a murmur, and although he was shiftless and loved to play poker he could always be depended upon when there was any fighting to be done. He was a brave man and a good soldier.

The army remained at Shelbyville, Tennessee, for some time, then moved on south by way of Tullahoma to Chattanooga and encamped there. Our individual regiment acting as scouts and guards for the rear moved leisurely along atter our army, delaying the enemy's movements as far as they might attempt to follow.

After we passed Tullahoma, I don't remember seeing another blue coat until the Battle of Chickamauga, which took place in the following September, the 19th and 20th. Our line of march was along the Nashville, Chattanooga and St. Louis Railroad until we reached Chattanooga. and then we were allowed to move down to Rome, Georgia, where we had a much needed rest of two weeks which, with a few days at Woodburn, Kentucky, constituted our entire rest up to this time.

It may be well at this time to mention the fact that while up in Kentucky General Forrest was taken from us and returned to Tennessee to raise a new command of cavalry. He took with him his old regiment and from that time up to the Battle of Chickamauga our regiment again acted as an independent command.

After our resting spell we were ordered to rejoin the army. Rosecrans with a large force had compelled General Bragg to retire towards Chickamauga a few miles south of Chattanooga. Here the two armies met in one of the bloodiest battles of the Civil War, continuing two days and resulting in a complete victory for the Confederates; but the victory was won at a fearful cost. General Forrest had by this time raised a new command and during this battle he and his men won immortal fame by fighting the enemy on foot and driving them, capturing their artillery and proving to all who were disposed to doubt the effectiveness of cavalry in warfare that they could vie with the infantry in infantry service when called upon. Someone speaking of

Forrest's success at Chickamauga said he had glorified the cavalry by showing they could win victories against great odds, on foot as well as on horseback.

Our regiment was engaged only twice during the battle and that was when Federal cavalry tried to attack our army from the rear. In one of these attacks, we met and defeated the Fourth Ohio Cavalry, mortally wounding their colonel and driving them off, leaving their dead and wounded on the field. We passed back over the field, and the colonel still living and gasping for breath was sitting with his back against a tree. Some of our boys approached him and said to him, "Well, Colonel, as you will not need your hat or boots any longer, we beg the privilege of exchanging with you," and as the colonel could not reply, the boys concluded that silence gives consent, and proceeded to make the exchange.

For the balance of the time our duties kept us policing and guarding during that battle rather than fighting. The Federal Army returned to Chattanooga and our army took position near there on Missionary Ridge and Lookout Mountain, where other battles occurred later on. Our regiment moved up on the Tennessee River, where we picketed on the river. On the opposite side at the time was the Fourth Ohio Cavalry also on picket duty. The pickets talked to each other across the stream and found out they were somewhat acquainted from personal contact at Chickamauga and some other point which I cannot recall; also feeling there should be no animosity existing between men who had faced each other in battle, they arranged for a truce, a suspension of hostilities until they could have a swim, a few yarns, swap tobacco for coffee, exchange newspapers and have a good time generally.

A Yank said to Johnnie Reb—these were the endearing names we were accustomed to give each other, "Where is Old Ironsides (our colonel) today?"

"At camp," says Johnnie Reb, "Where is Colonel So-and-so?" (Calling by name the colonel of the Fourth Ohio)

"Oh, the devil, you know where we left him over at Chickamauga," was the answer.

These truces were common in all parts of the army when it could be arranged without a commissioned officer being present. They could not afford to participate because of position and commission. I believed then, and I still believe now, if the terms of peace had been left to men who faced each other in battle day after day, they would have stopped the war at once on terms acceptable to both sides (except the civil rulers) and honourable to all alike. These men that always bore the brunt of battle never had and never will have any bad feelings towards each other.

Sometime in October news reached us that one hundred wagons, loaded with provisions for Rosecrans army had started from Nashville to Chattanooga to feed his army. Provisions had become very scarce, and the railroad was torn up so they could get nothing over it. Hence it was necessary for them to use wagons to transport their supplies. A brigade of cavalry was organised at once consisting of the 8th Texas, which was our regiment, the 11th Texas, 3rd Arkansas, and 4th Tennessee regiments and placed under command of, General Joe Wheeler. General Forrest was ordered to turn over his command to General Wheeler. This order aroused the wrath of Forrest, who contended that he should be in chief command.

General Wheeler started on a raid through middle Tennessee to capture and destroy that wagon train and to do the enemy any damage he could otherwise. We met the wagon train in Sequachie Valley, all loaded heavily, with four good mules to each wagon.

We burned the train, while the guards with the train deserted it for safety in the mountains close by. We killed most of the mules, amounting to hundreds, only saving a few to take the places of some worn-out horses in our commands and other needs we might have on the trip, such as substitutes for ambulance work and for artillery service when it became necessary to make such changes. This destruction of the train was a great waste of food and other army supplies, but we felt it was but just punishment for the invaders and destroyers of our country. We moved into middle Tennessee.

By the time we reached Warren County, General Mitchell (author of *Mitchell's Geography*) had gathered an army mounted infantry and was in pursuit of us. Once upon the mountains, Colonel Harrison had to form a line of battle and show fight to protect our rear guard who had been run into by Federals. We stood in line· some time for them to come in sight so we could charge them, but instead of coming on they stayed back in some bushes and ran up a battery of their guns and began to shell us pretty heavily. I was in command of Company F and while sitting on my horse in front of my company I noticed most of the shells were coming or seeming to come over my company and the shots were getting lower every time.

I looked for a reason and found that four of the men were riding white horses and had accidentally gotten bunched together in the line, this affording a fine target for the enemy's guns, so I ordered one, of these men to go quickly and ask permission of Colonel Harrison for me to dismount my men. I had ordered him to go quickly and he galloped or ran his horse up to head or right of regiment (my company being in left of same). In less time than it takes to write this my man returned and said "Colonel Harrison says 'No. Keep your men on their horses.'"

I called at once, "Attention, Company F; dismount, lie down flat on the ground and hold your bridle reins in your hand."

Just as the order was obeyed, a shell struck one of these white horses in the breast, tearing off his shoulder and doubtless would have taken off the leg of the rider if he had been on him. I had thus disobeyed orders, which is always dangerous and is condemned by the authorities on military tactics, but I found consolation in the fact that I had saved the life that would have been uselessly sacrificed, as I looked at it. Soon an order came from General Wheeler for us to fall back. Our loss was only one man killed in Company C, and some horses. This man might have been saved if Company C had been dismounted as was Company F.

The enemy didn't trouble us much more after this until we reached Farmington, in Marshall County, Tennessee. We had passed through Shelbyville the previous day and as Northern merchants had come into that town with an abundance of all kinds of merchandise, groceries, including liquors, wares, etc., our men considered that those goods were contraband, since they belonged to army followers, and they helped themselves liberally to such things as they thought they needed; the officers only forbidding the taking of whiskey.

But most of the soldiers managed to get some in their canteens to take with them for future emergencies; so, the next day the rear guard, imbibing too freely, got on a spree and while they were having the time of their lives the Federal Mounted Infantry ran into them, captured and scattered the whole guard and closed upon the moving column of General Wheeler's army, so that he had to give battle at Farmington to protect himself.

General Wheeler unlimbered his artillery near the pike and commenced a rapid fire. The enemy replied in kind with several guns. While this artillery firing was going on a courier was sent for us who were four or five miles north of Farmington near Duck River. The order was to come to Farmington double quick, which meant a gallop all the way. The enemy had moved a regiment in a column of two or double ranks close order up to within 250 yards of General Wheeler's battery and parallel to the pike and they were armed with Spencer rifles as we learned later on. This movement was being made on foot, notwithstanding they were mounted men. Their horses had been left in the rear.

Company F was in front that day at the head of the column of regiment and I was commanding the company. As we approached General Wheeler, he gave an order· to our colonel who was riding by my side to "form fours, move up the pike until you draw fire of the enemy, then charge them."

There was a drizzle of rain, the smoke from the artillery was lowering, and the enemy were obscured from our view until we were probably 75 yards from them. The enemy on our approach had formed along parallel the pike on the west side of it and fired a volley from their whole line into our columns of four, aiming at the sound of our horses' feet, for we were still obscured from their view by the smoke, but that volley found victims all the way down the regiment, striking every horse excepting one at the head of the column and about a dozen men in Company F. When that volley was fired Colonel Harrison ordered me to lead the charge; and with a yell, answered by many still unhurt along column, I shouted as loud as I could, "Charge them, Rangers!"

Colonel Harrison dropped out to one side and as the other companies came rushing on, he would say to them, "Follow Blackburn."

The yell and the rattle and roar of the horses' feet on the pike was too much for the enemy's nerves and they broke back up the pike. A high cedar rail fence along the pike on the side they were on kept them from scattering out far that way, and so they ran back like frightened sheep until they seemed to be twenty or more deep when we reached them and still pressing back away from us. When I had gone along the side of this fleeing mass as far as anyone seemed to be following me, I turned into the fleeing column with my six-shooter with all of the energy and expedition I could.

As I passed a small elm tree not more than four inches in diameter I think, where a few men, four or five, had stopped for protection, one of them put his gun within a few inches of my left thigh and fired. I saw the gun just as it fired, but not in time to knock it down. The bullet passed through both of my thighs, cutting a branch artery and fracturing the bone in my right limb, and as the bone did not break the ball glanced and came out on top of my leg. The blood from the artery followed, spurting for a short time. I had fired three or four shots up to this time at close range that enabled me to reach the men crowding against me, but when I saw the flow of blood following that wound, I had no inclination to continue the performance, so I turned my horse to ride to the rear. As I turned, I found my sergeant, Ledbetter, at my side engaged in the same game I was leaving, but before my horse could get a start the sergeant's horse was killed and fell suddenly, falling against my horse, nearly knocking him down with his fall. I saw Ledbetter was fastened under his horse, his foot having been caught under him. I rode to the rear.

Just at this juncture another enemy regiment came up on the right side and fired a volley into our regiment, which began to retire slowly and in order. I rode on through the village and on to a little creek nearby, where I found four of my men whose horses had been killed by the first volley of the enemy as we had charged. They had retired there for safety after being dismounted so unceremoniously. When I reached them my horse began to stagger and seeing he was going to fall I asked my men to take me off him and by the time they had placed me on a blanket on the ground my steed fell dead with six bullets in his body, anyone of which would have proven fatal, so my men reported. Noble steed, he had been with me in many battles, but this was his last one and I will say it was also my last battle, for I was a prisoner of war on parole of honour for the balance of the time.

The battle of Farmington was now over and the enemy held the field, but attempted no pursuit. Other Confederate commands had been fighting there before we came into fray, but had yielded to the onslaught of superior numbers. I do not know the losses on either side, but I saw an account of the Battle of Farmington a few days afterwards in a Northern paper which reported Wheeler's losses at 300 killed and wounded and Mitchell's losses at 180 killed and wounded. I know that was an exaggerated report so far as our losses were concerned and rather think it was concerning Mitchell's losses.

A just criticism of the regiment of soldiers we charged that day might be penned here. Situated and formed a they were so that their entire fire could be concentrated on the pike, and armed as they were with repeating rifles, they missed an opportunity that rarely comes to a command in warfare to annihilate a whole regiment of their antagonists by standing their ground and firing their guns already loaded in hand: for fourteen volleys well aimed as the first one would have destroyed our command without a loss of one of their own men. But their cowardly feet took them away and lost to them this opportunity.

Three or four men left on field were taken in by citizens close by, of whom I now call to mind, Steve and Dick Jarmon, and George Chandler. Ledbetter made his escape from under his horse in a miraculous manner. He said afterwards that he tried his best to pull his foot from under the horse, but as he had a new cavalry boot on that foot and that tied with a stout leather string above his knee as was the custom, he decided that it couldn't be done; so, he continued to shoot at this new command approaching from the east side of turnpike with his pistol, thinking he could surrender to them after his pistol was emptied.

As the enemy drew nearer, they discovered he was a red headed man and ordered him in a most indecent way to surrender "a red headed ————." They continued to fire at him, seeing he was not obeying their orders, when one of their balls struck him between the second and third fingers of his left hand, going through his hand and arm up to the elbow and coming out there. He said the pain seemed to give him the strength of a giant and with another trial he brought out his foot, leaving his boot under the dead horse. He rose and broke to run. W. H. Harris, another member of Company F as he slowly retired to the rear turned his horse and galloped back and met him. Ledbetter sprang on the horse behind Harris, and rode away in a gallop, out of danger. In the meantime, the enemy beholding the daring feat quit firing and cheered Harris for his brave act which saved a wounded comrade.

After my horse's death I turned over my pistols, saddle, bridle, blanket, etc., and another horse I had back with the baggage wagon to Sam Street one of Company F and asked him to take care of them for me. I was placed on a blanket and carried by four comrades to the rear to get beyond reach of the bullets which were still falling around us from the enemy's guns. As we moved along bunched up that way the enemy would fire at us, for we made a good target for them. I could hear the balls striking the ground around us and begged my men to leave me there and save themselves. They refused and said if I could stand if they could, and took me on and out of reach of the enemy's fire (for they did not follow us up) and found an ambulance, put me in that and carried me on about six mile further to Lewisburg, Tennessee.

Here they left me in the house of Mr. McKnight, who with his wife lived alone, both of them well advanced in years, but both a good and kind as possible for most people to be. Our surgeon had made only a casual examination of me, had given me a dose of morphine and a glass of brandy when I was first taken off my horse, and then went on to the other wounded, without seeming to realise I was bleeding so profusely as to endanger my life. But when we reached Lewisburg, I was so exhausted from loss of blood that Dr. McClure, a local physician there who looked at me, told my attendants it was necessary to leave me there if they expected to save my life. So, I was left there so weakened that I could not raise my head from my pillow.

That night Wheeler's command moved on southward five or six miles and camped. Next day about nine o'clock General Mitchell's army came into Lewisburg and halted there for some hours and while there his surgeon busied himself looking up the wounded who had been able to get that far from the battlefield, of whom there were several. When he came in to see me, he examined me pretty closely and said "This right thigh has a fracture and must be taken off at the hip joint."

I uttered my protest with all the strength I could command and said, "No, it will not be taken off."

He replied, "It will kill you if left on."

I said, "Let it kill me."

He replied "If you are fool enough to risk it, it is all right with me."

I said "I am fool enough to risk it for when that leg goes to the grave, I am going with it."

He asked my rank, I think and left.

Pretty soon Mitchell's adjutant general came in. He said he came over to parole me by Mitchell's order. I said, "Read me the terms and conditions of parole."

He read, "Pledge your honour never to fight anymore against the United States forces until you are duly exchanged. You report to the nearest United States forces as soon as you are able to walk. Will you sign it and keep it?" he asked.

I said, "I will," so he handed me the paper and pen and I signed, lying flat on my back. Of all the wounded left there at Farmington I was the only one paroled that I heard of.

My men left at Farmington were kindly cared for by the citizens and were constantly watched and movements reported to Federal authorities by Union men who were to be found in many sections, now that the Union forces had possession of the State. These Union men sympathised generally with the Yankees, and wished them success. Before these men of Company F were supposed to be able to travel, they escaped south by the aid of some secret scouts who were operating in the State on behalf of Southern leaders. Steve Jarmon the worst wounded one was put on a lounge or pallet on a mule's back and tied on and transported in that way south to his company while the others rode horseback by his side to their destination.

Steve recovered sufficiently for light service and remained to the end, but never got well and died from the effects of his wound many years after the war closed, so his wife afterwards told me. I recall a few names of the killed and wounded outside of my company in the Battle of Farmington. John Martin Lane of Company A was killed. He had a sister living in Pulaski, Tennessee, who came for the body and buried it at Brick Church, the former burying ground of his family. A. G. Love of Company C, I think, was killed and buried there. Some of his kinsfolk living at Culleoka came for his body, exhumed it, and buried it at Culleoka, Tennessee. Lieutenant Hunter was killed there and buried there. I think he belonged to Company H. Major A. P. Christian was shot in the mouth and several jaw teeth knocked out, and the bullet came out under his right ear. Jones, of Company A, was shot in the head, but not fatally wounded. About fourteen soldiers killed there were buried in one grave by the citizens of the neighbourhood, and they erected a monument over them, or for them since the war. This battle was fought on October 7, 1863.

Dr. R. H. Bunting was chaplain of our regiment and besides preaching and praying for us, one part of his work was to look after the mails—to send them out, receive them, and distribute them properly to the right parties. He also wrote regularly to the *Houston Telegraph* a letter to be published in that paper for information for our friends at home. This paper was published at Houston, Texas, and had a wide circulation in the State. In speaking of the Battle of Farmington and its casualties in our regiment he wrote:

> And the noble Blackburn, fell at the head of the column, leading a charge upon the enemy.

He never mentioned—and did not at the time he wrote know—whether I lived or died. My mother saw that news in the paper as soon as it arrived and after sitting some time in silence and agony of spirit, she remarked to those present, "Well, if he had to fall, I am glad he fell at the head of the column, charging the enemy of his country." My sister who was present at the time told me of this remark, showing the patriotic resignation of our dear mother.

Let no one conclude that I or Company F was selected because of our fitness for the undertaking to lead and make this particular charge and to gain this honour, for many other companies in the regiment could have done equally well or better. It was a mere chance that we were at the front, as you will readily see when I explain to you that the companies on the march alternated in service at the front, taking the place in regular rotation one day at the front, next day in the rear, allowing next company to be front and so on until every company had taken its turn at the front. All scouts, messengers, and pickets were selected from front company each day, hence the necessity of changing and alternating regularly from day to day. This day of battle was Company F's day at the front, and as I was in command of the company this honour of leading the charge and bearing the brunt of the battle was thrust upon us.

My experiences as a prisoner of war were for the most part very agreeable and satisfactory during the time I remained in middle Tennessee, which was about one year. I was feasted by the neighbours in the town and good people from the country would send in town and take me out to the country for a week at a time as soon as I began to hobble around on my crutches. The young people insisted on my attending all the little gatherings they had, and as there were many nice young ladies on every side it was quite a pleasant existence for me.

After about four months' time when I knew I must soon face the ordeal required by one condition of my parole—to report to the United States forces as soon as I was able—I began to make preparations for it. First, I asked Esquire Reed, a strong Union man living in Lewisburg and a man of influence with the Yankees, and a Mr. Idol Henderson, living at Cornersville a few miles away, with like qualifications, if they would accompany me when I went to make my report to the Yankees at Nance's Mills, just south of Cornersville, about one mile distant from there. They both consented very readily to do so.

They had both been to see me and made my acquaintance and seemed to like me and sympathize with me, and I had an impression that they might be able to keep me out of prison for a while at least, because I knew that clause was intended to make me take the oath of allegiance to the United States Government or go to prison as soon as I could travel. So, I set the day before I could walk without crutches. Esquire Reed took me in his buggy and Mr. Henderson was to meet us at Major Evans's headquarters, who was in charge of Federal forces at that place. He was using Nance's Flouring Mills to supply the Federal Army at different points in the State with flour and had a battalion of men, maybe more, about him for protection. We found Major Evans to be quite a nice man and a gentleman of quiet and friendly disposition.

We went in his office, and I presented my parole to him and told him I had come in to comply with condition of parole, and while I was not yet able to walk without my crutches still, I was able to report. Major Evans in a most jovial and affable manner said, "Why certainly, now let me administer the oath of allegiance to the United States Government to you, and as this country is full of pretty girls and a good country to live in you can have the finest time a young man ever had anywhere."

I shook my head and said, "No, I cannot do that."

Then with a saddened expression of face at my refusal he said, "It becomes my duty to send you to prison."

Up to this time my companions had not spoken, and I did not know what their plans were, for I had not discussed any plan with them, only asked them to accompany me.

They said, or one of them said, "Major, we would like a private conference with you in the other room."

The office was a two roomed cottage with a stack chimney in the middle, with doors and shutters between rooms. For half an hour or more they consulted, leaving me alone with my thoughts. After a while they came in and Major Evans addressing me said, "Your friends seem to have much confidence in you."

I said, "I am thankful, gentlemen."

He continued, "They proposed if I would let you stay in the neighbourhood that they would go on your bond for $10,000 for your good behaviour, and I have concluded to accept their proposition."

I said, "Many thanks, gentlemen, to you all."

The major continuing said, "The terms are agreed on. Who will write out the bond? Can you?"

I said, "I never did write one and I had rather not undertake it."

He then asked my two friends and his adjutant too, I think. All asked to be excused and he said he didn't know how to do it himself, and seeming to be at a loss as to what he should do he turned to me and said, "If I release you on your parole without bond will you pledge your honour to behave yourself and abide by the other condition in said parole?"

I said, "I surely will."

He said, "Will you promise to report to me once a week so I may keep track of you and find you when I have to?"

I said, "Yes, if you will allow a written report instead of a verbal one, as I have no means of transportation."

So, the agreement was made and I returned to my home at the McKnights at Lewisburg with a thankful heart, for I always had a mortal dread of prison life. This arrangement was satisfactory to the Federals and my parole protected me from molestation from the many passing commands I would see or meet almost daily.

I stayed at Lewisburg until sometime in March, I think. I had made the acquaintance of a young Presbyterian preacher named Ewing, at whose mother's house I had been a guest a time or two. He had a monthly appointment to preach at Brick Church, about fourteen miles south of Lewisburg, and asked me one time to accompany him down there. I accepted the invitation on condition I could get permission from Major Evans to do so. His route was right by Evans's camps, and I started with the hope that Major Evans would not object. He readily consented and I made arrangements to teach a little country school down in that neighbourhood, where the people were trying to get up one. At Mr. Ewing's next appointment down there I went, carrying my scant wardrobe with me, bidding *adieu* to many kind friends at Lewisburg, whom I had become very fond of. I kept up my reporting to Major Evans on and on until sometime in the fall.

General G. M. Dodge with a large force of Federals came to Pulaski, Giles County, and remained a while and was ordered from there on to Chattanooga, and took all of the troops from that section with him, including Major Evans, and his command. It was said that the major and his crowd got on a big drunk when they left that section. I know not how it was, but I do know that he went off without leaving me any orders, and now having no one to watch me I thought somewhat of my chances of going South and getting to my command and seeking a private exchange so I could take my place in my company. But the long trip seemed to be too much for me with one of my limbs still weak from the wound.

My school closed for a three month's term, and another one was offered me. I continued to teach for a while. One Sunday Doctor Gordon and I went to Cornersville to church to hear Dr. Stoddart of Presbyterian Church preach. On our return home we met General John C. Starkweather, who had taken General Dodge's place at Pulaski, on the pike with one or two regiments of cavalry, making a reconnaissance up towards Cornersville. He immediately arrested us, made us turn back and escorted us and several other prisoners he had arrested back to town and to Esquire Chafin's office.

He inquired of Chafin if he was a magistrate there and being told he was, he ordered him to enrol every one of these men in the State militia as required by the proclamation of the Military Governor of Tennessee, Andrew Johnson, and then left us under a strong guard while the magistrate should enrol us in the service to help to repel an expected invasion of the rebels from the South. I had made the acquaintance of a Mr. McBride who had deserted from a Texas regiment, joined Yankees in that section and was acting as pilot or guide for Federal scouting parties who might need such help, and while I never saw him or knew him before, yet he seemed to take some interest in me, probably because we came from the same State.

Not long after we were put under guard, Mr. Stoddart the preacher came to me, asking the guard the privilege of speaking to me, and said in a very low tone of voice, "McBride says, 'What are you going to do?'"

I replied in the same tone, "Tell him I am not going to enlist in the State militia."

That ended our conference and he withdrew. A little later Stoddart returned and said, "McBride says for you to ask for a guard to take you before General Starkweather and when you get there you show the general your parole, telling him who you are and he will excuse you from the enlistment, he thinks."

So, I asked for the guard and he marched me up to the general's headquarters, holding a gun with bayonet on it in his hands behind my back all the way.

When I reached there, the general had just had a good dinner and plenty to drink and was enjoying himself talking and chatting with members of his staff. I pulled my hat off, walked in front of the general, saluted with a military salute, and stood before his majesty. He stopped talking, returned the salute, and waited to see what I would do. I told him I was a Confederate soldier on parole, was one the men he had arrested and left with Esquire Chafin to be enrolled in the State Militia and I had come to tell him that I would not be enlisted and asked the protection my parole guaranteed me.

He asked for my parole and I showed it to him, and after a little consideration he said if I would report to him at Pulaski the following Wednesday, he would release me and let me return home. I told him I would if there were no providential hindrances. So, he dismissed my guard and gave me a pass to go home.

When Wednesday came, I asked Mr. Henderson to accompany me and he consented and I asked Mr. Lonnie Gordon to take me down and we three drove to Pulaski, went to General Starkweather's headquarters over on East Hill in Judge T. M. Jones' residence, and I presented myself before him saluting him. He didn't recognise me at first and I explained, "You arrested me last Sunday near Cornersville and released me with the injunction to report to you today and I am here according to promise."

He still remained in doubt. He pulled a memorandum book from his pocket turned his back to me to get a better light on his book and him to look over a list of names he had on it. He commenced at the top running his finger along slowly—and said when half way down "You say your name is Blackburn?"

I answered. "Yes."

He folded his book and remarked, "Major Alman gave me this list—a list of Confederates for me to look after."

Major Alman, it is needless to say was one of those Southerners who played both sides; always trying to curry favour with whomsoever controlled his section. Turning to me he said, "Won't you take the oath of allegiance to the United States Government?"

I answered "No." He asked why. I answered, "I cannot swallow it and besides I owe allegiance to another government."

He then said "It is my duty to send you to a Northern prison."

At this juncture my good friend Henderson, asked for a private interview with the general. These two retired to another room and were absent for some time. When they came back, I caught Henderson's eye and he slightly shook his head. I knew before the general told me that there was no hope in sight for me to escape prison.

The general said my friend was good enough to offer to stand for me, but he couldn't be bothered with such things, and he would do his duty and send me on to prison.

I said, "All right, but, General, it seems a long trip to make and a cold place to lodge for a man without a cent of money in his pocket." He agreed that this was true. I said, "General, I have one request to make you."

He said, "Say on."

I said, "I have been teaching a little school where I live and I'd like to have a few days before I start for prison to make some collections so I will not have to go without any money at all."

He said, "If I will let you off for a week, will you report to me here at Pulaski next Wednesday?"

I promised I would if the Lord was willing.

He ordered his adjutant general to give me and my two friends passes so we could go home, and this was the last time I saw General Starkweather, for before the next Wednesday came, he obtained a furlough for sixty days and went up to his home in Ohio for a rest and recuperation. I hadn't promised to report to anyone except General Starkweather at Pulaski, so when the next Wednesday came, I remained at home and didn't try to find him. By the time he returned from home, General Forrest who had taken Athens, Alabama, with about two thousand prisoners was marching up the railroad towards Pulaski, taking all the Yankee forces from stockades along the route and was now ready to lay siege to or capture Pulaski; and Starkweather was kept too busy to think of me. I knew he had returned, but as the time for my reporting to him at Pulaski had long since passed and no new date had been fixed for the report, I simply didn't seek to have another day set for our meeting, and remained at home.

General Forrest after shelling Pulaski for a while didn't deem it prudent to make an attack there on account of the strong fortifications; then retired south and joined General Hood, now approaching Tennessee with his whole army. As the Southern Army came in the State Federal forces in the southern portion of the State retired before it and pretty soon Giles County was under control of the Confederate soldiers and I was again in the hands of my friends.

I reported at once to General Hood, gave him account of my history as a prisoner, showed him my parole and asked him if he could arrange for my exchange so that I might enter the service again. He replied that he had a camp at Columbus, Georgia, where he made private exchanges of prisoners with the enemy, and he would furnish me with papers and transportation to that point, which would enable me to get the desired exchange.

So, he issued the necessary papers of instructions and orders for transportation on railway and for use of soup stands for my benefit, and taking the papers I returned home to make preparation for my trip. I purchased a fine mare from Dr. Gordon which he had bought to use in his profession, but found he would be unable to keep her from the raiding cavalrymen passing, often looking for and taking all the best horses wherever they found them. He was very willing to sell her to me for $125.00, taking my note for same. My intention was to get in as good shape as possible and to make the trip on horseback to Columbus, Georgia, and when I got the exchange, I would be mounted and ready for service.

While I was getting ready for the trip, General Hood pushed on to Franklin, Tennessee, and had one-third of his army slaughtered there, but held the battlefield and followed the Federal Army on to Nashville, where he was defeated by the Federals, they being reinforced by another army. (The Battle of Franklin was fought on November 30. 1864; that of Nashville on December 15-16.—C. W. R.) Before I was fully equipped for my journey General Hood was falling back south with his army. So, I delayed my start south, to see if I would have company for my trip. A few days more passed and Hood's army was passing through Giles County going south. I fell in with the rear, far enough from the extreme rear to be out of reach of the continuous fire the Federals kept up on the rear guard of that retreating army.

The weather was extremely cold, many of Hood's army were entirely barefooted and ragged. and some of them wounded at Franklin were trudging along, making their way south to avoid capture and imprisonment. I never saw an army so dispirited, so needy, and withal so determined not to give up the contest. I had read of Washington's army at Valley Forge, barefooted and leaving a trail of blood as they marched, over frozen ground, and I said within myself, "History is repeating itself before my very eyes." I travelled on and on and fell in with two more horsemen going southward and after dark came, we looked for a place to stop for the night.

I suggested that we get off of the main road for fear that some of these barefooted soldiers might find and borrow our horses while we slept. We turned east and went one half mile from the main road, found a house where lived a family by the name of Marbutt and soon we were made welcome and comfortable by being housed and fed and having our horses fed and fine prospects for a good bed and a fine night's rest. Our horses were put in the smokehouse very near the, house so that they would be safer than at the barn if anyone should undertake to steal them in the night, for there was much of that being done at this time. This was not very far from the Alabama State line, in Giles County, Tennessee.

Next morning on rising early I went to the smokehouse and found two of the horses gone, mine being one of them. Our saddles and bridles were undisturbed. We tried to trace them by following their tracks, but they had gone to the main travelled roads which were covered by millions of tracks of a passing army, so we had to abandon the search. I felt sure mine had been taken by some brokendown infantryman, who would think it fair to make me take turns with him in walking.

After our morning's search for horses had proven fruitless my two companions, one with a brokendown horse and outfit, the other one with outfit and no horse at all started out together to follow the retreating army, and I never saw them again. I was left alone at Mr. Marbutt's to consider my best course to pursue. I learned from some of the family, or by observation I don't know which, that there was a blind horse there in the barn, so I asked Mr. Marbutt if I could buy him. He said he was blind and didn't see how he would suit me, or really how he could do without him, but if I could raise thirty dollars good money, I might take him. So, I looked over my finances and found I was short two and half dollars. So, I told Mr. Marbutt I had only $27.50 and would give up every cent of it for his horse.

He said it was a trade so I handed him the money and took my bridle, saddle, and blanket, and put on him and took possession. He was four years old, good size, in fair condition, quite active, and not a blemish or defect except he was totally blind. I rode him all day following the retreating army until late in the evening, when I began to look out for a lodging place for the night. Houses were scarce and what there were in that section were mostly vacant. It was fearfully cold and I felt that I must be inside of some house or suffer greatly with the cold.

I saw smoke coming out of the top of a cabin about one hundred yards from the road, and I rode up to it to learn the chances of being sheltered for the night. I found five or six infantry soldiers had taken possession of the cabin, which was empty, had torn up the floor in the middle of the same, made a fire down in the ground underneath, and were warming themselves, sitting on the floor with feet down over the fire. I asked permission to join them for the night. They readily consented and I remained with them until morning, tying my horse to the log house on the south side to protect him from the cold, and he and I passed the night without supper and next morning without breakfast.

The lady with whom I had boarded in Tennessee had fixed many things for my comfort and protection from the cold. Among other things a pair of heavy woollen sock; to wear over my boots instead of overshoes, which were impossible to procure at that time. When we were dressing next morning, getting ready to move, a soldier remarked it looked hard to him to see a man with two pair of socks when he had none at all. I looked over the crowd a little bit and I saw they were all practically barefooted, so without a word in reply I stripped off these over-socks I had on, and handed them to the one speaking and said, "Gentlemen, I regret that I have not a pair for each of you."

Next day I continued my journey south and coming to the Tennessee River late in the evening, I crossed over on a pontoon bridge prepared for use of the army. The following night I fell in with some cavalry of the 11th Tennessee regiment, the same being Captain Andrew Gordon's company, then commanded by Lieutenant James Edmundson, now living in Marshall County, Tennessee, about four miles east of Lynnville.

I had been staying in the same neighbourhood where many of this company were raised, and knew their families and kinfolks, so they made me entirely welcome and shared provisions and horse feed with me, making me as comfortable as they could. And now day after day I journeyed with the army southward, keeping a sharp lookout for my valuable black mare, but without success, finally reaching Columbus, Mississippi, where the army entrained for the East.

The exposure I had endured and change of diet and climate and habits, brought on an illness that kept me laid up for some days, when I found I had to go to bed for an indefinite period. I went out of town to a country doctor with a small family, with plenty of the world's goods and fair practice, who had been recommended to me, and applied to him for treatment and lodging for myself and board for my horse. He kindly took me in and cared for me for some days until I felt myself able to travel again.

Then I told the doctor and family I must be off for Columbus, Georgia, my objective point; that they had been wonderfully kind to me, which I greatly appreciated, and that I didn't have a cent of money with which to pay them, but that I had a good blind horse there, saddle, bridle, and blanket, all of which I would give them to pay for the care, treatment, and lodging they have given me. The doctor said that would satisfy him, and so we settled the debt and we parted good friends and everybody satisfied.

But I was completely strapped, only having now a little bundle of underclothing and a pistol, which a friend up in Tennessee had given me, and my journey was hardly begun. But I went cheerfully forward, thinking "A bad start may have a good ending." The Confederate Government had established soup houses at convenient distances on the railroads to feed the soldiers in transit—I suppose for this particular army movement but I don't know. At any rate the train would stop two or three times each day for meals furnished free to soldiers. The meals were nearly entirely soup, pea soup or some other kind vegetable in season at that time of year.

Nothing of especial interest happened until we reached Columbus, Georgia, after two or three days' travel. As soon as we pulled into the depot, I asked the direction and road to the exchange camp, and with all the haste and speed I could muster, walked out to it, about one and one-half miles from town. When I reached there, I found the place very well provided with shelter, bunks to sleep in with long dining tables and other things for taking care of prisoners, but entirely deserted except for a coloured woman who was employed by the military authorities to cook for prisoners who were being kept for exchange. The cook announced to me at once that the prisoners were all exchanged and had gone and she was remaining there for a time to see if any more would be sent in. This was a sore disappointment indeed for me who had so constantly expected an exchange and freedom from further obligations imposed by my parole of honour.

I returned at once to town and hunted up the *commandant* of the post. At this stage of the Civil War the authorities had appointed at every principal city in the South a *commandant* of the post, and the whole country was under martial law and each particular section under the military control of the local *commandant* I showed my papers, my parole and papers from General Hood, and told him of my disappointment. He expressed his regret and seemed to sympathize with me. We talked over current events for a while and the gloomy prospects of our army's success at that juncture, and after a while he asked me what I wanted to do. I told him without hesitation and frankly I wanted to go to my command if he could tell me where to find it and could give me transportation.

He replied, "Your command is now north of Savannah, Georgia, across the river in South Carolina, confronting General Sherman's army, which is getting ready to move up through South Carolina for her destruction, and if you want to go, I will give you transportation wherever we have any. The railroads are torn up some places and you will have to do the best you can over those skips where there are no cars running."

So, I made another start eastward on a train and I don't recall just how far we travelled before we had to walk. Another straggling soldier or two had fallen in with me by this time, all trying to reach their command further east, and they walked with me for miles, ten or fifteen or more. Now a new trouble overtook me. One of my wounded limbs having not gotten sufficiently strong for the journey began to fail and I had to let my late companions in travel leave me alone, so I rested and limped on and on as well as I could until I passed over the gap. The soup houses had given out now, and I had to depend upon strangers in a strange land for support.

One night I stayed in a neatly built log house, two or three women and some children living there alone. I remember they used what they called "light'ud" for illuminating purposes. They seemed to have plenty of plain food to live on and some to spare. I recall a conversation occurring at the table at supper. The lady of the house asked me where I was from. I told her "Texas." She said, "Well, well, from the far Texas."

I said "Yes."

She replied that she always thought she would like to live in Texas. After a little silence she asked me if we had any "light'ud" there. I said not in the section where I lived, but in other sections there was plenty of it. She remarked she would not live in any country where there was no light wood.

Now my journey was one of variations, sometimes on a railroad, sometimes on a wagon going my way, and sometimes afoot; but I continued with a firm set purpose to reach my command and finally succeeded in doing so, somewhere in the southern part of the State of South Carolina. My comrades rejoiced at my return to them. They were all so blackened by pine smoke it was difficult to recognise them. My heart ached when I inquired for many with whom I soldiered in former times, when the response would be dead, or disabled from wounds, or disease and discharge. My comrade Street, with whom I left in charge my $250 mare, my saddle, blanket, spurs and pistols had been killed on a hazardous scout and my belongings had fallen into the hands of the enemy when he fell.

Many changes had taken place. Officers to fill vacancies caused by death, discharge or promotion were no longer elected by the men, but went up by virtue of seniority of rank. My old captain had been promoted to be major of the regiment, leaving the captaincy in the company vacant, and awaiting my return to fill it, as I was next in rank in the company. The second lieutenant, A. J. Murray, was in command of the company.

I reported my arrival to Generals Wheeler and Rampton, then commanding all the cavalry forces in South Carolina, showed them my parole of honour and gave them the details of my efforts to get exchanged and of my travels. They commended me for abiding by the terms of my parole and told me to remain with my company and they would arrange for a private exchange for me, so I could take charge of my company again.

Now commenced with me a new experience in my life. There were no wagons now belonging to the cavalry to carry their cooking utensils and camp equipage and to afford a safe refuge for the non-combatants as formerly, but each company had a pack mule upon which was carried the frying pans for the company and a soldier or a negro cook to lead the mule during the day, following the company constantly except when engaged in battle. An oil cloth was used instead of bread trays, and a flat rail or board used for the baker, and when a rail or board was not available a limb cut from any tree was trimmed up and held over the fire with dough wound around it to cook.

The potatoes, the only abundant article of food to be had, were roasted in the fire. I ate and slept with the company, and when the battle came on, I was herded with this frying-pan lead-horse crowd until the firing ceased. This was the most disagreeable experience I had during the war. I urged the officers to hasten the exchange if possible, and so they offered to exchange a major of Kilpatrick's staff for me; but General Sherman refused to do it when he learned what command I belonged to, remarking, as I heard, if he had anyone of that command fastened, he would not release him for anyone, and so I had another disappointment. Now it is proper and fair to tell why General Sherman should refuse to swap a Texas Ranger for one of his own men of higher rank.

Captain Shannon had become chief of scouts for the Southern Army, and he and his command were Texas Rangers, or most of them were, and were known as Texas Ranger scouts; and they became quite efficient in killing Yankees without capturing any they found burning houses or insulting women, which was the daily habit of Sherman's men as they marched through South Carolina with torch, rapine and devilish lust. General Sherman in retaliation for what the Texas Rangers were doing and had done put sixty prisoners in irons and threatened to execute them. General Hampton heard of this threat, sent a flag of truce to Sherman for a conference with a view of saving the lives of those prisoners in irons.

General Sherman complained that acts of these Rangers were not in accordance with the rule of international warfare, but uncivilized butchering. General Hampton's reply, as I now remember the published reports of the conference at the time, was that he had observed all rules of international or honourable warfare, but when his antagonists engaged in burning down the houses over the heads of women and children, and non-combatants, without provocation, and in insulting and raping the helpless women of the land, he would order his men in all such cases to kill without mercy everyone so engaged and if he wished to retaliate by executing prisoners, he (Hampton) would enter the same game, taking two of Sherman's men for every one Sherman executed and in every case giving his (Sherman's) officers the preference. (This correspondence may be found in *Official Records*, Series 1, Vol. 47, Part 2—C.W.R.)

General Sherman saw his bluff could not be carried out for the reason, perhaps, that twice or three times as many Yankee prisoners were captured daily as were taken from the Confederates, for our scouts were exceedingly active, being on all sides of the enemy almost daily, while the Federals were straggling all out from the main body, trying to desolate South Carolina, because they regarded her as exceedingly wicked in being the first State to secede from the Union. The irons were promptly removed from the prisoners and they were sent in to our camps without the formality of exchange.

These poor fellows came into the camps full of wrath against the Rangers for their murderous acts and said, "You men think it fine sport, but if you had to take our chances as hostages you would play the game differently." But their wrath and injunctions were wasted on their audience, for the Texans were fully decided as far as possible to protect the honour and property of helpless people against the vandalism and destruction of an unprincipled antagonist, whose main ambition seemed to be to make the Southern people realise that war was hell as their leader was accustomed to say to them. Just what there was in the truce conference held to cause the release of the prisoners may be only surmised, but why General Sherman refused to make the exchange sought seemed manifest at the time to parties most interested.

The ravages of war were fearful to behold. Anyone could stand upon an eminence in the morning and tell by the smoke from burning buildings just how far east and west General Sherman's line of march extended. From daily reports, which we believed authentic, every living animal for use or food was taken from the citizens, including all kinds of fowls, and their smokehouses and pantries were stripped, and when the women and children would appeal to General Sherman for food, he would tell them to call on their people in the northern part of the State. There was just one article of food they could neither destroy nor carry off and that was sweet potatoes, of which there was an abundant crop the season before which must have been the means of keeping the dependent population from starvation.

Of all the campaigns made, during the Civil War by either Northern or Southern Armies, none had more of devastation and cruelty and inhumanity than this one led by W. T. Sherman across South Carolina, during the winter and spring of 1865. And no other campaign equalled this one for its barbarity except perhaps Sherman' s march from Atlanta to the sea. After his army reached Savannah, Georgia, Sherman made his report to the Secretary of War, in which he said he had made Georgia realise that war was hell and that he had devastated a country fifty miles wide and two hundred miles long so completely that if a crow visited that section, he would have to carry his rations with him or starve. This report was published at the time and is now doubtless among the war records today. (For Sherman's account of his march to the sea, see his *Memoirs*, volume 2, also *Official Records*, Series 1, volume 44.—C.W.R.)

This incident will probably bring to the mind of the student of history how Nero fiddled and danced while Rome burned up. Sherman left Atlanta with an army of between fifty and one hundred thousand men for his campaign through Georgia and the Carolinas, opposed only in Georgia by Wheeler's cavalry, reinforced by other cavalry forces under General Hampton, McLaws and other local commands when he started through South Carolina, not enough at any time to resist his progress materially, but enough perhaps to delay his movements somewhat while he repaired the bridges destroyed by the Confederates and enough to keep his men reasonably closed up in solid columns and thus saving from destruction some of the districts near his line of march.

This marching of Sherman's army accompanied by the burning of houses in the country and of the towns and villages passed, and the general destruction of property, continued without variation or cessation worthy or mention until he reached the capital of the State, which shared the same fate as other towns in line of march.

But at this juncture General Sherman published a report in the papers that General Hampton had burned Columbia; and while no soldier in either army in South Carolina believed it, yet there were others who did give that published report credit. Of this latter class was one, writing in *Nelson's Encyclopaedia*, who in speaking of this destruction of Columbia said, "The charge that he ordered the burning of Columbia, South Carolina, has been completely disproved," leaving the impression on the reading world that Sherman's charge against General Hampton was true. It seems strange that one who presumes to write history should be so careless about facts.

Now why should anyone conclude that a man who had spent months in destroying and burning everything in a devastating campaign should be relieved or exonerated of the charge of burning Columbia, the goal, of his ambition and cherished conquest of his military career. Besides this process of reasoning, to fix the blame on General Sherman, I have seen published a report that I deem reliable, that General Sherman published in his *Memoirs* before he died that he charged General Hampton with burning Columbia in order to discredit him with the people of South Carolina, his native State. I have never seen these memoirs and cannot vouch for the truth of this report, but it seems reasonable and much in keeping with General Sherman's character. (This confession is in Sherman's *Memoirs;* Vol 2—C. W. R.)

John G. Haynie of Company F, as good a soldier as ever Texas sent to war, was drowned in Saluda River at Columbia the same day the city was burned. Haynie had rarely ever missed a battle, had been wounded two or three times, and had no hope or expectation of ever going home again, as he confided to me only a few days before his death. I asked him why he should take such a gloomy view of the future. His answer was, "This war may last ten years, and I am not going to shirk a duty or miss a battle if I can possibly help it; and I know it is only a. matter of a short time when everyone who does this way will meet his final call. Judge the future by the past. Look for the best soldiers of Company F. Where are they? Most of them have answered their last roll call, and I can't hope for a different fate."

While Sherman was making desolate these regions, the Army of Tennessee was collecting in North Carolina near Raleigh or rather in that section of the State, for the purpose of meeting Sherman's march northward. General Joe Johnston, who had been succeeded by General Hood at Atlanta, was restored to the Army of Tennessee while said army was near Smithville, North Carolina. I never saw a demonstration to equal that made in honour of his return. Nearly a whole day was consumed by the army in cheering and shouting over this event.

The army had nearly been destroyed by Hood's manipulation of it, and the remnants were wholly dispirited by the misfortunes that had befallen our cause, and having great confidence in General Johnson as a leader and successful warrior, they showed renewed enthusiasm and determination by the magnificent reception accorded him.

A week or ten days later General Johnston moved his army out to meet Sherman in his onward march and met him at Bentonville, North Carolina, and engaged him in battle which lasted two days, March 19-21, 1865. It was furious and bloody from the beginning and to a spectator it seemed that the Confederates had advantage on all parts of the field. I had no special duty to perform, being on parole. I was exposed several times to the enemy's fire when I ventured too far to watch the battle or to help carry the wounded from the field.

During the first day the Texas Rangers lost. In the first charge they made every field officer they had, Colonel Cook, Lieutenant Colonel Christian and Major Jarmon, was badly wounded. In after years Cook died from this wound. The other two recovered after the war ended.

Doc. Mathews, a mere boy, captain of Company K being senior captain now with the regiment succeeded to the command of the regiment and won unperishable fame by making a successful charge on the 17th Army Corps of the enemy driving them in great confusion from a bridge they were ready to seize. This bridge was the only available crossing of a deep sluggish stream around our army on its west and south sides, and in case of its capture by the enemy in front our army would have been cooped up and forced to surrender. Our ammunition and supplies had to come to us over that bridge. The enemy fully realised the importance of its capture and approached near to it without being discovered, with a whole corps of infantry.

The Rangers being the nearest Confederate troops to this point, were ordered by General Hardee, who was nearby reconnoitring that part of the field, to drive them back. With a charge rarely equalled and never surpassed in impetuosity and daring the Texans under Doc. Mathews' leadership threw themselves upon that corps of infantry with a recklessness that indicated do or die on their part. The enemy were greatly confused and wavered for a moment and then began to give back. The Texans still pressing were reinforced by Brown's brigade Tennesseans, I think, and the two commands combined drove the enemy clear off the field and the bridge was saved to us for our use.

The toll of the Texas regiment was heavy in the killed and wounded, but the charge was a success, as most of its charges were. It was reported that General Johnston said he would compliment that regiment in a general order, but owing I suppose to the great confusion in military quarters and the fast changing of operations just previous to final surrender, the complimentary order and the official report of this battle were never written so far as I know. This was the last battle of the Tennessee Army of any consequence.

In this last charge General Hardee had a son killed, about 17 years of age. The boy had been in military school at Milledgeville, Georgia. The dash and success of the Texas Rangers challenged his ambition. He left school without permission, came to the army, sought out the Rangers and offered his services in their ranks. His presence and desires were made known to General Hardee who sent him back to school at Milledgeville. He made his escape from school again and came to us during the Battle of Bentonville. He was again reported to General Hardee by Captain Kyle of Company D of the Rangers. Hardee said to Kyle "Swear him into service in your company as nothing else will satisfy."

Kyle enrolled him in his company. About four hours after this time this fatal charge was made and he fell dead in sight of his father, who had come out to see the charge made. Of course, I cannot recall many of the casualties that happened in that battle, but one other case is so fixed in my memory that I feel constrained to mention it.

Eugene Munger of Company B of the Rangers had escaped the missiles of death so long, not even receiving a wound from the enemy, though always in the thickest of the fight, that he had become a fatalist, and often said that he didn't believe a Yankee bullet was ever moulded to kill him. In that charge a bullet went crashing through his brain, and he never knew what killed him. So much for fatalism, so much sometimes in presentiment. I have known other cases where these things failed in realisation.

One other thing in connection with this famous charge. General McLaws from the Virginia Army witnessed it. He said he had soldiered with "Jeb" Stuart on his many exploits in Virginia and Maryland, but had never witnessed a charge equal in efficiency and results to this one.

The great Battle of Bentonville was now over, both sides badly punished. Sherman's hitherto unimpeded progress was checked, and he gave his time and energy to recruiting and repairing his army, and General Johnston to organisation and moving leisurely towards Greensboro, North Carolina. In the meantime, the Virginia Army was surrendered at Appomattox, and General Grant's army moved south to make a junction with Sherman's army and to force the surrender of General Johnston which finally took place at Greensboro. Just before the armistice between the two armies, Johnston's and Sherman's, took place, one other incident of interest might be related pertaining to the Texas Rangers.

They were camped out on Haw River, or some tributary of it, near a bridge over a stream. Pickets between them and the enemy had been removed during the night without their knowledge. Next morning about sunrise a regiment or more of the enemy's cavalry came across that bridge into the edge of our camps, while all the regiment were asleep except five or six men who had saddled their horses to go out for forage. These raised a shout, made a dash at the enemy, thus awakening the balance of the regiment, who instantly grabbed their guns without any orders; everyone for himself, and gave them such a reception as to send them pell-mell back the road over which they came. So far as I now remember this was the last firing by any part of Johnston's army, and so the Terry Texas Rangers had fought the first and last battles of the Army of Tennessee; the first at Woodsonville, Kentucky, the last near Haw River, North Carolina.

Not long after this Captain Doc. Mathews, now commanding the Texas Rangers visited General Hardee's headquarters to learn what he might about the current events of the day. General Hardee was a favourite of the regiment, and the regiment was a favourite of his. He told Mathews of the situation pending; that Grant was moving upon us from the north and Sherman's army had approached us from the south and east, and General Stoneman had 10,000 cavalry on Catawba River southwest of us, and that while he had nothing official on the subject, he felt satisfied the army would be surrendered right there.

He also advised Mathews to take his regiment away from there and join Dick Taylor's army then at Mobile, Alabama, and by thus adding strength from different sections to that army, under the providence of God victory might finally come to the Southern cause, and added, "I don't want to see your regiment surrendered to the enemy."

Captain Mathews returned to camp at midnight and had the bugler sound the assembly call for the regiment, and when it was assembled, he delivered Hardee's information and advice and concluded his remarks with these words, "I am too young a man to assume the responsibility of such an undertaking, but I now offer my resignation as commander of the regiment," asking each company commander to take charge of his company. "Hold a council to determine your course, and each company decide and act for itself regardless of what others may do."

Company F, my company, returned to quarters, held its conference and decided unanimously to go to Dick Taylor and to start at once. Some of the company, including the commissioned officers, were absent on police or scout or other duties or on account of sickness, and were not in this conference and hence were left behind when we started to leave. C. D. Barnett, our orderly sergeant, agreed to be commander and I agreed to be "counsellor" for the expedition. I never did learn definitely the course the other companies pursued, but had the impression fixed upon me that most of them made their escape and were never paroled until after all Confederates had surrendered, and some of them were never paroled at all, but are still, so to say, soldiers of the Confederate Government.

Some parties, making out as best they could a roster of the regiment, since the war, in speaking of this surrender of the troops said that two hundred and forty-eight Rangers answered to roll call the day before the surrender but only two of them surrendered next day. I think this is erroneous, but indicates how much the Rangers opposed surrendering to the enemy. Captain Tom Weston, last commander of Company H of the Rangers, wrote to me some years after the war closed and said among other things, that he had the honour of surrendering regiment at Greensboro, and that there were ninety men present who received paroles. I think this statement is reliable.

About fifteen or eighteen members of Company F at one o clock in the morning began their journey south for Mobile. We went through Greensboro. Brigadier General Harrison of our brigade heard of our movement and sent for us to come to see him, where he was laid up with recent wounds received in battle, and when we drew up in front of the house, he came out on his crutches and made us a speech. He commended our movement heartily and regretted only that he was unable to accompany us. Then with many tears and benedictions he bade us Godspeed with God's blessing and a loving farewell to his faithful comrades who were, according to his words, the heroes of 300 battles.

From Greensboro we went the most direct way to Catawba River. We employed a guide to show us a private ford, knowing that all public crossings were heavily guarded by Stoneman's cavalry. Our guide rode with us all night and towards daylight we left the main road, took a by-path which took us to the river by sunup where our guide pointed out to us the ford, telling us we would have to swim twenty or thirty feet in the middle of the stream, and ascend on far side up a little trail leading up the bank. Thus instructed we dismissed our guide and moved forward. Having crossed the river and ascended the bank we found a cabin up on the bank and a lane leading out to the main road, which ran up and down the river two hundred yards or more distant.

Soon after leaving the cabin, we saw about twenty Yankee cavalry coming in the other end of the lane meeting us. They were some of Stoneman's men patrolling up and down the river to intercept Confederate soldiers trying to make their way south. I was in the rear of our company, which halting for a moment asked me what to do, I said, "Move forward quietly and when within ten steps of them raise a yell and charge them with your pistols in hand and demand their surrender." They were surprised at the unexpected charge and surrendered without firing a gun. Now with twenty prisoners, well mounted, and well armed, we moved forward at a lively gait, crossed the main road, went through the woods, fields and pastures, until we had many miles between us and Stoneman's command.

We travelled on and on, going south until nine o'clock at night, when we began to feel the need of rest, and began to consider what was best to do with our prisoners. I suggested to my men to take their horses, arms and munitions, parole them, and turn them loose to return to the command afoot, so building up a fire of pine knots, the paroles were soon written for each one and signed up. We then took possession of their horses and equipage, bade them goodnight and we moved on several miles further and camped.

Next day we continued our travels south, taking from Confederate commissaries and quartermasters' stores in the towns we came to such food and feed as we needed. The officers in charge of such stores sometimes objected, saying that Johnston's army had surrendered and that they had been ordered to turn over these supplies to Federal authorities. I gave them choice of opening their storehouses where provisions were stored or having them broken open. They unlocked them and told us to help ourselves. I told them after they had supplied the Confederates' wants, they might turn over the residue to Federal authority; that we were regular Confederates and were eating Confederate food and using Confederate forage.

Not many days later we learned that General Taylor had surrendered his army, (May 4, 1865.—C. W. R.), to Federal authorities without a single battle, and we were confronted with new difficulties. Another council of war or of procedure was necessary on our part, so we decided to turn west and cross the Mississippi River by private ferries and offer our services to General Kirby Smith commanding the Trans-Mississippi department. Still another difficulty arose, for we had now reached that desolated strip which General Sherman's army had made on his famous march to the sea, and it was exceedingly difficult to obtain supplies for a company of men.

We then divided into squads of three or four men in each, with the promise to meet on the east side of the river to reunite there and go in a body across the river to General Smith's army. Being separated into smaller bodies we more easily found subsistence. Thus, we all travelled westward on widely differing routes. As we began to gather in Mississippi, still a new obstacle to our progress was presented. We had hoped to use canoes or skiffs in crossing the river, swimming our horses beside them, a custom that prevailed in that section after the the public crossings had fallen into the hands of the enemy.

This could be done when the river was at its ordinary stage or depth very successfully: but now what was termed the June rise was on caused by the melting of ice far up North and the spring rains, and the river was thirty to forty miles wide, making it impossible for our mode of crossing for a month at least, perhaps more. So, we must await the falling of the waters before we could crossover.

While lying up and waiting Tom Gill, Peter Arnold, John Justice and I concluded we would take a run up into middle Tennessee, where we all had sweethearts whom we desired to visit. So, after forging some paroles for Justice, Gill and Arnold we made our start for Tennessee. Now I don't wish to make the impression that I forged these paroles for the boy, for I did not, but they found other men on parole down there in Mississippi and copied them substituting their own names in place of the one on parole. Thus equipped, well mounted, and armed with our side arms we started for Tennessee.

As we approached Wayland Springs in Lawrence County, Tennessee, we unexpectedly, at a short turn in the road, rode into a regiment of Yankee cavalry who were dismounted and seemed to be resting under some trees by the roadside. We halted for a moment and I said "Forward boys, and look for commander of these troops."

So pretty soon Colonel Blank was pointed out to us by the troopers and we rode boldly up to him, all of us saluting, when Tom Gill became spokesman for us, and said "Colonel, we are Confederate soldiers on parole, going up farther in Tennessee to visit our friends before we proceed to our homes in the West." In the meantime, we all drew out our paroles for the colonel's inspections, and Gill continued his speech, saying, "You see, colonel we have our side-arms. These are for our own personal protection, as Federal officers in Mississippi advised us that if we came to Tennessee we would find bands of outlaws, horse thieves, etc., plentiful, and we ought to have some defence against these."

After examination of two of the paroles, the colonel bade us to proceed on our journey.

This was about six or eight miles south of Wayland Springs, which was the regular camping place for this regiment, as we learned later in the day. These springs as it happened were on the road we were travelling. After sundown as we approached these springs that evening, a sentinel on guard called out to "Halt! Halt!" several times, to which we paid no heed, but kept riding on towards him. When we drew near this sentinel was furious and cursed us vigorously and threatened to shoot us.

His calling to us and cursing us aroused the curiosity of his comrades back in camp, so they, eight or ten of them, came out to the road to see what the trouble was. They first discovered we were Confederate soldiers, and one discovered we were on McClellan saddles and said, "Why, they are using our saddles," meaning we were riding saddles the Federal Army used for their cavalry, and then another one called out, "Why, they are armed with pistols; look at them."

Then I said, "Yes, we have our pistols and all of us know exactly how to use them, so you need not trouble yourselves further about trying to halt us, for we are going on," and bade them goodnight, and rode on. It may be but fair to state that they had come out to the road without their guns and as the vidette only was armed and we had two six-shooters each, they simply acted wisely and judiciously by letting us pass on, without molestation. This was my last personal interview with the Yankee soldier.

Next day, we reached Giles County, and as some of the crowd wished to go on up to Franklin County and on to Maury County while I wanted to stop in Giles County, we separated with the understanding we would meet at my stopping place to begin our western trip after the Mississippi River had gone down sufficiently. Pretty soon, after this date, Generals Lee, Johnston, and Taylor, having surrendered, the future for our independence seemed so unpromising to General Kirby Smith's army that they simply broke camps and went home without awaiting any enemy to ask them to surrender. So, their final act in this fearful drama was called "The Breakup" and is still, (1919), so-called.

In our last contact with Yankee troops down in Lawrence County I did not endorse Mr. Gill's speech to them, for it was only one-fourth correct, since I was the only one that had a genuine parole, but he proceeded on the theory, I suppose, that "all things are fair in war."

The war was now over, our dream of an independent Confederate Government was passed. Overwhelming numbers with inexhaustible supplies had triumphed over a half-fed scantily supplied army, greatly inferior in numbers. I am reliably informed that war records of this period will show to parties seeking correct history that the Confederate enrolment of soldiers was 600,000 in all, while the enlistment on the other side was 2,800,000, or more than four to one in favour of the Northern Army. In addition to this, all Southern ports were blockaded by the Federal Government, so it seems wonderful even yet that this war could have continued four years with this great inequality of advantages.

Personally, I had been loyal to the Confederate Government, had done the best I could, had offered my life, endured privations and shed my blood freely: had no apologies to make for my action, and still believed and now believe we were right and engaged in the cause of human liberty as did our forefathers in other years. I do not know certainly, and do not want to know how many men I killed or how many I wounded. I only know I had many fine opportunities to do both. I wear four scars on my body from Yankee bullets that will go with me to my grave, but I regard them as scars of honour received in defence of the Southland, and am proud of them. I thank God that I can forgive and pray for my former enemies and that I entertain no ill will towards any of them at this time.

In the foregoing pages I have in a plain way told where I served and when I served in the Confederate Army, together with many incidents connected therewith. I have tried at all times to be accurate, and fair and loyal to the truth. It now remains for me according to first intention as announced in the beginning of this record to tell just why I served the cause with such fidelity. I might answer this question with one word "Patriotism." I believed the South right in her contentions and in her actions in seceding from the government and setting up for itself. According to the Constitution, Amendment X, the powers not delegated to the United States by the Constitution nor prohibited by it to the States were reserved to the States respectively.

These independent States never delegated their powers to make or unmake governments to the general government, so if they ever had the right of choosing in this matter and had not delegated it to others, they still possessed it. These independent Colonies, or States, had never lodged in the hands of the general government, so if they ever had right to make war on any one of its members. Secession it was said was advocated by Abraham Lincoln in a speech in Congress as a right belonging to the States respectively. Massachusetts threatened secession when the government purchased Louisiana from France, because, as her people argued, the price paid was extravagant.

Fanaticism in The Northern States caused them to pass fugitive slave laws in violation of the Constitution, in Article IV and latter part of Section II, and when reminded of this violation the usual answer was, "The Constitution is a compact with the Devil and in a league with Hell." They brought on war and bloodshed in Kansas because some United States citizens had moved to Kansas and took their slaves with them, as I now remember. The same fanaticism sent emissaries through the South to raise insurrection among the blacks, and to incite them to bloodshed and murder and when one of those was condemned and hanged for his murderous deeds, those fanatics held great public funerals over the North, proclaiming him a martyr to the cause of human welfare and to the holy service of God.

In addition to all of these things this same element increased in strength and power until it was able to elect a President and a Congress of the U.S. from its members and what could the South expect but humiliation and destruction of her institutions from such a set?

The time had come when we believed we could not live peaceably with them. Therefore, we preferred to secede and form a government of our own, which we thought we had a right to do. We did not demand any of the public treasure or public lands or any of the community property of the government of which we rightfully owned a part, but simply seceded from disagreeable company and set up a government of our own and asked only to be let alone. I doubt if a constitutional lawyer could have been found at that time who would have said we did not have a right to secede and I doubt if you can find a constitutional lawyer today who understands the organic law of the government who will say that we had no right to secede. Then where did this power lie or come from authorising Abraham Lincoln to make war on and devastate the Southern States?

There is another viewpoint that justifies the South in going to war. Self-preservation is the first law of nature and a people who would not fight to defend their homes and firesides are not worthy of freedom or respect. I love the South and her institutions and I went out to help defend them and to help, if possible, drive the destroyers from our borders, and old as I am now, if such a catastrophe should happen again to our beloved land, I am ready to offer my life, my fortune, and sacred honour in her defence.

Conclusion

It is self-evident from the foregoing writings in these sketches that if the writer were asked to fix the responsibility of Civil War he would say, without hesitation, Abraham Lincoln, his ill advisors and coadjutors were responsible for all the bloodshed, the deaths, the horrors and devastation of that war. But as another Judge, the Judge of all the earth who will do right, has jurisdiction over these and all other human affairs, the writer is willing to leave these and all other things for Him to adjudicate.

Diary of Ephraim Shelby Dodd

By Ephraim Shelby Dodd

Introductory Note in his history of *Terry's Texas Rangers*, Mr. L. B. Giles narrates the following tragic incident of the East Tennessee campaign:

> It was during this winter that one of the saddest events in all our career happened: the hanging of E. S. Dodd by the enemy. He was a member of Company D. He was of a good family and well educated. For many years he kept a diary, setting down at night the happenings of the day. He was taken prisoner with this diary in his pocket. On that evidence alone he was condemned and executed as a spy.

In January, 1914, the State Librarian received a letter from a resident of New York State, informing him that she had in her possession a diary found on the body of a Texas Ranger hung as a spy. Negotiations for its acquisition by the State Library were opened at once, and terminated successfully. The only information about the diary this person could give was that it "was found by a lieutenant from a N. H. regiment, who for years was a friend of our family, and some time before his death (which occurred six years ago) he gave it to me."

E. S. Dodd came to Texas from Kentucky late in 1860 or early in 1861. After visiting an uncle, James L. L. McCall, at Waco, he made his home with another uncle, Dr. John R. McCall, at Austin. He was teaching school near Austin, and was not yet out of his teens, when he enlisted in Terry's Rangers.

Ernest William Winkler

Texas State Library
November 5, 1914

Transferred from old *Diary*. December 4, 1862-January 1, 1864

Thursday, December 4th, 1862—I went out from M. to Mr.———, five miles from town. I went from there to Gen'l Morgan's Headquarters, leaving the Knox County filly at Mr. ——— and riding Walker's horse. I took supper at Lewis Black's, Morgan's Headquarters. The gen'l was in town but came in just after supper. I went on to Chenault's camp and staid all night with John and Van Benton.

Friday, 5th—Snowed all day. I rode to Alexandria and went out to Mr. Bass's, seven miles, got there about night. I found all well.

Saturday, 6th—I remained quiet today. Miss Frances came over. I staid all night and Sunday, 7th, I started on my return to camp. Came to Statesville, got pair of boots, $25. Came out three or four miles and staid all night.

Monday, 8th—I got some cloth and came to town (M.); stopped but a short time. I saw Miss Kate, received a nice present, a sack to carry tobacco, made of red, white and blue. I came out to Mr. House's and staid all night.

Tuesday, 9th—Came back to camp. Company on picket. Burke in command at camp. I was put on comm. guard.

Wednesday, 10th—Lieut. Ellis went on a scout, I went with him. Ten men detail went down on Wilson pike, turned off to left and staid all night with Mr. Smith, a clever man, nice family, daughters, etc.

Thursday, 11th—Crossed the railroad and went down near Franklin. Got a guide and went down country through farms, etc., to near Brentwood, stopped at Miss Mag. McGarrock's. Came back to Mr. Campbell's, two miles from Franklin, and staid all night.

Friday, 12th—This morning just at daylight, while in the act of eating breakfast, the fight commenced in town. We put out immediately; found the Yanks in possession of the town when we got there. Their pickets fired on us. We then crossed the creek to go round and get with Smith. Got into Mr. Baugh's lot and while there came near being surrounded by a hundred or two Yanks. Came cross-country to Hillsboro, got good dinner and came back to F. by night. Yanks left about 11 o'clock. Found Smith in possession. Came out two miles and staid all night.

Saturday, 13th—Came back to camp. I went on forage.

Sunday, 14th—Got a good dinner at Mrs. T.

Monday, 15th—I and Jeff Burleson went out and got a good dinner and my clothes. Came back and found the company in camp. Tonight I, Eslinger and Jessy Johnson went out cross the hills to preaching. Parson Bunting officiated. I went down with Eslinger and the girls to Mr. Page's, got some good apples, set till bedtime and came to camp.

Tuesday, 16th—Remained in camp.

Wednesday, 17th-Saturday, 20th—During this time had several false alarms amounting to a run down the pike and back to camp. Also, regular turns on picket.

Sunday, 21st—Go on the famous detail to M. after guns which cost me three days roots. I went to see Miss Kate, spent about three minutes; had to make flying visits. Called to see Mr. Lane's family. Coming back to camp, stopped to get supper and did not get to camp till after night.

Monday 22nd—Put on three days. A false alarm caused us to go to the front.

Tuesday, 23rd—Went on picket. I was put on at the Widow ——.

Wednesday, 24th—Was transferred to Black's picket at Holt's and stood tonight.

Thursday, 25th—This morning just after being relieved the Yanks made a break on us. We were fired on just as we reached the Com., fought them all day, falling back about four miles (Christmas Day). Returned to camp.

Friday, 26th—Were aroused early this morning with the word the Yankees are in Nolensville. Went up at double quick and found them there. Fought them there all day until night, falling back to our old camp at Mr. Page's. Staid there tonight. Our loss, one piece of cannon and a few men McClure of Company E killed.

Saturday, 27th—Commenced skirmishing early, falling back slowly; fought through Triune and beyond Mr. Perkins. Rained on us all day. After passing Mr. P's, we took up line of march, came up three miles and turned off for Murfreesboro. I stopped and spent the night in a kitchen; came on Sunday 28th and overtook the regiment. We came in five miles of M. Met the wagons, unloaded them and prepared to cook three days rations, but were ordered to saddle up and get out to meet the Yankees. A false alarm. Staid out until near midnight. Came back to where we left the wagons but they were not there.

Monday, 29th—Went out this morning to the end of the Wilkerson pike. Met the Yankees and skirmished with them all day, falling back gradually. Their cavalry charged us once but paid dear for it. A number of prisoners were taken. We fell back to our infantry this evening.

Tuesday, 30th—Rained today; all quiet till evening; fight then opened between the infantry and continued until dark.

Wednesday, 31st—The great day of battle commenced at day light and raged heavily all along the line until 3 o'clock. Yanks drove back four miles. Our boys took in prisoners by the hundreds. Captured twelve cannon and during the day about 2,000 prisoners, 160 odd beeves, some wagons, etc.

Thursday, 1st January, 1863—Went to La Vergne and pitched into their wagon train, captured and burned a good many wagons, 200 prisoners.

Friday, 2nd—Transferred to the right wing. Saw the fight this eve. Breckinridge had to fall back. Raining all the time.

Saturday, 3rd—Raining all day; sent out on a scout last night beyond Stone River to Mr. Black's. All quiet.

Sunday, 4th—This morn before day our army commenced to retreat. I left the regiment on the *plaza* in M. and went out to the end of the Wilkerson pike. Got my clothing and came across to the Salem pike, found a number of unparoled Yanks on my way. I met Gen'l Buford but he would not send back to parole them. I went on to town, went to see Miss Kate, took a bite to eat and bid them goodbye. Went up to Mr. Lane's and from there out to Col. Smith's Regiment and back to Col. Cox in town. He promised to attend the Yanks. I then started for the command. Came out to Col. Lytle's, stopped, found Morton of the battery there. I took supper there but did not know where I was until the young ladies came down. Miss Mollie came in glad to see me, was then introduced to Miss Mollie Turner and Miss Alice Hord, staid till 11 o'clock, time passed very pleasantly. Came on to camp.

Monday, 5th—Fell back to Old Fosterville, remained 6th-10th.

Sunday, 11th—Came out on a reconnoitring expedition, past Col. Lytle's. I stopped on return and saw Misses Mollie and Alice. Miss Molly T. had returned home. From this time until the 27th we did nothing but picketing. I piruted a little on Duck River, spent a night or two with Mr. Stewart, took dinner twice at Mr. Wilhoit's and thus the time passed. On 27th came in to camp and on 29th we were relieved by Wheeler's Brigade and with three days rations started on a scout down on Cumberland, passed through S. and out on Eaglesville pike to E. Camped near the place.

Friday, 30th—Came through Triune and out to Franklin, got there 4 p.m., went out one and a half miles on Columbia pike and camped. I and Oly Archer went out to Mr. Baugh's and took supper, staid till bedtime and returned to camp.

Saturday, 31st—Details sent out to get all the provisions possible and return by 12 o'clock. I went to town, but did not get my horse shod, met the command as I went out, coming in. Went some ten or eleven miles and camped on creek on steep hillside. Rained all night. I and John Henry slept dry in my Yankee tent. Most company got into stable and crib.

Sunday, 1st February—Rained all day, came within four miles of Charlotte. A very poor country. I and Reuben Slaughter went out and staid all night with Mrs. Hood. Her husband had been conscripted. She boiled a ham, baked some pies, filled our haversacks and started us on our way rejoicing. Came down to Mr. Ventress.

Monday, 2nd—Froze up and snowed today and night.

Tuesday, 3rd—Started before day for Fort Donelson. Had to walk to keep from freezing. Got to the fort about three hours by sun. Our regiment sent on Fort H. road to prevent reinforcements from coming to D. Reached our position and the fight commenced and continued till dark. We cut the telegraph at all points, fight resulted in capture of about 100 prisoners, 50 negroes and same number of horses, one twelve-pound brass rifled cannon. Gunboats came up after dark and commenced shelling and we had to get. Came back to the forge, two and a half miles, and camped.

Wednesday, 4th—Came back to Ventress's on creek. Snowed tonight awful time.

Thursday, 5th—Boys had grand snowball. Gave Col. Harrison a taste. Came up Columbia road, twenty miles, to little village of Wharton, took up quarters. We went up creek three miles and back close to headquarters and camped in road, making fires of the fence. I got fodder and we spread it on the snow and blankets on fodder; slept comfortably.

Friday, 6th—Came to Vernon and camped. I went out and got some fodder and made beds, but did not get to enjoy it long. 'Bout 1 o'clock started and came to Duck River, built fires of the fence on river bank. Our squadron sent on scout eight miles, got back just after day. Found them swimming the horses and taking the rigging over in a boat flat. We were then sent on picket. A ford was found and the brigade crossed over. Camped one mile from the river. Crossed near Centerville.

Saturday, 7th-Sunday, 8th—Came up to Columbia pike, ten miles from town. Once more in pretty country. Camped in woodland blue grass pasture.

Monday, 9th—Moved up in five miles of town.

Tuesday, 10th—Remained in camp.

Wednesday, 11th—Sent to headquarters to draw ammunition as A. O. S. Gen'l Wharton had a ball tonight.

Thursday, 12th—Came up to within seven miles of Lewisburg.

Friday, 13th—Came up to L. I went with Aaron Burleson to the fortune teller's; had our future destiny read to us; then to Mr. Lane's and listened to Miss Jennie paw ivory awhile. Miss Mattie Long present.

Saturday, 14th—Remained quiet today. I and Nix went to see Miss Jennie Lane. Miss Mattie still there.

Sunday, 15th—Moved camp out seven miles on Franklin pike near Berlin. I went out to Mr. Sewell's and got dinner; piruted around and came back to camp with two dozen eggs.

Monday, 16th—I went out piruting again today. Wagons got in today. I was put on camp guard; roots for being out. Soon after dark a detail was called for to go to Lewisburg; 'twas raining; I was detailed. Doak in command. Got there about 11 o'clock, could find nobody, went into Court House and slept in the bar.

Tuesday, 17th—Received twenty-four boxes, saddles, bridles, halters, etc. Sent to camp. Got a detail and put them all in a house and locked them up. We took charge of the clerk's office to sleep in, tied our horses in court yard and got our forage from the farmers around. Secured boarding at Maj. Holden's, a clever gentleman and nice family; has one grown daughter, Miss Emma, a nice young lady. Remained here Wednesday, 18th-Monday, 23rd. During this time had nothing to do but write letters, visit MY GIRL THAT PAWS IVORY, and make acquaintances. Among them Miss Lou Hill I prize highest. We had prayer meeting and church. I purchased four books and left them with Miss Emma: *Mormon's at Home, Pilgrim's Progress, Bayard Taylor's Travels* and *Bible Union Dictionary*.

Tuesday, 24:th—Just before leaving a couple of young lady equestrians passed out of town from Mr. Fisher's. I jumped on H. Emnoff's horse and overtook them, rode out a mile with them and turned off pike. If I should ever get back to L. I intend seeking them and make their acquaintance. After dinner we bid our kind friends *adieu* and put out, overtook the command about eleven miles from Shelbyville.

Wednesday, 25th—Came through Shelbyville today. Commenced raining on us just as we got to town and continued. Came out on road to Beech Grove, ten miles, as wet as water. I and Albright went cross Wartrace Creek and staid all night with Mr. Fork a nervy layout.

Thursday, 26th—Still raining. Went over to Mr. Hancock's, intending to cross Wartrace at a bridge above but gave it out as it was pouring down rain. Found Charley Pellam there at Mr. H's.

Friday, 27th—All start this morning for camp, find the wagons close to Fairfield, the Regiment three miles further on. I was sent after corn over the highest mountain in the country as soon as I got in.

Saturday, 28th—Moved camp out near Beech Grove. I and Polk Kyle sent on forage, bought a stack of hay. Staid all night with Mr. Carlisle.

Sunday, 1st March—Get his wagon and hauled one load to camp. Camp moved three miles further up the pike. I went up creek and got

Mr. Jonichin to start with his wagon. Went on top the mountain to get two more wagons and as I came back the Yanks ran our pickets in. I came near being caught by them. Came back down creek and told J. He turned back. I and Polk then went on to camp. After going to bed, all waked up and fell back to the other camp.

Monday, 2nd—I and Polk go out again. Get Mr. Ashley's wagon and Mr. Carlisle's; send in two loads. Camp moved up pike again. Go into camp.

Tuesday, 3rd—Company went on scout. Unshod horses did not go, so I staid.

Wednesday, 4th—Company on picket. All gamblers and pirutes put on roots. I came under the latter head.

Thursday, 5th—Still on picket.

Friday, 6th—Relieved by K. and F. Raining all day and night. Sent on bread detail with Big Ugly, got back after night, raining.

Saturday, 7th—I went out to Widow Ewell's to get some bread. Regiment relieved and went into camp. I got there after night.

Sunday, 8th—Went on forage; got back in time for preaching.

Monday, 9th—Remained in camp tonight. Rained.

Tuesday, 10th—Could not get forage.

Wednesday, 11th—Went after forage. I and Reuben Slaughter went together, did not find the squadron, piruted around and came back to camp after night.

Thursday, 12th—Came (regiment) down through Shelbyville to near Dolittle. I stopped at Lee Stewart's and got dinner. Came on to camp.

Friday, 13th—Went on bread detail, saw Mrs. Billington at Widow Clardy's, her mother; took dinner with them. Met Miss Ore and Miss Patton.

Saturday, 14th—Squadron went on scout. I went to shop and on bread detail.

Sunday, 15th—Remain in camp.

Monday, 16th—Last night had a meeting of the Lodge; passed two and raised one; made the acquaintance of Dr. Moore and lady, also Miss Stern, a niece of the doctors.

Monday, 16th—Another meeting; one passed and two raised.

Tuesday, 17th—I listened to some delightful music this morning by Miss Stern, particularly the Texas Rangers, dedicated to Mrs. Gen'l Wharton. I started back to camp but met the Regiment going out on picket. I fell in and went out and had to come back or go back and get my blankets. Came out half a mile from D. and camped.

Wednesday, 18th—Remained in camp all day. I am very unwell.

Thursday, 19th—Came on picket this morning.

Friday, 20th—Our squadron sent on post this morning. I joined Tom Taylor's mess; Jessy also. I and Tom went out to Mr. Elmore's and got some bacon and milk. I stood tonight.

Saturday, 21st—Brigade went out on scout. Our company supported battery, drove the Yanks back to their main camp and returned.

Sunday, 22nd—Parson Bunting preached for us today. Nothing occurred to change monotony of camp. Sick, and time drags slowly with me.

Monday, 23rd—A false alarm tonight, and rain.

Tuesday, 24th—In camp quiet.

Wednesday, 25th—Roll call five times a day, arms and horses inspected in the morning and dress parade in the evening is the order of the day.

Thursday, 26th—Drill two hours and dress parade. A document from Gov. Lubbock of Texas read, giving an account of presentation of flags of 4th and 5th Texas Infantry of Virginia to the State. Also, one or two captured by our regiment.

Friday, 27th-Monday, 30th—Nothing of importance occurred.

Tuesday, 31st—Went on a scout out to Eaglesville. Met a Yankee scout just this side of E. We charged them and run them one and a half miles, capturing six and wounding several.

Wednesday, 1st day of April—Yanks brought up three or four thousand to E. and shelled our boys for some time.

Thursday, 2nd—Went out beyond Maj. Winn's, brought his family and negroes out, skirmished with the Yankees for some time, nothing serious.

Friday, 3rd—I went out piruting this evening, came back to camp and went in to Dr. Moore's, sit till bedtime. Miss Nannie made some music for me; the evening passed pleasantly.

Saturday, 4th—The Grand race between Wharton and Harrison came off this morning. All the regiment that wished to went out. I remained in camp. I and Reubens went over and got dinner at Mrs. Blanton's. Came back and the regiment was getting ready to leave. I and Lonnie Logan came on to town and stopped at Dr. Moore's. Miss Nannie made some music for us. We bade them goodbye and overtook the regiment. After we got to camp, I took John Rector's horse and went up to Mr. Stewart's; found Dan at home. I took supper and staid all night; got some provisions fixed up and left before day. Came down to camp and started soon after up country.

Sunday, 5th—I came by Dan's and got my clothing, overtook the command at town. Came up to Fairfield, crossed Bell Buckle Creek, went three or four miles and camped.

Monday, 6th—Came up near Jacksboro and camped.

Tuesday, 7th—Marched on way to Liberty far enough to consume the day when we turned back in getting to camp; had to go down and up a pretty steep mountain. The Yankees had possession of Liberty; drove Morgan's men out. We came back to Ballou's (Blues) and camped. Nothing for our horses to eat or ourselves.

Wednesday, 8th—We came down to the forks of the pike two miles from Liberty. I and Reuben Stroud stopped and got supper and our horses fed. Found four companies on picket, ours among the number.

Thursday, 9th—I, Tom Taylor and Stroud came on to Alexandria and shod our horses. The regiment passed on and left us. We came on and got our dinner at Mr. Neal's living near Mrs. Grandstaff's and came on to camp at Spring Creek.

Friday, 10th—I was very sick last night and hardly able to ride this morning. Command left before day, got to Lebanon at daylight. Dr. Hill could not get the medicine for me but gave me a pass to return to the wagons. Near McMinnville I came out to Mr. Bass's and staid all night.

Saturday, 11th—I felt better this morning but very weak. Francis came over this morning or evening. George Tracy was over in the morning, I believe.

Sunday, 12th—Rained last night. Very pleasant this morning. I remained quiet today. Three or four soldiers came by; found our brigade had come back about Spring Creek.

Monday, 13th—My mule taken scratches or something else badly, cannot ride her. Pretty day today. Aunt Nancy came over this evening.

Tuesday, 14th—Rained last night again and cleared off this morning. I remained quiet today. Rained again tonight.

Wednesday, 15th—'Twas misty and damp this morning. I fixed up and went up to Mrs. Tarpley's, bidding the folks good bye at Mr. Bass's. I found the way pretty easy. Killed a squirrel and took dinner with them. Staid an hour or two and started; came on through Commerce and out two miles to Mr. Davis and staid all night. The mist finally turned to rain.

Thursday, 16th—Cleared off this morning. I remain with Mr. Davis today; very pleasant day.

Friday, 17th—Lieut. Davis and Emmet Trammel came by today and took dinner. Learned all about the Regiment from them. Camped at A. Today was a beautiful day. I did not feel so well as I have for a few days before. Fine time for farmers to work.

Saturday, 18th—Hermosa mañana. Nothing unusual occurred this morning. I passed most of my time reading; still gaining in strength.

Sunday, 19th—Rained last night; beautiful spring morning this. Rained again all morning till 12 o'clock and cleared off.

Monday, 20th—I leave Mr. Davis this morning for camp. Go out by Rainey's. I got my cartridge mended and came up to Mrs. Grandstaff's and got my dinner. Came on to A.; met the regiment just at camp, on their way to Lebanon. Our squadron on picket. Sent after them. As soon as they came regiment started. Got to Lebanon about 11 o'clock. 'Twas two before the last of the column passed. A train of wagons was along after the Com's. We stopped on street and the train passed on. We picketed all the roads and remained. I slept on street, my head resting on kerbstone for a pillow, but one blanket and got very cold before day. At daylight I went down and washed my mule off and warmed in blacksmith shop. Started back and Ferrill being drunk, had me arrested. Kyle had me lay off my arms, but soon after regiment all went to water and I was released. I eat breakfast and went over to Mr. Davis. Cousin Mec and Miss Fannie were at home. Mr. Davis down in town.

Tuesday, 21st—I remained in town some two hours. Went over to Camp, moved my mule to where 'twould be safe in case of a move and went down to Mrs. Jordon Stokes. I had a good long conversation with her. Got a paper from her and just as I was leaving Kyle came in. I loaned him the paper and went over to Cousin Mec's to take dinner. Hank Sullivan came in after dinner. Fox Trammel and Jim Davis came for dinner. The Miss Thompsons, sisters, came in. I went into the parlour with Hank and was introduced to them. We then had some music.

An hour or two passed rapidly. We took leave. I promised to call again in the evening. I went over to Mrs. Stokes and after making addition left a letter which she kindly promised to send to Nashville and mail for my father. I got some more papers. She and Mrs. Muirhead, her mother, tried to make a proselyte of me to Lincolnism or Unionism, as they would term it. Commenced raining. We left soon after I got back; came out near Cherry Valley and camped. I was on picket; the reserve in a barn; the videttes in a blacksmith shop; a good time of it.

Wednesday, 22nd—Rain ceased; bright and clear this morning. We came on to Alexandria. I spent the evening working with my mule's feet. After supper I went over to Lodge to assist in conferring some side degrees. I took 1,001; staid till 11 o'clock. Came back and went to bed. In a few minutes ordered to saddle up. Yanks coming down on us like thousand of brick from Liberty, Snow Hill and all around. We marched all night. I and Jack and Bill Kyle got together. Couldn't keep up with regiment. Stopped at daylight, got breakfast, fed horses and travelled on. Crossed river nearly swimming. Came out three miles and camped.

Thursday, 23rd Friday, 24th—Remain in camp this morning, all day nothing of interest.

Saturday, 25th—Start at 3 o'clock for the wagons at Yankeetown. All horses unfit for duty sent there under Lieut. Gibson of 11th Texas. Regiment went to Rock Island. We came in fifteen miles of Sparta and camped. Men and lame horses straggled all along the road for miles. I and McFarlan bunked together.

Sunday, 26th—Came on by Mr. England's; stopped on mountain at Airs. Lowe's and got some bread baked and duck cooked; took dinner and came on to camp. Found the wagons camped near Yankeetown.

Monday, 27th—Remained in camp all morning; then started as John Rector had come in to see Cousin Jim Hawkins; found he had moved camp. I went up to Mr. Johnston's and took dinner; saw Mr. Denton of Mike Salter's Company there. Sent note up to Jimmy by one going up.

Tuesday, 28th—James Hawkins came up today to see me; staid all day with me. After he left, I and Frank McGuire went out to Mr. Bradley's and got supper. I got some bread. We then went and got twenty bundles fodder apiece and came back to camp.

Wednesday, 29th—Remained in camp today; horses inspected. John R. left me to go to the command. Albright bunked with me tonight. I went up with him to Mr. Williams and got supper.

Thursday, 30th—Came up, I and Albright, to Brown's Mill. Regimental wagons ordered to Sparta. Regiment on detached duty; spent night with Cousin James Hawkins.

Friday, 1st day of May—Spent this day with Jimmy.

Saturday, 2nd—Went to Granville. I rode Jimmy's grey horse and left my mule with his boy. Staid all night with Capt. Trousdale; had to paddle over the river in a canoe and swim our horses.

Sunday, 3rd—I went on by Duke's and to Squire Bennett's on Buffalo Creek. Took dinner and remained till near night. Then crossed the pike at Hogg's Store and up to Billy West's and spent the night.

Monday, 4th—Came on to Abel Smith's and to Widow Ballou's and took dinner. From there to Womac Parker's on Dixon Creek, and staid all night.

Tuesday, 5th—Came to Gifford's blacksmith shop. Albright had swapped horses, had two shoes put on, got dinner and came on to Joe Carter's. A. had two more shoes put on. Went on to Griggs and got supper. A. and Maze of Petticord's Company came on. We came four miles to Joe Sullivan's; left A. there. I and Maze went over to Jordan Carr's. Yanks all through here yesterday.

Wednesday, 6th—Left Carr's and came up to John Mitchell's. Came out to Stinson's on to Giles Harris. From there to Scottsville and Gallatin. Crossed at Coatstown, went on to John Rippy's, got supper and fed horses. Went on in rain to the Webb's, Maze's uncle, found the Yanks so close by that we turned and went back to the hills.

Thursday, 7th—While at John's, Green Crews and John West came in. I went with them over to Mrs. Dinah Huffey. A. soon came, said Yanks were about. I staid all night. He went to John West's. Miss Polly is a fast one.

Friday, 8th—I went to John Mitchell's to meet A.; was not there. I went on to John West; saw Miss Jane Wiley; came back to D s; found A. there. I came back to John West, and on to Dots Belt's; staid all night; on to Green Crews this morning.

Saturday, 9th—Start this evening, six of us, to Allen County, Ky. Went up in eight miles of Scottsville; stay all night or day in woods. Tonight, go by Ayres, Will Span's and old man Span's. At the latter place we got into hot water. Bush whackers attacked us, killed my horse, stampeded all. I got separated from the rest, went one mile, got two horses, came on through to New Row Monday, 11th, and on across to Coatstown. Find Will at Mrs. Huffey's, shot. Miss Sallie Key there on visit. I stay all night.

Tuesday, 12th—I and Will Rogers went over to Green's and Bass's; met by John M. Green getting in. Met Al bright, went back to D's and stay all night. S. K. there.

Wednesday. 13th—I met some of Morgan's men; Harper with them. I joined them and went cross railroad at Mitchellville over to Wickwire's, eight miles from railroad. Stopped at Mr. Simpson's and got breakfast. Miss Sue Offutt, Miss Jimmy Wickwire there. After breakfast went to the woods and staid all day.

Thursday, 14th—This evening we all went in and got supper then down to Mr. Wickwire's and got supper and the supper is a mistake; danced until 12 o'clock. I and Miss Jimmy danced two sets. I enjoyed it finely, then bid them *adieu* and came out to Pete Laurence's by daylight. Birch swapped horses on the way. Pete's sister brought us provisions.

Friday, 15th—Tonight stopped to see two Lincolnites; got six shooter from one, single barrel from the other; stopped at Squire Henry's; got some cherry bounce; played off Yankee on him; got all the information we wanted and went on to Wickwire's; fed at Mr.

Simpson's; girls got up, chatted them awhile. I, Harper and Gibson then left the crowd, crossed the railroad and bought two horses and came on to Bracken's and got breakfast. From there to Ashlock's and got dinner. Came cross the pike and I left them, went by Bass's and on to Crews and staid all night.

Saturday, 16th-Sunday, 17th—Came to Mrs. Huffey's, found Albright.

Monday, 18th-Tuesday, 19th—Yesterday went to Tompson's shop; not at home. This morning to Hughes; gone to Gallatin. Came by Jordan Carr's, got dinner and on to Moss's. Found Jim Berryman there. Harper came soon. Went down to Sullivan's, fed and I left. Went on to John Stewart's, staid all night.

Wednesday, 20th—Down to Hughes, got my horse shod, came back, and nine of us started. Came up near Epperson Springs, found the Yanks were there and at Scottsville too strong for us. Got supper at Stinson's, a regular tory. Lamb swapped horses with him. Then started for New Row. Came across to Bracken's, got breakfast, three of the boys had left us.

Thursday, 21st—We came this evening out to where the others were; Yanks in New Row; so, we could not go there. Came to Widow Hodge's. Five of boys went on; two slept in bushes; I and Jim Berryman slept in house.

Friday, 22nd—Came cross the pike to Meadows, fed our horses. I, Jim and Lamb started back to Kentucky. We came cross pike to Mr. Hodges and got supper, then cross railroad and out through Mitchellville to Norris ten miles from railroad; staid all day and tonight.

Saturday, 23rd—Went down to Finch's and got a horse. Mr. Finch came out with us some distance. Came back to Norris; staid all night; nothing to eat.

Sunday, 24th—Tonight went down near Redman s; run into Yankee pickets, and started back. Came cross railroad and out to Sherwin's, got breakfast and on to Boss Meadows. From there to Hughe's Shop; got two shoes and nails made. Went down to Essick's and got supper and on top Mountain and staid all night.

Monday, 25th-Tuesday, 26th—This —— got my mare shod, went on, found A. at Henry Mitchell's came back to Hardy Silver's, found the boys and started back to the railroad to get some boots. Took supper with Mr. Hodge and on to Rodimore's; had not the boots; then came back cross pike. I went with Berryman to shop; Hughes not there. I left him, came on to Jack Stewart's. I, Albright and Lamb started back for Granville this evening; came on to Griggs, got supper. From there to Staffords and staid all night.

Wednesday, 27th—Met Thompson's and Staley's men.

Thursday, 28th—Came to Montgomery's. Lamb left us. We came on to Widow Ballou's. Yanks close at hand. We staid in bushes tonight.

Friday, 29th—Went to Dixon Springs today to get a Yankee saddle; had to wait until the two regiments of Yankee cavalry and train passed out. We then went in, I and Ward. I went up to Mr. Alexander's; Miss Mollie knew me, Miss Nannie did not. I took supper and staid till 10 or 11 o'clock and left. Came back to Mrs. Ballou's.

Saturday, 30th—Came to Mr. Beasley's and staid all night.

Sunday, 31st—Met up with Parker as Lieut. Brown. I got a horse for Mason Rector. Came on to Granville, found Company D there, and that we were published as deserters. Came out near Cookville tonight.

Monday, 1st day of June—Came to Mrs. Brown's, took breakfast, got our clothing and came on to camp. Camp moved this evening. Proceedings stopped until Kyle comes up. Our names sent with others to be published in *Houston Telegraph*. Came out tonight to pasture and turned in.

Tuesday, 2nd—Came in to camp, find that my name has been sent on with others to be published as a deserter.

Wednesday. 3rd—Ordered to remain in camp.

Thursday, 4th—Wm. Hamby got in from Austin, Texas; staid all night with me. We went out to a private house and spent the night.

Friday, 5th—William left me this morning. Tonight, I and Reuben went out to Mr. Mills and staid.

Saturday, 6th—Lieut. Black took all men able for duty and started to Sligo this morning. Tonight, the company got in from G.

Sunday, 7th—Started for left wing, went to Sparta, halted there hour or two; came on to Cany Fork and camped.

Monday, 8th—Came to McMinnville this morn. Ordered regiment to Hoover's Gap to picket; wagons to Manchester. I went to the wagons to get a saddle, stopped with Dave Nunn, staid all Tuesday, 9th. Came to camp, rigged my tree and Wednesday, 10th, came to the command, camped near Beech Grove on pike.

Thursday, 11th—Came on picket.

Friday, 12th—On picket duty; camped at our old stand.

Saturday, 13th—Company go on picket.

Sunday 14th—I and Capt. Hill go out after provisions, stop at Mr. Mankin's, Prayter's, Jacob's, Mankin's and return.

Monday, 15th—I took dinner today with Mr. Guess. Relieved this evening. Five of us went on scout; got supper at Mr. Mankin's. I left my valise at Mr. Guess's. I forgot to note leaving undershirt and pair of drawers at Mr. Brown's on Falling Water.

Tuesday, 16th—Regiment relieved and came into camp.

Wednesday, 17th—Drill morning and evening inspection. Received two letters, one from Cousin Jennie, one from Tom Maxwell.

Thursday, 18th—Review of brigade by Gen'l Hardee.

Friday, 19th—Regiment came to Fairfield and from there to Bell Buckle and camped. I went out to Mr. Suggs and got some bread baked and returned.

Saturday, 20th—Remained in camp today. Three of the Arkansas Post boys came up from Wartrace and among the number was Doc. Norwood. Staid with us tonight.

Sunday, 21st—Came over to Old Fosterville to picket.
Monday, 22nd—All quiet.

Tuesday, 23rd-Wednesday, 24th—Company on picket. I came back to attend a court martial; staid all night in camp.

Thursday, 25th—Rained all day. Yanks made a general attack on our pickets. I went out to the company about 11 a. m.; fell back to Ransom's; went over to Bell Buckle; travelled all night. Came on to Fairfield; staid a short time and came on back to Ransom's and camped.

Friday, 26th-Saturday, 27th—Came to Bell Buckle this morning and from there to Wartrace, our infantry falling back to Tullahoma.

Went a short distance beyond Wartrace; 11th Texas and 4th Georgia skirmished with them a little; a few wounded. We came to Duck River and camped.

Sunday, 28th—Came on today to Tullahoma; continues to rain night and day. I saw James Maxwell, Billy Dunson, Julius Lensing and Doc. Norwood.

Monday, 29th—I was detailed to go to the shop; came on to town, found Stroud and came out five miles to shop. Still raining. We spend the night at the shop.

Tuesday, 30th—Our work finished and we return to camp at Tullahoma. Regiment came in soon after. I got a letter from Miss S. A. Jourdan. I went over to the Texas Brigade, saw Doc. Norwood, George Holman, George Jourdan, Frank Wilkes and Billy Dunson. Came back and our regiment moved out on the right and camped. I went on a scout with Black to Hillsboro; went within one mile and came back; no Yanks there. Travelled all day or I should have said all night. Got back and found the army on the retreat.

Wednesday, July 1st—Army in full retreat. Came on to Alisony 'bout 11 o'clock. While on the move from that point my mare fell and broke her left foreleg just below the knee. John Henry was left with me. We came on short distance and went to sleep. I left my mare where the accident happened.

Thursday, July 2nd—Came on to Deckerd this morning. From there took wrong road and came up Cumberland Mountain to the University with Hardee's Corps. Found there that we had taken the wrong road. John went down to the house to get some information and I lost him. I came down to the railroad and staid all night. Folk's Corps crossing all night.

Friday, 3rd—I waited until our wagons came up and put my luggage on them and rolled on. Came to foot of mountain tonight.

Saturday, 4th—Came down to Battle Creek from head of Sweden's Cove; portion of Folk's Corps crossed pontoon at mouth of Battle Creek and cross the river. We came on to Bridgeport. Crossed this evening. Met Bob Ship here.

Sunday, 5th—Came up to the foot of the mountains and camped.

Monday, 6th—Start cross the mountains. Came up, I and Paul Watkins, to Nicka Jack, staid all night with Mrs. Porter.

Tuesday. 7th—Came cross the mountain through Hamburg, got dinner there at Mrs. Reeves and came on to Camp within one and a half miles of Trenton.

Wednesday, 8th—Remain in camp.

Thursday, 9th-Saturday, 11th—All quiet. Put on one month's roots for the Kentucky trip; read at dress parade yesterday evening; commenced this morning.

Sunday, 12th—Start this morning for Rome, Ga. Came on top Lookout Mountain; rained tonight.

Monday, 13th—Came on through Lafayette and six miles beyond. I and Bob Ship, Tom Peterson and Jim McGuire stayed all night about one mile from camp. Rained very hard for a while. Music tonight.

Tuesday, 14th—Came to within fifteen miles of Rome, passed through Chanyville.

Wednesday, 15th—Came to Rome; pretty place for the country. Camped two miles from town and spent all day in town.

Thursday, 16th—Remain in camp all day.

Friday, 17th—All quiet in camp. Brigade officers had a ball in town last night.

Saturday, 18th—Moved camp down on Silver Creek four miles from town.

Sunday, 19th-Friday, 24th—Usual routine of camp duty. A protracted meeting going on, conducted by Parson Bunting and others, commenced Sunday. I am on duty every other day Weather warm and dry.

Saturday, 25th, to 1st day of August—All quiet; usual routine of camp duty. Two days since, while out on forage, I saw Miss Anna Ransom at Mrs. Garrett's a great pleasure to meet with them.

3rd, 4th, Wednesday, 5th—The barbecue and presentation of the horse to Gen'l Wharton came off today. Jno. Rector made the presentation speech. Gen'l W. replied. Harrison made a few remarks; dinner was then announced. After dinner Billy Sayers and Adams of Company C made speeches. Everything passed off finely; quite an array of beauty present. The Misses R. and G. present. I paid my respects to them.

Thursday, 6th, to Friday, 14th—Nothing but roll call, inspection, dress parades and drill. We are living high on peach pie. I have made a few acquaintances, but don't find the hospitality that we did in Tennessee. I was over at Mr. Bryant's today. Can't say that I enjoyed it very highly.

I pass from 14th to 20th. Nothing stirring. Oh! yes, the wedding Charley Littlefield to Miss Mollie Maddry, by the Rev. Mr. or Lieut. Simpson of Company B *alias* Sim Bruce of Company E. My time passes very pleasantly.

25th—Went to town today. Passed the day pleasantly; took dinner with —— Rome. Saw Cousin Mollie; came out to Mr. Mobley's; took supper. Met with Col. Cox, Mr. Barrick of Glasgow, Ky., and Mr. Johnson and Lady of Nashville. Miss Mobley was very sociable. I sit till bedtime. Time passed pleasantly. Now, that we are acquainted, have become attached to the folks, we have to leave; always the case. I made the acquaintance of Miss Maggie Ezzell, Miss Mattie Sommers, Miss Fannie Summers and Miss Mollie Robert and enjoyed myself with them finely.

Friday, 28th—We bid our friends *adieu* and came out eight miles above Rome. I got my hunting shirt as I passed through town, cost me sixty-eight dollars.

Saturday, 29th—Remained in camp.

Sunday, 30th-Monday, 31st—Moved four miles this evening. I and Jim McGuire went out and spent the night with Mr. Anderson.

Tuesday, 1st—Came on today to Mrs. Partain's where we stopped as we went down; found Mr. Sewell there still mending clocks; the girls looking charming. Staid all night. Music and mirth.

Wednesday, 2nd September—Came on to Lafayette, camp one mile from town. Had a meeting of the Lodge this evening; I attended.

Thursday, 3rd—Remained here today; met again this evening at the Lodge in town.

Friday, 4th—Started for Alpine; came out twelve miles and camped.

Saturday, 5th—Reached Alpine, left one wagon to the regiment, and with the rest the dismounted men started for Rome. Came eight miles and camped.

Sunday, 6th—A number of us started at two o'clock this morning and came on twelve miles and got breakfast. I and Oly Archer turned off at Coosyville and came by Miss Ransom's. Miss Anna and Miss Fannie were there, also Mr. and Mrs. Settle of Murfreesboro. We spent the day with them and came to camp in the evening.

Monday, 7th—Camped at Col. Shorter's; one brigade of infantry near us.

Tuesday, 8th—All quiet. I went off over to John's last night, but big Cousin was not there.

Wednesday, 9th—Quiet today.

Thursday, 10th—I went over to Whitehead's to get some raw hide to cover my saddle. I stopped at Mr. Mobley's and took dinner, chatted Miss Metta a while and went over to the Mill and on to the tan yard and back to the mill; found Dr. Neely there. I staid till bout 10 o'clock and came back to camp. Time passed pleasantly, "on Angels wings," while with Miss Mag.

Friday, 11th—Remained in camp.

Saturday, 12th—I played off on an old Georgian as captain or with captain's uniform, got a buggy that a private could not have reached with a twenty-foot pole. I and Oly Archer rode out in it to Mr. Ransom's. Took Mr. Jackson along with us. We took supper and sit till bedtime. Time passed delight fully. Pleasant drive back to camp.

Sunday, 13th—Moved eight miles from Rome out on the Kingston road to where the 4th Tennessee camped near a mill on the river.

Monday, 14th—Remained in camp all day.

Tuesday, 15th-Sunday, 20th—During this time I made the acquaintance of Miss Mary Reece, Miss Mary Davis and Miss Eugenie Holt. I spent all my leisure time visiting them. Very nice ladies indeed.

Monday, 21st—I and Mr. Nolin went up to the tan yard this evening and took supper and sit till 10 o'clock. Miss E. was looking very nice indeed.

Tuesday—Reading *My Stories of Court of London.*

Wednesday, 23rd—Reading *Tempest and Sunshine.* Went up to see Miss E. tonight. I spent a few hours at Mr. Davis; Miss Mollie and Cousin looking charming.

Thursday, 24th—Start this morning for Tunnel Hill. Came by T., left G. T. McGehee, got my boots $75. Bid Miss E. good bye and in company with Capt. Hill and Wm. Nicholson came on eight miles and staid all night at Mr. Brownlee's.

Friday., 25th—Passed through Calhoun this morning, twenty-one miles to Dalton. Came on through D. to Tunnel Hill, seven miles from D.

Saturday, 26th—Came on to Ringgold and six miles beyond to Chickamauga. When we got in three miles of R. we struck the main Yankee line of invasion; from there on the country is destroyed fencing burned, everything eat up and destroyed.

Sunday, 27th—We start up the railroad this morning but turn back and camp on Chickamauga. Here we remain.

Monday 28th-October 1st, Thursday—Rain last night and still continuing; truly refreshing. First, we've had for an age. All quiet in front. Well, I've missed being in one battle, that of Chickamauga.

October 2nd—Continued to rain all day.

3rd, Saturday—Moved camp this morning to Cherokee Springs one and one-half miles from Ringgold. Cousin Jimmy Hawkins met me and went to camp with me.

Sunday, 4th—I, Jim McGuire and Jimmy went out beyond Catoosa Springs and staid all night. A mistake. *Saturday Eve.*

Sunday, 4th—Took breakfast at Mr. Maston's this morning. Came by the Springs and stopped to see Miss Kate Shamblin. On to camp.

Monday, 5th—Remained in camp.

Tuesday, 6th—I and Jimmy went out to the Springs; spent the night at Widow Conner's.

Wednesday, 7th—Piruted around generally. I left Jimmy at Mr. Smith's and went over to see Miss Kate.

Thursday, 8th—I came into camp this morning, was appointed Adjutant of the Preps! Preps!

Friday, 9th—Jimmy came in this morning but did not stay long; was to be back in the evening.

Saturday, 10th—Jimmy did not come.

Sunday, 11th—I went out to see Miss Kate this morning, but heard nothing of Jim. Went by Mr. Shamblin's. Miss Eva and Miss Nannie were at home; two of the prettiest girls I've seen in Georgia. I went over to Mr. Smith's and heard of Jimmy; had gone on to camp. I went back to camp and found him there.

Monday, 12th—I went out this evening and staid all night with Mr. Cannon, at Mr. Smith's.

Tuesday, 13th—I started by daylight this morning and came to camp. Raining.

Wednesday, 14th-Thursday, 15th—Nothing but rain, night and day.

Friday, 16th-Sunday, 18th—I went out to Catoosa Springs and to Mr. Shamblin's and back to camp.

Monday, 19th-Wednesday, 21st.

Thursday, 22nd—This morning we start for Kingston. I came on in advance of the train to Tunnel Hill, saw all the boys and called around to see Miss Kate and Miss Nannie. They had moved down a few days ago. We came on four miles below Dalton and staid all night, I and Paul, Jim.

Friday, 23rd—Came on through to Calhoun and six miles below and staid all night. Raining all day and night.

Saturday, 24th—Came to Adairsville. Camp three miles from the village. Tonight, I went to Mr. Green's, one mile from A. with Wm. Campbell. Left my horse and went to town and took 10 o'clock train and went to Kingston. I staid but a few minutes; did not find what I went after. Came up at 12 o'clock to A., went out to Mr. Green's and staid all night.

Sunday, 25th—Went to town this morning and sent a letter to Tunnel Hill by Harper to Miss Nannie.

Monday, 26th-Wednesday, 28th—Nothing worthy of note.

Thursday, 29th—I went down to our old stamping ground today. I stopped to see Miss Eugenie Holt; had just returned from a visit to Marietta and was looking very pretty; stopped but a short time. Went on to Mr. Davis's; nobody at home but Miss Mollie. Crossed the river at Freeman's Ferry and went to Mr. Somers. Miss Maggie's husband at home. I staid all night. Miss Mattie came down this morning. I staid till 'bout 10 o'clock.

Friday, 30th—I came back to Mr. Davis; Mrs. D. and husband just starting to Rome. I took dinner and left. Came in to Mr. Green's, near Adairsville, and staid till bedtime and came to camp.

Saturday, 31st—Remain in camp.

Sunday, 1st November—I went to town and mailed some letters, and out to Mr. Mooney's, the tanner, and got dinner; came by Mr. Green's, stopped awhile and on to camp.

Monday, 2nd—Remain in camp all day.

Tuesday, 3rd-Friday, 6th—Start this morning I and James Pickle down the country, stopped at Mr. Gillam's and took dinner. From there to Mr. Kit Dodd's and staid all night.

Saturday, 7th—I met Mr. Gore there, promised to write to Cousin Serena. Came on to Mr. Somer's and then to Van Wert; staid with Col. Jones tonight; met Mr. Jones and Lady, Mrs. Cullin and Miss Lou, daughter of the Colonel. Had a candy pulling.

Sunday, 8th—Came or went to Mr. Carmichael's and back to Van Wert before we found him. Jim left his leather with him and we came on to Capt. Wimberly's and staid all night.

Monday, 9th—Came in to Cedar Town this morning. Stay all night at the hotel, ten dollars apiece. Sold some tobacco to him.

Tuesday, 10th—Came out with Clan Blakemore and Fuget to Mr. Thomas. I spent the night at John Hatchers. Miss Jane Simpson was there tonight. James Pickel was not with me; the other boys went back to town.

Wednesday, 11th—I spent the day and night at Mr. Hatchers.

Thursday., 12th—Went over to Mr. Thomas's. I made a girth for him. From there to Miss Kate Carter's. Mr. Shirry and two other gents came in, gentlemanly, merry.

Friday, 13th—I came over to Mr. Hatcher's.

Saturday, 14th—Left Mr. Hatcher's and came up to Cave Spring, saw Jenkins and Capt. Hooks. Mart Lee was there but I did not get to see him. Came on to Dr. Richardson's near Cedar Town and staid all night, a very fine family indeed. Has one grown daughter. Met Col.

Bryant, a Kentucky refugee.

Sunday, 15th—Came on to Van Wert. Jim stopped at Carmichael's and got his boots. Came on to Mr. Peck's and to Mr. Somers; stopped and spent Monday.

November, 16th—Came this evening to Adairsville; found our Train gone to Charleston. Slept on the ground.

Tuesday, 17th—Went to Grandpaps this morning and got breakfast. Jim stopped at Mr. McDow's to see Reuben Stround. Came on and we started from Grandpaps. Came up to Mr. Curtis and turned off to the right. Came up to Silvacoa and camped; got corn from a field.

Wednesday, 18th—Got breakfast, paid two dollars for it and crossed the river. Came on to Spring Place, got heel plates put on. Came out seven miles and staid all night. Camped.

Thursday, 19th—Came on today to Charlestown and six miles above to Mr. Galloway's and staid all night.

Friday, 20th—Came on through Athens, Sweetwater and Philadelphia; came out one and one-half miles and took supper at a very nice place Virginians. Met McMahon of Company H. I and Jim came on to camp near London.

Saturday, 21st—Jim went to the Com. this morning. I had an offer for my mule this eve and sold him.

Sunday, 22nd—We remained in camp.

Monday, 23rd—Moved camp to within two miles of Lenoir on Little Tennessee River. I went out to Mr. Vassey's; let my clothing.

Tuesday, 24th—All quiet in camp. Firing at Kingston, Wheeler and Wilder.

Wednesday, 25th-Thursday, 26th—Went to a dance tonight. I only danced two sets. Dr. Bob was with me. Came back about one o'clock.

Friday, 27th—Remained in camp all day.

Saturday, 28th—Started this morning on a scout through Blunt—Charley Mason, John Kelison, Jessy Kirkland. Met up with Charley Pelham and Sam Piper.

Kirkendol of Company G was with us. Found Steve Gallagher and Jim with Mr. Upton. Jim was wounded; Steve came on with us. We crossed the river at Niles Ferry and staid all night at Mr. Norwood's.

Sunday, 29th—We went up the road two or three miles and found all the troopers leaving Blunt. We turned and came back to Mr. Norwood's and took dinner and came cross the river to Mr. Curtis and staid all night.

Monday, 30th—Charley Pelham came down this morning and told the Yanks were upon us and to fall back to Mr. Upton's. Kirk was pretty merry. Went down to Hawkins to get Sam Piper and Kirkland. We came up to Upton's, met Maj. Stevens, took dinner and sent after whiskey. Upton called up his negroes and gave them some whiskey and commenced the preparation for the move. I staid with them until they started. Four of us went to Cunningham's and staid all night.

Tuesday, 1st December—We came to Mr. White's this morning and there left Mr. Upton and started for the Telico Plains, I, Mason and Kelison. Met Kirkland, Piper and Kirkendol; then came up to McDermot's and staid all night.

Wednesday, 2nd—I and Kirk went to Cagle's and got his horses. I paid 200 to boot. Met at McD's. Four of us staid at Mr. Hunt's.

Thursday, 3rd—I came over to the shop and had my horse shod, and I and Kirk came on to Carmichael's. Found Pete Kendall there. The other boys had gone. Met Bulger Peoples. Went on to Hawkins; found all the boys there; staid all night.

Friday, 4th—Started for Motley Ford. Heard the Yanks were there and started for Carmichael's. Came on five or six miles and met up with Dick Tainter of Scott's Louisiana Regiment. Came on to C. and there divided; Sam Piper going to Mr. Shaw's with me and T. Had not been there long till the other boys came on. We got ready to start, and they refused and Sam Piper with them. I and Tainter then left them and came on to Mr. Donohue's and staid all night. I have never taken such a pirute before nor never will again.

Saturday, 5th—Left Mr. Donohue's with Dick Tainter and came down to Mr. Carr's on the river, five miles above the mouth of Citico. Found them all gone up the river for North Carolina. Dick did not want to go to Blunt. We went across the river to Bright's and found several men, Briscow of Company K among them. We staid all night.

Sunday, 6th—We started for Holloway's with two of the boys. We got there. Dick would go no further. Mint and Drew and Meroney all turned back.

I, Hugh Singleton and Briscow started for L. Came out to Old Major Pugh's and found the Yanks had prowled him of beehives and everything. Then came on cross Motley Ferry road and through a camp they had just left. Some Yankees on the ground laying up fences with the negroes.

We came on cross Morgantown road, found all the roads travelled by them. Came on to Capt. Dyer's, fed our horses and got supper and on to within one mile of Louisville. Stopped at Old Man Dyer's; found the Yanks in large force near him. Stopped, and fed and walked down to within three hundred yards of their camp fires. Could not get to the Planters Hotel. Came back; six of our boys were laying out in the woods near Mr. D's. We fed and slept in the barn till nearly day. Old Man woke us up, found two of the men were Carlton and Patton of Company F; others were Morgan Men. All came out to a thicket and spent the day.

Monday, 7th—Came in this evening to Mr. Dyer's, found the Yankees all gone, got supper and went down to the Planters, spent two or three hours. Gardner sold them a horse. I must take Miss Kate one. Came out tonight to Mr. Dyer's, warmed and came on to Lige Jim Henry's. I passed as a Yankee with Mrs. Henry. Came on to Mr. Holloway's and to Mr. Bess's and got dinner.

Tuesday, 8th—Came on to Mr. Bright's and staid all night; rained all day.

Wednesday, 9th—All quiet today. Didn't move.

Thursday, 10th—We start for Longstreet for or *via* Sevier. Gave it out and started for the vicinity of Bess Mill. Went to see Mr. Jo Gray, a lieut. in the Yankee Army. He was not at home; took two horses and a negro. Came on to McCully's and got two of them, two guns and one pistol, two horses. Came on to Bess but found them all gone, then came back to Mr. Bright's.

Friday, 11th—Started this evening for Sevier, got as far as Little River at Mr. McClane's and turn back. Two Yanks rode right through us. Came on by day near Mont Vale Spring. Stopped and got breakfast. Saw two bushwhackers but could not catch them. Met Mr. King at the Springs. Came on over to Mr. Gomly's.

Saturday, 12th—I staid all night at Mr. Cutchberson's.

Sunday, 13th—All started tonight for Louisville. Rained and we separated; I, Smith and Alexander leaving the crowd at Mr. Everett's. We stopped at Mr. Best's and staid all night and all day.

Monday, 14th—Start tonight for Sevier; ran into the Yanks at Maryville; my saddle turned; I lost my horse. The boys abandoned theirs and we made our escape on foot. Worked our way out to McClaine's on Little River just at daylight, but he would have nothing to do with us; could get no assistance from him. Came down the river and lay out in a little mot of timber.

Tuesday, 15th—Came to Hiram Bogle's, crossed the Little River at Finley's, the Sheriff of the County. Got to Bogle's and got a snack to eat. Mr. Bogle had taken the oath and would give me no information, only directions to Tim Chandler's.

Tuesday, 16th—Came on to Chandler's, got lost on the road and had to stop and inquire at a house (John Robinson's). He told me about the Home Guards being in the neighbourhood. I or we went on until we got to the house where they were camped or near it.

****

There is confusion of days and dates from "Tuesday, 16th" to "Thursday, 25th;" for the 16th is Wednesday, the 17th is Thursday, etc.

****

The road forked and I went up to inquire about the road. Found 'twas not a dwelling and saw the Home Guards through the window. Went on to the next house, Mr. Johnson's, and got the information and travelled on. Got to C's 1 o'clock at night, found Mr. Houck there.

Boys staid at the house while I went to the house. I took supper with them and got some meat and bread for the boys. Miss Rogers was there. I could get but little information from Chandler. I went to the barn and we went into the straw to stay next day and cross at Bradson's next night.

Wednesday, 17th—This morning the Home Guards got on our tracks, and by the aid of citizens found us and carried us back to the Academy. Randell is Capt., Cresivell first Lieut., Rose 2nd, Moore a Private, Ingle, Keener and others.

Thursday, 18th—Start this morning for Knoxville; get in bout 1 p.m. Capt. Barnetts takes charge of me and sends me to prison.

Friday, 19th—I find one of the 11th Texas here, three or four of the 2nd Georgia. I send out a summons to the Lodge for assistance; two members call on me and promise to attend to my case, but I hear no more from them.

Another squad of 96 prisoners came in, also three of Morgan's men, Messrs. Church and Smith.

Maj. Smith of Wheeler's staff called on us. Two other squads came in. With the last came Will Morton of the battery or Company F. Alexander takes the oath and left us. Morton, myself, the two Churches and two Smiths form the mess.

Sunday, 21st—Parson ———— preached for us this evening.

Thursday. 25th—A dull Christmas. Receiving one-quarter pound bread a day and 'bout one pound beef, no wood hardly—freezing and starving by inches.

All this brings me up to the 29th Monday. Morton tried to get to see his sister but could not. The parson came in and informed him that she died at 3 o'clock this morning. Such is the fate of war. In 150 yards of her and yet could not get to see her.

Wednesday, 30th—Morton out on street parole.

Thursday, 31st—Miss Anna Brooks came around, Miss McMullin with her, brought me a pair of socks. I sent a note to Mrs. House by Hupplits tonight.

Friday, 1st day of January, 1864—Received one pair of drawers from Miss Nannie Scott, two shirts from Mrs. House. One hundred and fifty of the prisoners start today for Strawberry Plains. We go tomorrow.

★★★★★★★★★★★★★★★★★★★★★

Dodd was sentenced to death on or before January 5th. An extract from a letter by the general commanding and dated at Knoxville, Tenn., January 17, 1864, reads:

> I also avail myself of this opportunity to forward an order publishing the proceedings, findings and sentence in the case of Private E. S. Dodd, Eighth Texas Confederate Cavalry, who was tried, condemned and executed as a spy.
> I also enclose a copy of an order which I have found it necessary to issue, in regard to the wearing of the U. S. uniform by Confederate soldiers.

★★★★★★★★

"Enclosure No. 7 (here omitted) contains General Orders, No. 3, Department of the Ohio, January 5, 1864, promulgating charges, findings and sentence to death in the case of E. S. Dodd, Eighth Texas Cavalry, arrested and tried as a spy." *War of the Rebellion*, Series III, Vol. 4, p. 53.

★★★★★★★★★★

ALSO FROM LEONAUR
AVAILABLE IN SOFTCOVER OR HARDCOVER WITH DUST JACKET

AN APACHE CAMPAIGN IN THE SIERRA MADRE by John G. Bourke—An Account of the Expedition in Pursuit of the Chiricahua Apaches in Arizona, 1883.

BILLY DIXON & ADOBE WALLS by Billy Dixon and Edward Campbell Little—Scout, Plainsman & Buffalo Hunter, *Life and Adventures of "Billy" Dixon* by Billy Dixon and *The Battle of Adobe Walls* by Edward Campbell Little (*Pearson's Magazine*).

WITH THE CALIFORNIA COLUMN by George H. Petis—Against Confederates and Hostile Indians During the American Civil War on the South Western Frontier, *The California Column, Frontier Service During the Rebellion* and *Kit Carson's Fight With the Comanche and Kiowa Indians*.

THRILLING DAYS IN ARMY LIFE by George Alexander Forsyth—Experiences of the Beecher's Island Battle 1868, the Apache Campaign of 1882, and the American Civil War.

THE NEZ PERCÉ CAMPAIGN, 1877 by G. O. Shields & Edmond Stephen Meany—Two Accounts of Chief Joseph and the Defeat of the Nez Percé, *The Battle of Big Hole* by G. O. Shields and *Chief Joseph, the Nez Percé* by Edmond Stephen Meany.

CAPTAIN JEFF OF THE TEXAS RANGERS by W. J. Maltby—Fighting Comanche & Kiowa Indians on the South Western Frontier 1863-1874.

SHERIDAN'S TROOPERS ON THE BORDERS by De Benneville Randolph Keim—The Winter Campaign of the U. S. Army Against the Indian Tribes of the Southern Plains, 1868-9.

GERONIMO by Geronimo—The Life of the Famous Apache Warrior in His Own Words.

WILD LIFE IN THE FAR WEST by James Hobbs—The Adventures of a Hunter, Trapper, Guide, Prospector and Soldier.

THE OLD SANTA FE TRAIL by Henry Inman—The Story of a Great Highway.

LIFE IN THE FAR WEST by George F. Ruxton—The Experiences of a British Officer in America and Mexico During the 1840's.

ADVENTURES IN MEXICO AND THE ROCKY MOUNTAINS by George F. Ruxton—Experiences of Mexico and the South West During the 1840's.

AVAILABLE ONLINE AT www.leonaur.com
AND FROM ALL GOOD BOOK STORES

www.ingramcontent.com/pod-product-compliance
Lightning Source LLC
Chambersburg PA
CBHW030229170426
43201CB00006B/156